CHILDREN OF THE DARK GHETTO

CHILDREN
OF THE
DARK GHETTO

A DEVELOPMENTAL PSYCHOLOGY

BARRY SILVERSTEIN / RONALD KRATE

THE WILLIAM PATERSON COLLEGE OF NEW JERSEY
WAYNE, NEW JERSEY

PRAEGER PUBLISHERS · NEW YORK

Published in the United States of America in 1975
by Praeger Publishers, Inc.
111 Fourth Avenue, New York, N.Y. 10003

© 1975 by Praeger Publishers, Inc.

Library of Congress Cataloging in Publication Data

Silverstein, Barry.
    Children of the dark ghetto.
    Includes index.

    1. Negro children—New York (City)   2. Harlem, New York (City)—Social
conditions.   3. Negroes—Race identity.   4. Socialization.   I. Krate, Ronald, joint
author.   II. Title.
F128.9.N3S52   370.15   74-23264
ISBN 0-275-50370-4
ISBN 0-275-84800-0 pbk.

Printed in the United States of America

To the children of Central Harlem
and
to Jane, Judy, and Stephen
with hope for the future

Contents

ACKNOWLEDGMENTS

The inception of this project was made possible by grants to the authors from the Carnegie Corporation of New York and the Anti-Defamation League of B'nai B'rith. We received encouragement and support for our efforts from Fredric A. Mosher of the Carnegie Corporation and Oscar Cohen and Stanley Wexler of the ADL. The views expressed herein, however, are the sole responsibility of the authors, who contributed equally to the authorship of the book.

We wish to thank those who contributed in various ways to the book. Naomi Grasso shared with us her experiences as a teacher in Central Harlem and, later, as a psychologist in the Head Start project; her clinical observations and insights were invaluable during the initial phase of our work. We thank Professor James Houston, of William Paterson College, for his early encouragement and support. Professors Daniel Skillin, Fort P. Manno, and Kathleen Leicht, all of William Paterson, graciously provided useful critiques of early drafts of the manuscript, as did, at various phases of the work, educators Michael Padva and Stephen H. Klein. We received patient and enthusiastic editorial assistance from Gladys Topkis of Praeger and from Frances S. Krate and Patricia Sampson Kahn. The readability of the book was immeasurably enhanced by their work. Typing assistance was tirelessly supplied by Claire Silverstein, Patricia Kahn, Agatha Botterio, and Lucille Schwartz. Our wives' contribution was of vital substantive aid; their patience, faith, and good spirits were taxed more than we or they could have imagined when we first embarked upon this project.

PREFACE

We have seen children full of life while overwhelmed by grief. Each day they face direct encounters with man's inhumanity to man. Yet many of the poor black children we knew in the inner city also experienced joy, excitement, and—a small number of them—a special kind of happiness. Otherwise more fortunate children in America are sometimes deprived of the electricity many ghetto black children know from time to time, the feeling that sometimes springs from young lives in spite of physical deprivation and economic precariousness. But in a place like Central Harlem, where childhood can be a cruel encumbrance, generations come up quickly.

We did not enter the elementary schools of Central Harlem with the specific intention to study the children we found there and to put our observations into a book. This is not to say that our motives were purely altruistic. During the early 1960's, both of the authors were graduate students in psychology who intended to become developmental psychologists but who needed jobs that would enable us to support ourselves while, we hoped, also providing an opportunity to learn something about children. We therefore became elementary school teachers in Central Harlem, expecting to stay in the schools for two or three years. One of us stayed six years; the other, five.

Our decision to write about our experiences in the schools and about the psychological development of poor black children arose relatively late in our careers as elementary school teachers. We read the exploding literature on "disadvantaged children" and constantly compared the descriptions with the children we saw daily. To us, the children were not abstractions, as they seemed to be to some of the "experts" on "the disadvantaged." We decided to write about the children we knew because we could not find in the literature any description that was entirely true to our experiences.

As elementary school teachers, we did not come to know the children of Central Harlem in the ways that psychologists who study children typically come to know them. We did not set up controlled situations, nor did we carry out systematic programs of observation. We did not execute test and measurement programs. We could not separate ourselves artificially from the children so as to deal with them as objects of detached study and manipulation. We were participating with the children in a variety of real-life situations, and we shared with them many "warm-blooded" experiences: joy and sorrow, pride and shame, achievement and failure. But if during this period we could not be detached participant-observers, we nevertheless were able to function as observant participants. We came to know many children in a personal way on the basis of our shared experiences.

We spent at least six hours a day with the children in our classes. Through this sustained, intensive interaction, we came to know about two hundred children in our combined eleven teaching years. We saw these children in a variety of situations, one day after another. We came to appreciate them as people and to understand their behavior in the context of their intentions, goals, desires, and fears—the reality of their lives.

Each of the authors later taught in a different elementary school in Central Harlem. Thus we came to know children in more than one school setting. Further, our knowledge of poor black children is not limited solely to school situations: One of the authors worked on the streets as a recreation worker in a number of poor black and Puerto Rican communities before becoming a teacher and subsequently served as a consultant to Harlem Youth Opportunities Unlimited (HARYOU), frequently meeting black youth at the HARYOU center. Both authors spent time with their pupils in playgrounds and parks and on the streets of Central Harlem. We also visited the homes of some of the children.

One of the authors worked for two consecutive years with the same group of children (fifth- and sixth-graders). This two-year relationship provided a fruitful opportunity to get to know the children well and to observe their development during the important transitional period from childhood to early adolescence. It also provided an opportunity to know some parents, grandparents, and siblings on a personal basis. An additional opportunity arose from the fact that we often had more than one child from a given family in our classes over the span of years we spent in Harlem. We came to know the siblings of some of our fifth- and sixth-graders (the grades where the bulk of our teaching experience was gained) when they were in first, second, or third grade, and we had a chance to watch these children develop until they reached the age to be in our fifth- or sixth-grade classes.

We began to consider writing about the development of black children shortly before our last year as elementary school teachers. During that year, we set out deliberately to gain a broader, more systematic knowledge of black school children. To this end, each of the authors worked as a substitute teacher in schools with populations of poor black children in the southeast Bronx and the Lower East Side of Manhattan, as well as in Central Harlem and East Harlem. We devoted the year to more systematic observation of children, teachers, and schools than we had attempted previously.

After we left elementary school teaching, both of us became college instructors in psychology. Our commitment to writing about the development of poor black children grew as the literature on this subject (particularly by psychologists) grew and became, in our view, farther and farther removed from the reality of the children. Aided by a grant from the Carnegie Corporation, we kept in touch with the children and the schools. We visited schools. We observed younger children by visiting Head Start programs. We spent many hours in discussions with teachers and psychologists employed in elementary schools and by Head Start. And we held many individual and group discussions in our developmental-psychology classes with students, black and white, who were employed as teachers in inner-city neighborhoods.

At no time in our observations did we use tests and measurements. Rather, we watched children in action to see what they did and how they went about it. We supplemented observation by discussing with the children (as well as with parents and teachers) their feelings, thoughts, and activities.

Although much of this book is an attempt to present a heuristic portrait of the children we knew in Central Harlem, the basis of our discussion extends beyond our own observations and the limited size of our population sample. We have carried out a thorough review of the behavioral-science literature relating to black children, and throughout our presentation we have integrated observations and ideas from this literature with our own observations. The literature reviewed was written by blacks and whites of various theoretical persuasions, operating from a number of frames of reference and reporting on black children in many cities. Noting the similarities and differences between such observations and our own enables us to discuss the development of urban black children more broadly than our own findings permit.

Although Harlem has a long-established cultural life and a sense of community not equally present in all urban black neighborhoods, we believe that, in its essential aspects, growing up poor in Harlem is the same as growing up poor in other black urban communities outside the South. Accordingly, we often present observations of black children from other cities alongside our Harlem observations to document patterns of development that we believe are experienced by most poor black children in the major cities of our country. In presenting extended descriptions of children, we have tried to allow their special, idiosyncratic natures to shine through. Most of our work, however, is an attempt to delineate several (largely) socially determined patterns of development common to sizable groups of children.

Some features of our heuristic presentation may offend those who insist upon strict adherence to scientific method. As it is usually interpreted in American psychology, scientific respectability means the testing of specific hypotheses, the presentation of data in numerical form, and statistical analysis of such data. Armed with this narrow conception, many American psychologists have tended to break life down into small, observable, measurable, controllable bits and pieces in order to get answers to questions about the relationships between artificially isolated bits of experience. This obsession with measurement and precision ("objectivity") has caused them to fragment real human concerns and problems into considerations of simple, isolated processes that do not add up to an understanding of more complex human experiences and social processes. Through our attempts to comprehend the complexity of what we saw and felt in Central Harlem, it became clear to us that behavioral scientists cannot afford to rule out immediate and direct experiential knowledge as a basis for grasping reality, emotionally as well as conceptually.

The blending of description, conceptualization, and speculation that follows might be classified as representing "theories of the middle range." We have not always differentiated as clearly as some might desire between our observations as evidence and our conceptualizations and speculations concerning the significance of these observations. Nor have we separated systematically our relatively subjective feelings and emotional insights, developed directly through interaction with black children (and adults), from our relatively objective intellectual insights, derived more from calculated observation and after-the-fact reflection concerning our experiences. We chose to present our work in this manner, mindful of its limitations, because we are most concerned with helping the reader to see the "big picture," the complex set of interrelated processes and factors that comprises the course of development for poor black children in urban communities. We wish to avoid the typical procedure of fragmenting the children into isolated phenomena for abstract consideration of, for example, their intellectual faculties, their self-esteem, or their attitudes toward school, so that the reader can see *chil-*

dren emerge from the following pages, not disembodied intellects, feelings, or attitudes. But, at the same time, we want the reader to share our conceptions concerning the interactive relationships among various processes or functions—the cognitive, the emotional, and the social—in the development of poor black children. These processes or functions have been discussed at length in many other sources in relationship to the development of poor black children, but usually not as interactive phenomena in a holistic context, the framework within which we shall discuss them.

We also want the reader to consider such larger realities as the relationships between various patterns of development in the ghetto and the quality of interaction between children and adults in family and school, the relationships of family and school to the black community, and the relationships of institutions in the black community to the larger society. We are not so much obsessed with being "right" on all issues as we are committed to stimulating the reader to feel and think deeply about the issues we present. On the one hand, this may stimulate further studies to assess the validity of the relationships discovered or conceptualized. On the other hand, to the extent that we are accurate in our assessments of the children, our work may help to identify some of the issues that must be dealt with in practical terms if the children are to live more satisfying and rewarding lives.

The main focus of this book is on the behavior of urban black children in school. However, our concern extends far beyond the classroom and the schoolhouse. We have attempted to paint a comprehensive portrait of the development of these children and to relate their school experience to the rest of their lives.

In Chapter 1, child development and socialization are considered as against ethnicity, socio-economic class, urbanization, South-to-North migration, and time. Chapter 2 considers the development of black children within a series of expanding contexts: the family, the black community, and the encompassing white society. Chapter 3 focuses more closely upon some of the socialization experiences common in the early lives of the children and considers the impact of such experiences on the behavior of developing children.

Chapter 4 continues our exploration of black socialization and psychosocial development, focusing on issues of personal and racial (group) identity and the process of children's identification with the adults in their lives. The effects of recent widespread changes in black consciousness upon young children's attitudes toward their racial group and toward themselves receive special attention. Chapter 5 considers the role of peers in socialization. Chapters 6 and 7 deal with the cognitive and linguistic abilities of low-income urban black children.

Chapter 8 presents our conclusions about the behavior of black children in nursery school and elementary school. In that chapter we introduce a typology of observed behavior patterns as budding life-style adaptations to the socialization experiences the children have had at home, on the street, and in school. Chapter 9 focuses on the school as a socializing institution and the functions of schooling in shaping and reinforcing children's life-styles and opportunities within the social order. Chapter 10 continues the analysis of relationships between psychosocial characteristics, life-style adaptations, and achievement into the later school years and adulthood, relating our typology of behavior patterns to historical, political, and economic forces.

The final chapter focuses primarily on identity development among poor urban blacks and the actual and potential transformations of black identity brought about by long-range demographic and political forces, as well as by the dramatic events of the 1960's and early 1970's. In that chapter we offer our thinking concerning the crucial role of black ethnicity as a basis for local political and economic organization and the transformation of socialization practices.

CHILDREN OF THE DARK GHETTO

1 / INTRODUCTION AND PERSPECTIVE

The children we write about were growing up in a world that may be viewed from many perspectives. The children were black, and their lives were enmeshed with black ethnicity. Yet they were Americans. They were poor, from the lowest socio-economic strata. They lived in the North, and they lived in the inner city. The children grew up during the 1960's and early 1970's. Our analysis, then, must take into account the ethnicity, socio-economic class, region of socialization, and urbanization of a particular group of children, and the historical period in which they live. In this chapter, we offer perspectives on each of these factors to provide a basis for the analysis that follows.

ETHNICITY

The total black community in America may be seen as an ethnic sub-society, a relatively large group that is distinguished by a shared "sense of peoplehood."[1] This "sense of peoplehood" derives from both ancestral and future-oriented identification with the group. To a member of the group, other members are the people of his ancestors—therefore, his people, and the people of his children and their children. Ethnic identification strongly influences contemporary social relationships by building a special sense of kinship with fellow group members:

> With members of other groups I may share political participation, occupational relationships, common civic enterprise, perhaps even an occasional warm friendship. But in a very special way which history has decreed, I share a sense of indissoluble and intimate identity with *this* group *not that one* within the larger society and the world.[2]

This conception of ethnic group appears to capture not only the reality of existence for black people in America but also the awareness of identity and peoplehood that is increasingly becoming legitimated in black communities throughout the country.

Black ethnicity derives in large measure from the African (non-Western) identity of black people everywhere and, specifically, from black adaptations to white racism in America. Although acculturated to the dominant modes of American (white Western) cultural experience, many black Americans continue simultaneously to exhibit modes of relating and communicating that have their roots in the African heritage of the group. Some African elements can be identified in contemporary black-American forms of social interaction, linguistic performance, music, and art (to give but a few examples).[3] The continuing salience of discrimination and hostility toward blacks in white America has forced blacks to develop adaptive survival strategies and skills, including styles of coping with such social-psychological functions as the handling of contradictions and language systems, interpretations of the meaning of work and the role of the hero, and the like, which differ profoundly from white (especially WASP) forms.[4]

The idea of America as a "melting pot" in which diverse peoples blended together to form one homogenized American people has long been part of our national mythology. In fact, the descendants of European immigrants generally were able to acculturate rather successfully to the dominant institutions of the society, but, for many of them, no widespread structural assimilation ever took place:[5] Various European ethnic groups became "Americanized" in their cultural practices to a great extent, but the limitation of primary-group relations to fellow ethnics of the same class status is still a prominent feature of American society, though possibly of declining significance for contemporary youth. Even though the dominant white, Anglo-Saxon, Protestant groups were not inclined to share wealth and power or socialize intimately with European immigrants of different backgrounds, these groups nevertheless insisted that all newcomers to America must strive to eliminate their distinctively ethnic practices and identities, work hard, and become "good" Americans (that is, WASPS).[6] This was supposed to lead to full social acceptance and equality as well as economic security. In spite of their "Americanization," many white ethnics today do not feel either socially or economically secure.[7]

The discrepancies between the promised rewards for embracing WASP cultural referents (to the exclusion of non-WASP referents) and the limited economic and social gains (together with considerable loss of personal and group esteem) that attempts to meet these demands actually brought have become heightened in the consciousness of white ethnics in recent years. But such contradictions have been salient aspects of the experience of nonwhite ethnics in America for hundreds of years. Since the end of slavery, blacks have been exhorted to "whiten" themselves as a prerequisite for acceptance as "real Americans" by whites, despite the clear evidence that most whites will accept blacks only to a limited degree and despite the persistence of institutional racism, particularly discrimination in employment and housing. The effects of such cultural pressures on black identity in America were pointed out by W. E. B. DuBois in 1903:

> It is a peculiar sensation, this double-consciousness, this sense of always looking at one's self through the eyes of others. . . . One ever feels his twoness—an American, a Negro; two souls, two thoughts, two unreconciled strivings.[8]

Historically, many blacks defensively identified with white cultural referents and sought to suppress their own black identities.[9] Black behavioral adaptation in America, including modes of socializing children, have often had the character of responses to oppression, though these adaptations were strengths in that they made survival possible; at the same time, they were weaknesses in that they sometimes prevented the development of positive black group consciousness and effective social action toward collective ends because many of these techniques were predominantly individualistic in orientation. The 1960's and early 1970's saw a number of attempts by blacks to cope with their "double consciousness" more effectively by promoting a synthesis of positive individual identity and positive group identity, group cohesion, and collective action for group goals.

SOCIAL CLASS

According to the sociologist Andrew Billingsley, the black community in America is much more complex and highly stratified than is generally realized. Using criteria of income, employment, and education, Billingsley divides the black community into three social-class groups, each comprising several subgroups. The upper and middle classes account for approximately 50 per cent of black families (10 per cent and 40 per cent, respectively), according to Billingsley. The various subgroups of the lower class, differentiated on the basis of occupational history and security of the heads of families, income, and education, consist of the "working nonpoor," the "working poor," and the "nonworking poor."[10] The heads of working poor families are employed in semiskilled, unskilled, or service occupations and have marginal incomes; by 1975 standards this would mean yearly incomes in the $4,000–$6,000 range, on the average. A simple fact of life is that a large proportion of black parents who work do not and cannot earn enough money to support their families adequately. In 1970, for example, the Bureau of Labor Statistics estimated that a family of four needed at least $7,183 per year to sustain a "decent mini-mum" standard of living in New York City (the necessary national urban average was $6,960). This sum would require the family income-earner to work fifty weeks a year, forty hours a week, at a rate of $3.50 per hour. But 60 per cent of the manufacturing jobs in New York City—jobs filled to a great extent by blacks—paid less than this hourly rate.[11] And most low-income families are unable to find enough work to occupy more than one "full-time-equivalent" member. By 1972, the Bureau of Labor Statistics had increased the yearly income needed for minimally decent living by an urban family of four to $7,386; yet at that time 54 per cent of the four-person black families in the nation's cities had gross yearly earnings of less than this amount (and this does not account for families with more than four members).[12] This means that 54 per cent of such families were unable to achieve what the government defines as the threshold of *decent* urban poverty and thus might be classified as poor. (Our focus here is on children from working poor and nonworking poor families, those segments of the black population that are most often written about.[13] We hope to portray the diversity and complexity of these children more adequately than has been done to date.)

The working poor and nonworking poor black families we knew varied both in their level of income at any point in time and in the stability of income over time, two factors contributing to a relative sense of economic security or insecurity. In addition, these families varied in their ability to cope with problems, on the basis of such criteria as: Are the children being adequately fed, though not necessarily on a particular schedule? Is the family meeting its obligations so that it is not forced to be rather continually on the move? Are the relationships between children and the adults who care for them relatively enduring? Is there a relative predictability or pattern in the placing of children in the care of adults other than biological parents? Are the relationships between the adults in the children's home relatively enduring? Are the children getting into much more trouble than other children in the neighborhood? Variations in income level and stability did not appear to be necessarily related in a causal manner to variations in these life-style phenomena.

ETHNICITY AND CLASS

The children we shall discuss live in a world in which ethnicity and class intersect. That is, they experience the world simultaneously as black Americans and as poor Americans, and, as they grow up, they come to see a connection between the two statuses—that to be black increases the likelihood of being and remaining poor. Of course, there is a difference between being poor and feeling poor. By the standards of Calcutta, the families our children came from may not be poor, but, measured against the standard of living supposed to be typical of Americans, as evidenced by families on television (especially the commercials), the families our children came from are poor.

After World War II it became fashionable to describe America as an affluent society and to believe that the vast majority of Americans enjoyed such material abundance that poverty was no longer a serious national problem.[14] But, in the early 1960's, poverty was "rediscovered."[15] And in the late 1960's and early 1970's, national attention focused increasingly on the fact that most Americans don't feel affluent after all— that, despite the unprecedented wealth of the country as a whole, most Americans are having a hard time making ends meet and staying out of debt.[16] In 1972, 44 per cent of urban white families and 74 per cent of urban black families were unable to achieve a yearly income of $11,446, the level the Bureau of Labor Statistics set as the lower limit required for a "moderately decent" urban life.[17]

Although many white families in our cities have risen above the income level required for a "minimally decent" life, they remain trapped between poverty and affluence. Many of them feel resentful toward blacks because they believe that most blacks are on welfare and are getting for nothing something for which the whites work hard. On the other hand, many whites also feel hostile toward black workers who compete with them for jobs or toward black school children and youth whom they see as threatening to take over their schools and disrupt their neighborhoods.

Although millions of whites have many real grievances relating to the distribution of wealth and power in America, market conditions and salary scales for black workers generally remain worse than those for white workers. The dollar gap between black and white families increased from about $2,500 in 1947 to about $3,600 in 1969. For young husband-wife families in which only the husband worked, the ratio of black median income to white was 71 per cent in 1969, no significant change from the 75 per cent observed in 1959. During the 1970's incomes have been rising for both races, but the gap between the races is nevertheless widening because the income of whites is accelerating at a faster rate than that of blacks—and the buying power of the dollar is falling as prices rise rapidly. So much for "benign neglect."[18]

Discrimination in hiring and in wages contributes significantly to the relatively disadvantaged position of the urban black family as compared to whites. Although it is true that the poor school records of many blacks hinder them in finding well-paying jobs, it is also true that the educational prerequisites for many jobs are unrealistically high, unrelated to success on the job, and often designed to exclude blacks and other minorities.[19] The myth persists in America that white ethnics used schooling as a route to economic upward mobility. In truth, most white ethnics, as we have noted, remain trapped between poverty and affluence, and the route used by those who have achieved higher economic status usually was not schooling (Jews are a possible exception) but, rather, participation in the organized labor movement and employment in civil-service occupations.[20]

American trade unions, especially those in the skilled construction trades, succeeded in obtaining continuing increases in wages, but the higher-wage (more skilled) unions have always been more receptive to white workers than to blacks.

In Northern cities, European immigrants were hired preferentially over blacks as they arrived in large numbers during the late nineteenth and early twentieth centuries. Commenting on the position of black workers in the North, Mary Ovington observed in 1911, "If they are the only available source of labor, colored men can work by the side of white men; but where the white man strongly dominates the labor situation he tries to push his black brother into the jobs for which he does not care to compete."[21] And by 1968, the National Advisory Commission on Civil Disorders reported, "Employment is a key problem . . . despite continuing economic growth and declining national unemployment rates, the unemployment rate for Negroes in 1967 was more than double that for whites."[22]

The continuing association between black ethnicity and a seemingly permanent condition of urban poverty had many grim overtones in the lives of the children we knew. The shadows of unemployment, underemployment, and low wages haunted many families. While the number of children in families increased, family incomes often did not. The result was that many families grew poorer relative to the percentage of total income available for each person as more of their children reached school age. Many eventually arrived at the point where they could not make ends meet without public assistance. But welfare-eligibility rules often required that, in order for a family to receive aid, the father must have left the home. As a result, many fathers did leave (at least on paper) to make public assistance possible. Harlem school records indicated that there were more fifth- and sixth-grade children from homes with no fathers present than there were kindergarteners and first-graders in this predicament.

REGION OF SOCIALIZATION

Although the children we write about came up in cities of the Northeast, we believe that poor black children in the West and Midwest develop in essentially similar ways. Throughout this century, a large proportion of the black population left the South and settled in Northern and Western cities. During the same time, the Southern black population also became increasingly urban. Migration from the South increased during periods when economic opportunities in the North and West opened up for blacks and decreased (or reversed) when economic opportunities closed down.[23]

One of the most important effects of the Northern move is the changing behavior of low-income black parents toward their children. As blacks moved North, there was a relative decline in socialization practices designed to make black children fearful of whites, deferential toward them, and inhibited in expressing aggression or self-assertion around whites.[24] These changes in socialization practices, reflected especially in the experiences of young black males, were a response to the change from the overt racism of parts of the South to the more covert, ambiguous forms prevalent in the North. The Northern variety of racism generally was less stultifying in its effects on black behavior.

Northern socialization during the 1960's was related to more open expressions of anger or even rage than were seen in the South. The Southern civil-rights movement of the late 1950's and early 1960's was aggressive but rather moderate compared to the riots of the mid- and late 1960's in Northern and Western cities. The earlier Southern black protest appeared to draw its participants from the better-educated, upwardly mobile sectors of the black community. In contrast, the urban riots of the North and West increasingly involved a wide spectrum of low-income black youth. Riots and other forms of protest and ideological rhetoric apparently contributed to an atmosphere that became more open to self-assertion and expressions of antiwhite anger. At another level, these phenomena may have created a climate in which personal identity development was increasingly wedded to rising political and ethnic consciousness. This atmosphere had to have an impact upon black children.

ENVIRONMENT OF SOCIALIZATION

The children we shall describe lived in the densely populated inner-city areas of large urban complexes. A number of factors associated with living poor in urban communities appear to be significant influences upon the behavior of these children.

One such factor is housing. Most of the children we knew lived in old buildings in need of significant repair and renovation, often lacking heat or hot water. In the cold Northern winter, many inner-city apartments were freezing. In the hot summer, they were sweatboxes, and often there was no running water at all. We do not know the precise effects on children of months of living in an extremely cold or hot apartment, but we believe that housing temperature can make children listless or irritable.

Many of the children we knew lived in crowded apartments and attended crowded schools. They seemed accustomed to continuous contact with other people, but there were times when they wished to be alone.

A by-product of crowding is noise. Many of the children lived in very noisy apartments. Sometimes a television set was left running continuously to amuse small children while a radio or phonograph played loudly in another room. Apartment walls did not stop assorted sounds from neighbors' apartments or the streets from penetrating one's own apartment. It was not uncommon for children to come to school very tired in the morning and inform their teacher that they had not slept well the night before because it was too noisy in their building or on their block. Together with the overcrowding, the noise of their immediate environments probably overstimulated many of the children.

Compared to small towns, cities have always been places where behavioral norms break down or are harder to enforce. The children we knew were exposed to much behavior considered deviant by the larger society and by many in their own community. They saw junkies, pushers, winos, hustlers, pimps, prostitutes, and an assortment of other "street people" in their neighborhood. Some of these people had been defeated by life and sought escapist solutions. Others were "making it" and might be regarded as heroes by many children. Street life provided excitement, entertainment, and camaraderie; it also provided violence, trouble, and pain. Children flirted with street danger, experimented with street stimulation, developed street awareness and smartness. Their attraction to the pernicious environment of the streets worried many parents, who sought to prevent the children from being lost to them. But the streets were there, and they played an important role in the socialization of the children.

The few children we knew who did not live in old buildings lived in densely populated high-rise city projects. Although project apartments were usually more comfortable than those in old buildings, and many of the more upwardly mobile families lived in the projects, the high-rise buildings themselves seemed to foster a peculiar sense of alienation. The apartments seemed to be both havens and fortresses for many families frightened by activities in project corridors, elevators, stairwells, and courtyards, where people could be caught alone and defenseless and could become victims of the considerable criminal activity in the area. The high-rise projects, though densely populated, seemed to produce a sense of isolation among tenant families, rather than a sense of community. Parents often were particularly anxious about permitting younger children to play unsupervised in project courtyards. The children would be "too far away," out of sight many floors below.

The children we knew spent a great deal of time in the company of their peers, in the streets as well as in school. The peer group became a potent socializing force quite early in the children's school years. This force soon overshadowed the influence of parents and teachers for most of the children.

The urban communities in which the children lived were inhabited mostly by black people. In the early 1960's, however, most of the property in these communities was owned by whites, and most of the institutions were controlled by whites. Since the mid-1960's, there has been considerable progress toward creating or restoring black ownership of local business establishments and local community control of such institutions as schools. In the economic and political spheres, however, blacks still lack effective control over such community institutions as housing policy and law enforcement. Many blacks are convinced that whites may try to force them out of inner-city areas if they decide that they want the property for themselves because of its strategic location in relation to midtown business areas. Urban renewal in that case could mean black removal. In this view, scatter-site housing could be a political move to disperse the more upwardly mobile blacks and thus weaken promising concentrations of black political power. Many blacks see political and cultural genocide as the inevitable outcome of such "integration." In their own communities, many blacks see the hard-drug epidemic and the seeming inability (unwillingness?) of law-enforcement agencies to stop it as symptomatic of the desire of whites to continue to enslave black minds, to discourage black youth from striving for independence by keeping them nodding on the corner or locked in prison cells—the Master's way of cooling reform or revolutionary ardor in the inhabitants of his interior colonies.

TIME

The time dimension is related to our study of black child development in two ways. First, in contrast to the static approach typical of American psychology, we view the children over a period of time; thus we see them in the process of becoming, moving from early childhood toward adolescence. Although we shall describe the children as we saw them at various points, we shall go beyond these descriptions to consider possible lines of differentiation in the children's development. The first time dimension, then, concerns changes in individuals related to the passage of time.

The second time dimension concerns the relationship of individuals and groups to their historical time period. The 1960's was a time of rapid social change. As a result of such events as the civil-rights movement, the urban riots, the black power movement, and the assassination of Martin Luther King, many black people were drawn into a process of change that might be called the Negro-to-black revolution. This movement involves a change in self-definition and affirmation of new cultural referents and values. We are concerned with it here in two senses. First, how did this cultural movement affect children when it first caught them, in the mid- to late 1960's? How did they change in response to the historical and cultural changes going on around them? Second, what is the effect of the revolution on urban blacks growing up today? Young black children today have available a wider array of visible black role models and heroes as figures for identification than did children who grew up in an earlier time. Older blacks often had to discover their blackness in an emotionally tumultuous manner, throwing off previously accepted antiblack identifications and referents during adolescence or adulthood. Today the more psychologically liberated blacks present new role models, as parents and teachers, enabling young black children to discover their blackness in a positive context early in life.

The Negro-to-black revolution is an on-going movement, still affecting many adults who have reached different levels of black awareness. Most pertinent to our concerns, it is a movement that has effected, and continues to effect, changes in the familial and community atmospheres in which urban black children are being socialized.

Although we have focused here on some of the factors that make life difficult for low-income urban blacks, we do not view their lives as necessarily characterized by constant turmoil or perpetual grimness. Many low-income blacks display considerable strength in coping with urban stresses—not only reactive fortitude and intelligence, but also an openness to feeling. The children we describe are complex personalities with skills and deficiencies, hopes and fears, joys and sorrows. We hope that we neither exaggerate their difficulties and weaknesses nor romanticize their world and their strengths.

NOTES

1. Milton Gordon, *Assimilation in American Life* (New York: Oxford University Press, 1964).
2. *Ibid.*, p. 29. Emphasis in original.
3. See Vernon J. Dixon and Badi G. Foster, *Beyond Black or White: An Alternate America* (Boston: Little, Brown, 1971); see also Ivan Van Sertima, "African Linguistic and Mythological Structures in the New World," in Rhoda L. Goldstein, ed., *Black Life and Culture in the United States* (New York: Thomas Y. Crowell, 1971), pp. 12–35.
4. See Joseph White, "Toward a Black Psychology," in Reginald L. Jones, ed., *Black Psychology* (New York: Harper & Row, 1972), pp. 43–50.
5. See Gordon, *Assimilation in American Life.*
6. See *ibid.*, and also Lewis H. Carlson and George A. Colburn, eds., *In Their Place: White America Defines Her Minorities, 1850–1950* (New York: John Wiley & Sons, 1972).
7. Andrew M. Greeley, *Why Can't They Be Like Us?: America's White Ethnic Groups* (New York: E. P. Dutton, 1971).
8. W. E. B. DuBois, *The Souls of Black Folk* (New York: Fawcett Publications, 1961; originally published in 1903), pp. 16–17.

9. See William E. Cross, Jr., *"Discovering the Black Referent: The Psychology of Black Liberation,"* in Dixon and Foster, *Beyond Black or White,* pp. 95–110, and Albert Memmi, *The Colonizer and the Colonized* (Boston: Beacon Press, 1965).

10. Andrew Billingsley, *Black Families in White America* (Englewood Cliffs, N.J.: Prentice-Hall, 1968); see also Herbert B. Hill, *The Strengths of Black Families* (New York: Emerson Hall, 1972).

11. William Spring, Bennett Harrison, and Thomas Vietorisz, "Crisis of the Underemployed," *New York Times Magazine,* November 5, 1972, pp. 42–60.

12. *New York Times,* August 26, 1973, p. 44.

13. For information on urban black families at higher economic levels—the working nonpoor and the lower middle class—see John H. Scanzoni, *The Black Family in Modern Society* (Boston: Allyn & Bacon, 1971), which focuses exclusively on conventionally stable families: families with a husband in the home.

14. See, for example, John Kenneth Galbraith, *The Affluent Society* (Boston: Houghton Mifflin, 1958).

15. Michael Harrington, *The Other America* (New York: Macmillan, 1963).

16. See Richard Parker, *The Myth of the Middle Class* (New York: Liveright, 1972).

17. *New York Times,* August 26, 1973, p. 44.

18. U.S. Department of Commerce, Bureau of the Census, *The Social and Economic Status of Negroes in the United States,* Special Studies, No. 103 (Washington, D.C., July, 1971); *New York Times,* July 28, 1974, p. 9.

19. See Ivar Berg, *Education and Jobs: The Great Training Robbery* (New York: Praeger, 1970).

20. See Colin Greer, *The Great School Legend* (New York: Basic Books, 1972), and Michael B. Katz, *Class, Bureaucracy, and Schools: The Illusion of Educational Change in America* (New York: Praeger, 1971).

21. Mary W. Ovington, *Half a Man: The Status of the Negro in New York* (New York: Schocken, 1969), p. 93.

22. *Report of the U.S. National Advisory Commission on Civil Disorders* (New York: Bantam Books, 1968), p. 13.

23. See Karl E. Taeuber, "Negro Population and Housing: Demographic Aspects of a Social Accounting Scheme," in Irwin Katz and Patricia Gurin, eds., *Race and the Social Sciences* (New York: Basic Books, 1969), pp. 145–93.

24. See Robert L. Crain and Carol Sachs Weisman, *Discrimination, Personality, and Achievement: A Survey of Northern Blacks* (New York: Seminar Press, 1972); David O. Sears and John B. McConahay, "Racial Socialization, Comparison Levels, and the Watts Riot," *Journal of Social Issues,* 26 (1970): 121–40; and T. M. Tomlinson, "Ideological Foundations for Negro Action: A Comparative Analysis of Militant and Nonmilitant Views of the Los Angeles Riot," *Journal of Social Issues,* 26 (1970): 93–119.

2 / SOCIALIZATION AND ITS DISCONTENTS: A MACRO VIEW

The child-centered orientation characteristic of middle-class white America, stressing the importance of a long, protected childhood, developed as increasing numbers of whites moved up economically. But until three centuries ago Western children were not typically sheltered from "real life." Not seen as particularly different from adults—"special"—they entered the adult world when they could do useful work. Even during this century, the labor of children was an important source of income for urban families; instead of staying in school, they worked.[1] Even today, it is not uncommon for working- and lower-middle-class boys to be employed for wages after school and on weekends during the late elementary and junior high school years.[2] As the productivity of the American economy has increased, fewer young laborers have been needed. Thus, the children of a large portion of the white middle class have become able to enjoy lengthy periods of dependency even to young adulthood.

The seemingly permanent state of poverty in which large numbers of urban blacks find themselves does not encourage a sentimental view of childhood. Parents cannot protect their children from many of the harsh realities of life for low-income blacks. They often have to depend upon the children to help in the care of younger siblings, housekeeping, marketing, and other domestic responsibilities. Partly because of the stringency of life for the urban poor, and perhaps partly because of a continuing non-Western orientation, there is relatively little separation between adults and children in many realms of experience in poor black communities. Many Harlem children we knew frequently shared adult responsibilities and worries over survival problems, such as family illness and the lack of money for needed items. They also participated with adults in parties and other "good times" in which various dimensions of adult behavior were open to the eyes and ears of the children.

We observed many behaviors among young children in Harlem that were imitative of what they saw and heard among adults and youth. Children in kindergarten classes, for example, often skillfully imitated the latest dancing style current among youth and adults in the community. It was not uncommon to hear kindergarteners discuss boy-girl pairing off—who was "going with" whom. On one occasion we watched two prekindergarten girls playing in a household corner. One of the children told us that the conically shaped blocks they were using in their play represented wine bottles. "We gonna drink some wine," she said.

The children also learned, at an early age, that they could not long remain very dependent upon adults for emotional support. Some of the children, as early as their elementary school years, attempted to relate to adults as equals, increasingly asserting their independence over crumbling adult authority.[3] Another group of children tended to withdraw from people and to become rather submissive. But most of them seemed to cling ambivalently to adults and to make great demands for adult attention, demands that were frequently frustrated. Whatever the dominant mode of response, almost all the children faced the common situation of limited opportunity to be dependent upon adults, to be cared for and protected in a warm and consistent manner.

Through their elementary school years, we observed the children's development of a pervasive mistrust of adults. This mistrust extended not only to the white adults in school, as it gradually became clear to the children that whites frustrated and oppressed blacks in this society; even earlier, mistrust was focused upon adults much closer to the children, who, the children came to realize, were unable or unwilling to provide the nurturance and protection the children desired.

As they progressed through the elementary school years, many of the children appeared to be less strongly attached to, or emotionally dependent upon, adults than their middle-class counterparts, black and white. This characteristic probably derived, at least in part, from the fact that in many cases the mother worked full time, often without a husband to share the burdens of financial and emotional support for the children. It was common for the children to spend the hours between school dismissal and bedtime in the care of a grandmother, an aunt, an older sibling, or a neighbor.

The children experienced a variety of family arrangements to provide and care for them. Some came from two-parent nuclear families; some came from one-parent families in which the mother's boyfriend might live, regularly or irregularly; some came from homes in which relatives other than biological parents lived; some came from families that had mutual-helping relationships with unrelated residents or members of other families living outside the household. All these arrangements could, and did, supply physical care for children. Many of the children had a number of adults or older siblings who served as parents, as potential sources of support, guidance, and protection. For some children, having many parent figures to rely upon provided enough security so that reduced opportunities to be dependent upon a mother did not produce severe distress. For most of the children, however, relationships with adults seemed to be predominantly ungratifying, and emotional bonds with adults appeared to be rather tenuous.

Most of the children we observed changed moods frequently and pouted or appeared sullen and dejected a great deal of the time. This was true even of children who were well dressed and physically well cared for. The children's tendency toward sullenness and dejection was exacerbated by their often frustrating school experiences. However, we saw the same mood shifts in playgrounds, parks, and the streets, though the children generally appeared to be livelier there than inside the school setting. We therefore concluded that they cannot be dismissed simply as a reaction to school.

Although they were nominally supervised by a relative or neighbor, many of the children typically spent most of the time between school dismissal and bedtime in the streets in relatively autonomous peer groups. In a study of the afterschool and home activities of inner-city children (black and white) in New York City, Suzanne Keller found that both first- and fifth-graders showed a pattern of little sustained contact with adults and little shared family activity.[4] Urie Bronfenbrenner argues that such a pattern characterizes the lives of school-age children from most urban and suburban American families today and cuts across ethnic and class lines.[5] Our observations lead us to conclude that this pattern begins to be apparent at a younger age and becomes more intense during the elementary school years in poor inner-city families than in more affluent urban and suburban families.

The parents of children in our fifth- and sixth-grade classes in Harlem commonly complained that they seemed unable to exert any continuing strong influence over their children's behavior or development. Fathers as well as mothers expressed their frustration in attempting to control their children. The parents complained that the children, particularly boys, would not "listen" to them, that they were spending too much time with "bad" boys and girls, that parental warnings and beatings seldom seemed to change the children's behavior in the desired direction. Several grandmothers who were responsible for watching the children while their daughters were away from home complained about the "bad disposition" of a grandchild (usually male), remarking that the child had never known his daddy, but it looked as though he was nevertheless turning out just like him.

Similar observations regarding parent-child relations in low-income urban black communities have been reported by researchers in other cities. For example, Hylan Lewis, a black sociologist, found that in Washington, D.C., influences outside the family were more important and became effective earlier in the socialization of children of low-income families than of adequate-income families:

> In many study families, the effects of external influences are reflected in the strikingly early appearance of cut-off points in parental control and emotional support—in the falling off of parents' confidence in their ability —as well as in their will to control and give attention to their children. For practical purposes, the immediate point of interest is that changes in control, and in self-estimates of ability to control, occur when the children are as young as five or six.[6]

The early exposure of children to influences from outside the family and severe strains in parent-child relationships are also reported in a study of a predominantly white sample of "disorganized" lower-class families in Boston.[7] These phenomena appear to be largely a function of the severe stresses that characterize a life of urban poverty, cutting across ethnic lines. Nevertheless, we believe that the combination of black ethnicity and urban poverty creates some special socialization requirements that might not be apprehended by focusing only on the commonalities of low-income life.

The children's sullenness and their early assertions of independence from adult control disturbed most of their parents; yet these characteristics seemed to derive mostly from the socialization practices the parents typically employed. The children seemed to mistrust adults because they saw them as unreliable sources of nurturance and protection. This perception coincided with a sharp decrease in the individual attention, nurturance, and protection offered by adults as the children grew older. In our judgment, the parents' behavior in almost all cases was not a reflection of lack of love and concern for children but seemed to be determined by several factors, often in interaction with one another.

For one thing, the heavy burdens the parents carried in attempting to fulfill their responsibilities in the face of economic difficulties, interpersonal conflicts, and racist institutions seemed to drain their energy supplies and their ability or willingness to pay attention to their children. Another important factor relates to the parents' concern about the future prospects for their children in an economically exploitative and racist society. Parents who expected the society to close many opportunities to their children and frustrate their aspirations because the children were black did what seemed necessary to them to prepare their children for a life of hardship. Many parents, by withdrawing individual attention somewhat abruptly while the children were still young, taught them a bitter but adaptive lesson—to be suspicious of the goodness of others, to anticipate disappointment. In low-income families with many children, these factors might be exacerbated by the need for young children to become able to care for themselves as quickly as possible so that the mothers could devote their attention to still younger children and infants.

Compared to typical middle-class children, black and white, the elementary school children we observed in Harlem generally appeared to be remarkably self-reliant and independent. Low-income black children in inner cities generally grow up fast; they develop characteristics that are functional and help them adapt to a life of hardship. But many seem to pay a price for their success in adapting in the form of ambivalence toward adults (and toward people in general) and the development of a sullen disposition in which feelings of frustration and rage are contained but are often easily triggered into explosive outbursts.

Joyce Ladner, a black sociologist, observed the development of low-income black children in St. Louis. She faced the same problem we did in describing such children in Harlem; how to present the children in such a manner that the characteristics that result from their successful adaptation to a difficult life are not described as unqualified strengths or weaknesses but, rather, as strengths that can be weaknesses and weaknesses that can be strengths. She notes the

> . . . great need for a new perspective and definition on what consequences for particular types of behavior should be viewed as healthy and which ones as pathological. Such a reinterpretation should enable social and behavioral analysts to view the black child, whose life has often been an unrelenting series of harsh experiences, as a more emotionally stable and well-integrated personality than his white middle-class counterparts, whose protected, sheltered lives are representations of the most fragile personality the society could produce.[8]

But adaptation to the "unrelenting series of harsh experiences" exacts a price:

> The societal canon of "childhood" is often unobserved to varying degrees because it is a luxury which many parents cannot afford. Parents in the black community are often unable to protect their young children from harsh social forces, which protection would ensure that they grow up in this "safe period" emerging relatively unscarred.[9]

Like Ladner, we found that many Harlem children developed resources of strength, toughness, callousness, and even brutishness, which equipped them to survive. But these very characteristics had the effect of interfering with adult control and influence over the children. Neither the threat of withdrawal of emotional support nor fear of a beating (after a while) could make many of the children obedient to adult direction or keep them away from the peer and street influences parents feared.

SOCIAL CLASS AND SOCIALIZATION

The characteristics of low-income urban black children described above are congruent with the attitudes toward parents typically expressed by children from lower-class groups in America. One study revealed that lower-class children were the most ambivalent in their feelings toward parents.[10] Upper-class children were more variable; some expressed highly positive attitudes toward parents while others expressed highly negative attitudes. Lower-class children more often see their parents as repressive, uninterested in the needs of the children, severe, and unreasonable; thus, lower-class children are more likely to be ambivalent toward authority figures in general than are middle-class children. Middle-class children generally express the most positive attitudes toward their parents and people in authority positions.

Family size is a factor that can exacerbate these trends. As the number of children in a family increases, mothers necessarily become less attentive to, and indulgent of, the individual children.[11] This finding corroborates the earlier conclusions of James Bossard,[12] who found that in large families the emphasis is on the group, not the individual. From this tendency may come both deprivation and security: When questioned, large-family children seldom mentioned parents as the source of their security; rather, they found security in their siblings, who formed a cohesive group for defense, playing, confiding, teaching, even plotting against parents. For children from small families, security came directly from parents, from what they did for and gave to the child.

A sentimental, child-centered orientation to socialization gained widespread acceptance among American middle-class families after the end of World War II. This trend was associated with the movement toward smaller families in the 1950's and 1960's, the rise of many families out of the stringent economic circumstances of the Depression years, the increasing educational level attained by mothers, and the impact of child-rearing experts (such as Dr. Spock) who advised a more child-centered, permissive approach. Mothers from middle-class families, who tended to have more schooling and to live more comfortably, were more likely to read and heed the advice of experts counseling a child-centered approach than were low-income mothers, whose economic circumstances remained more precarious and whose socialization techniques remained more traditional.[13] During the 1960's, white middle-class mothers were regularly exposed to literature giving advice on childrearing. This trend seemed to be less pronounced for the black middle-class and the white working-class, and it was clearly more the exception than the rule for the black working class.[14] Given the need to socialize their children so that they might survive hardship, it is unlikely that many low-income urban black mothers would perceive much of the child-centered, permissive approach as functional or realistic for themselves and their children.

It is important to relate modes of socialization to social class because, even though classes are not clearly discrete or discontinuous groups in America, differences in the amount and stability of income, nature and security of employment, area of residence, and level of education all contribute to different basic conditions of life for families, which the term *class* implies. Melvin L. Kohn argues that, although middle-class and working-class parents share many core values, there are characteristic clusters of value choice in the two social classes: "Members of different social classes, by virtue of enjoying (or suffering) different conditions of life, come to see the world differently—to develop different conceptions of social reality, different aspirations and hopes and fears, different conceptions of the desirable."[15] Working-class parental values center on conformity to external prescriptions; middle-class parental values, on self-direction. For working-class parents, it is the overt act that matters; the child should follow externally imposed rules. To middle-class parents, it is the child's motives and feelings that matter; he should learn to govern himself.

A comparison of the socialization practices valued and used by two groups of black mothers, a lower-lower-class group (receiving public assistance) and a middle-class group (defined according to husband's occupation), yielded some differences in line with the class distinctions proposed by Kohn.[16] Although the basic child-rearing goals and values of the two groups were quite similar, middle-class black mothers expected obedience to be combined with considerateness, an internalized moral orientation, whereas low-income black mothers stressed complete obedience to those in authority, a more external orientation. Middle-class black mothers were observed to reward children for behaving in desirable ways considerably more frequently than did low-income black mothers. The middle-class mothers were more likely to initiate interaction with children and to communicate affection verbally and nonverbally. These differences represent differences in the probability of behaving toward children in a certain way; they are not absolute differences, since mothers from each group behave at times in a manner more typical of mothers from the other group. A factor that may have affected the behavior of the mothers was the presence (or lack) of a husband to share childrearing responsibilities. A husband was present in all of the middle-class homes, but in only 25 per cent of the lower-class homes. (Our observations in Harlem, as well as research carried out in a large city in northern New Jersey,[17] indicate that such factors as the availability [or absence] of a male to share responsibility and variations in family income contribute to subtle but significant differences in childrearing practices.)

When the low-income parents we knew in Harlem directed individualized attention to their children, it was often in the context of attempts to control and regulate their behavior, and often through the use of physical punishment. Working mothers who had to be away from their children all day quite commonly threatened them with severe beatings if they should find out upon their return that the children had misbehaved in any way. Threats of beatings followed many children through the day like dark clouds over their heads. Often, when a young child soiled his clothes or committed some other transgression, one of his peers would call out, "Oooh—you gonna get a beatin'!"

Parents used threats and physical punishments freely in attempting to control their children—the traditional lower-class approach. The parents focused upon overt actions and demanded obedience far more than they concerned themselves with the children's motives and feelings. Certain conditions of their lives made this approach seem to them necessary and functional to ensure the well-being of their children. Parents frequently worried that their children would be tempted or hurt by the dangers of inner-city streets (drugs, crime, traffic) and used methods that were sometimes quite harsh to restrict the children so as to prevent such encounters. In addition, many parents attempted to suppress the self-assertive tendencies of children, especially boys, lest they get into trouble with white teachers or police. The parents knew that their children could afford such trouble less than white children. They did not attempt to make the children as passive or deferential to whites as was traditional in the South, but the need to prepare the children to cope with white racism nevertheless affected their socialization practices. From the mid-1960's to the present, we observed a significant increase in attempts by parents to actively socialize black children into self-assertion.

Many Harlem parents had little patience with noisy, active children. A threat or a smack often was employed as the quickest method to force compliance with a directive. All parents employ these methods on occasion, but low-income parents in Harlem used them frequently.

Because they are "tuned in" to children's motives and feelings, more educated mothers frequently feel inadequate or guilty about threatening or hitting children, and they try to rely upon other methods.[18] Many working-class mothers also express regret at times about their tendency to be impatient with their children. But it appears that middle-class mothers perceive a greater obligation to be emotionally supportive of their children; lower-class mothers perceive a greater obligation to impose constraints. Middle-class mothers seem more likely to see their children's behavior as complex, requiring understanding; lower-class mothers see the children's behavior as mysterious, beyond understanding. Lower-class mothers are thus more likely to rely extensively upon authoritative guidance, threats, and beatings, hoping that they will influence the children to proper behavior, while middle-class mothers are more likely to try to make children think about the consequences of their behavior and accept responsibility for self-direction.[19]

Middle-class mothers may sometimes become so concerned with a child's inner dynamics that they attach unwarranted psychological significance to normal difficulties in child development and needlessly blame themselves for children's characteristics that they find upsetting. On the other hand, lower-class mothers are likely to overlook emotional difficulties of children, to perceive as unworkable any alternative to threatening and hitting children, and to feel bewildered and helpless if the children persist in disapproved behavior in spite of the employment of these methods.

In trying to determine the meaning of such parental behavior, we must consider the possibility that there may be different levels of meaning that all apply to the same behavior. Beyond the various socially shaped cognitive factors that guided the socialization practices of low-income parents in Harlem, there were, in our judgment, deeper emotional factors at work in at least a sizable minority. Perhaps because of the diminished emotional support that may have marked their own upbringing and the extensiveness of their contemporary burdens, some of the parents we knew apparently could not afford to give much attention and emotional support to their children. For such parents, the demands of growing children for personal attention rapidly drained their capacities for caring and giving. It is possible that physical fatigue from coping with high levels of environmental stress, exacerbated by vitamin and iron deficiencies, also reduced the energy level of many mothers and forced them to limit their energy allocation to the immediate demands of family survival and management. Such parents gave what they could to their children, but often they could give very little. The perception that the children's behavior was beyond their control or influence sometimes was in accord with the facts of the situation, but at times it seemed to be a rationalization for decreased involvement with the children.

For a variety of reasons, then, the parents of many of the children in our classes in Harlem seemed aware of, and bewildered by, their loss of effective control over their children and the increasing influence of peers and elements of street life. They usually did not regard themselves as rejecting parents, nor did they see any clear connection between their socialization techniques and the problems they were having with the children. The children, on the other hand, commonly mistrusted adults, experienced highly ambivalent feelings concerning dependency and affiliative desires in relation to adults, and saw adults as repressive and frustrating.

ETHNICITY, CLASS, AND SOCIALIZATION

Now that we have surveyed some of the characteristics of lower-class socialization, we shall consider some of the particular manifestations of these patterns within black communities and the relation between class and ethnicity in the socialization of low-income black children.

We do not know how the children we knew in Harlem were treated as infants. The mothers we talked to generally expressed confidence in their ability to take care of babies and did not seem to find baby care problematical. In the homes we visited in which babies were present, it appeared that they were offered abundant social stimulation by mothers, other adults, and siblings, who regarded babies as cute and interesting. A perception of children as difficult to cope with appeared to be reserved for older children, particularly later elementary school children, perhaps because older children resented the loss of attention when babies were brought home and the childrearing responsibilities were often thrust upon them.

Commenting on low-income black mothers in St. Louis, Rainwater observed:

Lower-class Negro women do not show the deep psychological involvement with infants and young children that is characteristic of higher social classes. They rarely manifest the anxious attention to children, the sense of awesome responsibility, along with the pleasure, that is characteristic of many working-class women. Nor do they have the sense of the instrumental, almost occupational, challenge of rearing children properly that is characteristic of the middle class. Among lower-class Negro women, taking care of babies is regarded as a routine activity which is not at all problematic.[20]

The main thrust of socialization of low-income toddlers and preschoolers in Harlem appeared to be to make them obedient, to control and regulate their functioning. This trend was particularly evident in large families in which growing children were expected to be obedient so as not to cause trouble for others in the home or disrupt the functioning of the household.

From about age three onward, low-income children in Harlem typically lost much of the attention and affection they had been receiving from adults and older siblings.[21] They appeared increasingly bothersome and annoying to adults and older siblings, and what attention they did receive was commonly nongratifying and frustrating, in the context of attempts by older people to suppress and restrict the young ones. The levels of emotional support available from adults showed a sharp decline as children grew out of toddlerhood, leaving many preschoolers apparently "starved for affection" and eager to gain almost any positive attention from an adult they could.

After age five or six, Harlem children commonly became more openly mistrustful and suspicious of adults. Much of the friendly, attention-demanding, clinging behavior of the younger children was superseded by ambivalent approach-withdrawal behavior toward adults. Many children seemed to be so mistrustful of adults that they often struggled to conceal their own desire to receive affection. Sullen withdrawal and avoidance behavior, marked by suppressed anger, became an increasingly typical response to adults as the children moved into the upper elementary school grades. This progression from open dependence and attention-seeking to increased separation from adults is partly a function of increasing maturation and has parallels in many communities. However, the intensity of the growing mistrust of adults, of ambivalent emotions, and of sullen, suppressed anger must be viewed in the context of coming up poor and black in an inner city in America.

During the preschool years, it appears, low-income children in Harlem commonly experience negative reactions from adults and older siblings to their attempts to gain attention and approval. Bids for recognition and affiliation often lead to verbal or physical rebuff. Exploration, manipulation of objects, and expressions of curiosity often are strongly discouraged by parents.

Restrictive and punitive treatment of children can occur in any American community. In fact, extremely punitive treatment of children is so widespread that, by conservative estimate, 2,000 to 3,000 children are injured and 40 to 60 are killed each month through mistreatment and abuse. The number of children under five years of age killed by parents each year may actually be higher than the number who die from disease.[22] The parents of such children come from a wide variety of educational, socio-economic, racial, and ethnic backgrounds; no one community has a monopoly on severe handling of children. In fact, Billingsley has reported that physical abuse of children is more common among the white low-income or welfare families he investigated than among the black low-income or welfare families in his sample.[23]

Although traditional interpretations have stressed the "mental illness" of the child beater, it may be that a high level of child abuse persists in the United States because, in spite of the child-centered orientation of many parents, there nevertheless remains a widespread belief in the use of physical force as a legitimate procedure in raising children. Many cases of injured children may be unintended consequences of traditional disciplinary measures taken by angry parents in response to perceived misconduct of children.

Even though Billingsley reports that low-income white parents are more likely to abuse their children physically than are their black counterparts, it was our observation that many of the parents we knew in Central Harlem used physical force frequently in attempting to restrain younger children and punish older ones. Children in our classes had been beaten with ironing cords, belts, clothes hangers, and shoes. The practice seemed to be so accepted among low-income black parents that they employed such methods without attempting to conceal the practice or its results. Parent-aides from the community who worked in Harlem schools often hit children who misbehaved. Parents who came to our classes often hit the children in front of their teachers and classmates. As the children grew older, some seemed so accustomed to beatings from adults that threats of further beatings (and the actuality of beatings) had little or no dissuading influence on the children.

Speaking to William Moore, Jr., a black social scientist who studied the everyday life of low-income blacks in an urban housing project in the Midwest, one mother expressed her view concerning beating children in public:

> As long as I feed him, I don't plan to use no psychology. I going to use this (ironing cord)! . . . and when he gets too big to whip he can get out and feed hisself. So why should I be embarrassed about where I make him mind? I'd be more embarrassed about standing in front of some judge somewhere begging him not to put him where his oldest brother is.[24]

We have observed the reactions of many Harlem mothers to their two- and three-year-old children in the family rooms of prekindergarten (Head Start) centers while waiting for their older children in classes nearby. During the time of observation, the mothers spoke very little to their younger children other than to say "stop" or "don't." Many of these mothers tried to restrain the children from using the toys in the room, left by the staff precisely for the children to play with. One mother, for example, held a rolled-up newspaper in her hand with which she would poke her little boy when he tried to move away from her in the direction of the toys. Other mothers took a variety of actions that seemed designed to repress movement, exploration, and vocalization in their young children.[25]

Several times we watched mothers visiting the prekindergarten classrooms of their four- and five-year-old children both in Harlem and on the Lower East Side of New York. On a few of these occasions the mothers stayed for an entire morning (about three hours). Unlike the lower-class Puerto Rican and Chinese parents or the few white parents (of varying social-class backgrounds) we observed in these classrooms, the black mothers typically engaged in very little verbal exchange with their children. Mothers of other ethnic groups spoke to their children more often, and in a manner that demanded a response. The black mothers did relatively little questioning of their children about how they were feeling or what they were doing. When the children were playing with toys or blocks, the black mothers commonly sat at the side of the room and watched the children without interacting with them.

On days when mothers did not stay in the pre-K classrooms, we observed another phenomenon. Lower-class black mothers typically brought their children to the door of the classroom and simply left them there; by contrast, other mothers generally brought the children inside, unbuttoned their coats, talked with them, and left them with some open display of affection.

This behavior of low-income black mothers has to be viewed in context. The mothers typically felt ill at ease in the school. The presence of whites may have been inhibiting, and the lack of affectionate displays, verbal instigation, and supportive interaction on the part of the black mothers toward their children may have been, in part, a reflection of a long-standing orientation to behave cautiously, with controlled emotions, around whites. On the basis of a participant-observation study in the homes of low-income black families in Washington, D.C., Camille Jeffers, a black social worker, reported that low-income black mothers may equate overt demonstrations of warmth and affection with spoiling children.[26] She argues, however, that such behavior has to be viewed in the light of the childrearing values to which the mothers give priority and weight. The values that take precedence for low-income black mothers are often related to independence training; as we have noted, mothers may withhold affection, not because they reject their children, but because they want to train them away from depending upon them, often in anticipation of another child's coming along.

In spite of their punitive orientation to children, low-income black mothers are not likely to threaten children with withdrawal or to withhold parental love as punishment.[27] Usually love, or at least family acceptance, is given unconditionally. Children simply are expected to adapt to demands for early self-reliance in a context of little opportunity to remain dependent upon adults, combined with adult punitiveness. This situation is made more difficult by the parents' inconsistency; at certain times the mother may be very harsh and inflexible in demanding obedience, while at other times she pays little attention to her children, who run wild without direction or punishment. It seemed to us that such inconsistency was due, at least in part, to the emotional swings of some mothers as well as to the waxing and waning of energy supplies in these overburdened women.

Studies indicate that white middle-class parents rely more on withdrawal of love in punishing children than white working-class parents, who rely more on physical discipline.[28] The effectiveness of withdrawal of love in influencing children's behavior depends upon the amount of nurturance; the less a child has to lose, the less effective the technique.[29] Moreover, middle-class parents' tendency to encourage emotional dependency is a mixed blessing, for it often becomes a tool for psychological manipulation of children. Threats of withdrawal of love for transgressions can stimulate deep anxieties in middle-class children. The low-income children we saw in Harlem were less frequently subjected to this threat and less susceptible to it, since they were less emotionally dependent upon their parents—who encouraged self-reliance rather than prolonged dependence. The most distressing aspect of physical punishment to a middle-class child might be the implied loss of love rather than the physical pain involved.

Parents' discouragement of emotional dependency generated ambivalent feelings in many low-income Harlem children, but the children generally learned to do without extensive emotional support from adults (though most would have preferred to receive more than they did).[30] Harlem schoolchildren, as a result, were generally less anxious about pleasing adults than most middle-class children are. They had less to lose emotionally by displeasing adults. Although the black children were frustrated and embittered by the physical punishment they often received, such punishment, particularly when it was administered inconsistently, did not make the children more eager to please.

The older siblings who frequently cared for younger ones generally had parental permission to discipline their charges. It appeared to us that these older siblings often reacted rather severely to the slightest "disobedience." This repressive treatment, which the younger siblings often seemed to resent, weakened the security that children in large families might have derived from dependence upon siblings in light of their highly restricted opportunities for dependence upon adults.

In order to appreciate the relationship between ethnicity, class, and certain socialization patterns, we must consider the special features of black American history. The brutal experience of slavery and continuing racism have made poverty different for blacks from poverty for white ethnics and have required special adaptations. During the years of slavery, black mothers had to live with the fear that their white owners might separate them from their children or husbands. This threat may have created a special need to socialize children away from dependence on one particular parent as soon as possible. Whether or not it originated in slavery, an orientation to push children away so that they could quickly learn to function independently served the contemporary needs of many low-income black mothers by preparing the children for a life of hardship and helping overburdened mothers to avoid emotional bankruptcy. These contemporary problems result from the continuing manifestation of the racism and economic exploitation that made American slavery possible in the first instance.

If various adults other than biological parents, and even older children, assumed parental roles and responsibilities toward children in slave communities, the child's relative inability to remain highly dependent upon one parent would not necessarily have left him with unmet dependency needs. Children thus reared might develop less intense dependency needs for one parent than a child reared in an isolated nuclear family, and they might derive security from the multiplicity of parent figures. Such a pattern of extended and augmented family relations, while adaptive to the American slave experience, might also have seemed natural to people with cultural ties to West Africa, where family life tends to be integrated with widening levels of kinship and community.[31]

In the rural South today, many black families continue to live in extended and augmented families. Cooperative helping relationships between families are common, and older children participate responsibly in the rearing of younger ones. Such sharing of activities, hardships, and pleasures gives children a feeling of community acceptance and belongingness, which mitigates any insecurity related to a lack of opportunity to be dependent upon one particular parent.

In the rural South, there tended to be a common denominator to low-income black family life; various members of a family tended to share the same activities and views of reality, and from family to family, life was lived in much the same way.

With migration to Northern cities, some of the positive features of life in the rural South are lost to low-income black children, or at least diluted. Although contemporary low-income black families in Northern cities may have relatives or friends living in the same house or neighborhood, and even though mutual-aid arrangements are worked out pragmatically, the adolescent and adult members of a given household often go their separate ways, and family solidarity often is quite elusive.[32] Mutual-aid patterns within and between families often are based more on economic necessity than on a shared value system:

> The behavior of the bulk of [urban] poor Negro families appears as pragmatic adjustments to external and internal stresses and deprivations experienced in the quest for essentially common values. A seeming paradox is that affirmation . . . of some of America's traditional virtues and values . . . is found to be strong and recurrent among even the most deprived of Negro families.

The question of the existence of a shared value system as a basis for urban black family life is more complicated:

> [T]here are several modes or styles of family living and child-rearing rather than a single or basic mode or style among urban Negroes. We are especially impressed by the range of behavior within the low-income category of Negro families. . . . Our view is that it is probably more fruitful to think of different types of low-income Negro families reacting in various ways to the facts of their position and to relative isolation rather than to the imperatives of a lower-class or significantly different ethnic culture. It is important that we do not confuse the basic life chances and actual behavior of the contemporary Negro parent with his basic cultural values and preferences.[33]

Commenting upon the strength of value commitment of low-income blacks to ghetto-specific life-styles and behaviors, such as extended and augmented family arrangements, Hannerz argues that they may be learned through incidental observation of personally significant ghetto residents, thus becoming part of one's possible behavioral repertoire—through cultural transmission—even if one does not strongly value them.[34] And yet personal observations of such frequently occurring ghetto-specific modes of behavior are apt to increase a child's readiness to accept such modes as morally appropriate, as well as useful. Hence, the simultaneous presence of both mainstream and ghetto-specific household arrangements in low-income black communities may enable (or force) some developing individuals to refrain from sustained strong commitment to either one. Movement between these choices is therefore probable when social and economic circumstances fluctuate.

A recent strong argument for the existence of collective adaptations to poverty among urban black families arises from Stack's anthropological study of "domestic strategies" of second generation urban blacks, many of whom were reared on public welfare. They, in turn, are raising their own children on public welfare in the poorest section of a black community in a Midwestern city. The web of family life characteristically is spread over several kin-based households; fluctuations in their composition do not seriously affect cooperative family arrangements:

> A consequence of the elasticity of residence patterns is that, even when persons move to separate households, their social, economic, and domestic lives are so entwined with other kin that they consider themselves simultaneously a part of the residential groupings of their kin. Kin expect to help one another out. That one can repeatedly join the households of kin is a great source of security among those living in poverty, and they come to depend upon it. The loyalties toward kinsmen offset, to some degree, the self-defeating ordeal of unemployment and poverty.[35]

The number of people who take on a parental role expands to close kinsmen and friends. Close kin may fully cooperate in childrearing at times when they are living apart. Moreover, children are sometimes given to nonrelatives "who express love, concern, and a desire to keep the child." In general, Stack asserts, what may appear to be a random movement of individuals between dwellings and a randomizing of parental rights and responsibilities is not in fact haphazard.

Perhaps this cooperative kin system represents a model of creative adaptions to racism and poverty. Extended and augmented familial networks ensure that children are systematically cared for in some way, even though such arrangements evidence much tension and strife. Nevertheless, our observations and our reading of Stack's data suggest that many ghetto children experience strong feelings of ambivalence and insecurity arising out of a relative lack of consistency, stability, and predictability in their daily lives.

Like family solidarity, community solidarity also may seem elusive in inner-city areas, where a variety of black family types—two-parent nuclear, one-parent, and extended and augmented—often live side by side, some on welfare, some working poor, and some working nonpoor. Families with different income levels and structural forms do not necessarily identify with one another. Families with differing life-styles may view one another suspiciously, even antagonistically.[36]

In low-income black households of the urban North, the needs of adult members of the household tend to become the focal points of many household activities rather than those of children.[37] Grandmothers and older children may assume primary childrearing and domestic responsibilities while older adolescents and young adults participate in social (as well as work) activities that either exclude old folks and children or simply ignore them. The mutually supportive atmosphere of rural Southern extended families is seriously weakened in the urban North; hence, school-age children in the North are more likely to have a sense of being on their own. The sense of being on one's own may be mitigated by sibling interdependence, if the relationship is not marked by frequent punitiveness. Early peer associations and affiliations also seem to offer young school-age children an opportunity for social acceptance and support.

During slavery, slaveowners held the power of life and death over black children. Slave mothers had a special need to suppress initiative and aggression, particularly in male children. And although slavery ended more than a hundred years ago, continuing white racism, aggression toward blacks, and economic exploitation of blacks, particularly in the rural South, kept elements of the slave-mother orientation alive, particularly the need to suppress male initiative and aggression. In the early 1960's, a black mother in the South expressed to psychiatrist Robert Coles her perception of the need to restrain the behavior of her children and to demand severe restraint and obedience, particularly when in the presence of whites:

> White people are a real danger to us until we learn how to live with them. So if you want your kids to live long, they have to grow up scared of whites; and the way they get scared is through us; and that's why I don't let my kids get fresh about the white man even in their own house. If I do there's liable to be trouble to pay. They'll forget, and they'll say something outside and that'll be it for them, and us too.[38]

In a study in the late 1960's, black mothers in the rural South said they whipped their children for aggressive behavior more than for any other reason.[39] A larger proportion of black than white mothers reported whipping their children for being aggressive (61 per cent *vs.* 37 per cent, respectively). Inconsistent with the traditional view, however, was the finding that mothers of black girls reported whipping them for aggression more often than mothers of boys (65 per cent *vs.* 56 per cent, respectively).

Although social patterns are changing, even today many poor black parents in the rural South are still "cutting down" their young children, largely from force of habit.[40] Even though extreme suppression of the spontaneity of black children is no longer necessary, rural black parents, particularly older ones, are not always convinced that this is the case and often deal with the children as if they had to spend the rest of their lives on the white man's plantation.

Although blocked from expressing overt hostility toward whites, blacks in the South developed many means of expressing hostility covertly. The more ambiguous forms of racism of the Northern cities offered greater independence from whites and more opportunities for open displays of hostility with less fear of reprisal.[41] Children in Harlem were encouraged to defend themselves against aggression, to hold their own without depending upon adults. Nevertheless, as we have noted, the Harlem mothers we knew appeared to be particularly anxious that their children appear well behaved and obedient when in the company of white teachers, white administrators, or other parents. They were more restrictive of their children and less openly supportive or affectionate than other mothers in the same setting.

Commenting on the bitter burden of preparing children, particularly sons, to face the hard life even in the North, Grier and Cobbs, two black psychiatrists, made the following observations in 1968:

> . . . who would say it is so very different now? Must not the black mother warn her child against travel to certain parts of the nation? Does she not fear that any involvement with the police may result in the forfeiture of his life? And does she not know that there remains a national purpose to keep him poor, ill housed, ill trained and available for the exploitation of his labor? The differences are quantitative, not qualitative, and the mother now and then takes a long, hard look at her world, and a long look at her son, and makes the decision. While she will give him life, she must wound him deeply so that he can survive and pass on the gift. In so doing she forfeits his love for her. She must hurt him first, then he will live, but there will ever be a hatred for her.[42]

We believe that Grier and Cobbs are overstating the prevalence of this hatred for the mother as the black male's reaction to maternal restriction of initiative and aggression. Robert Staples, a black sociologist, agrees that black mothers traditionally had to repress the self-assertive tendencies of their sons to protect them from white retaliation, but he argues that, since the withdrawal of emotional support and the restrictiveness are motivated by concern for the boys' safety, hatred of the mother is an inappropriate and improbable response.[43] We suspect that the ability to understand the seeming contradiction between the mother's actions and her feelings without resentment may be beyond the mental or emotional capacities of children. The low-income children we observed (girls as well as boys) generally did not come to hate their mothers as a result of their restrictiveness and the early withdrawal of emotional support, but they did, as we have said, experience a heightened ambivalence toward them.

This ambivalence may have been somewhat adaptive in preparing the black children to live with the contradiction between a black self and an American identity with stoic strength and resignation. The social movement of the 1960's and 1970's, the Negro-to-black revolution, has influenced black parents to change their traditional practices so as to try to socialize children for more self-assertion and collective solidarity, rather than for passive resignation to white oppression. Previously, the emotional scars inflicted early upon black children generally functioned to prepare them for the assumption in adulthood of the traditional Negro role behaviors then required for survival.

One can see in the lives of some blacks who came to manhood during the 1960's the need to face up to the conflicts engendered by a traditional early socialization experience. George Jackson wrote:

> It always starts with mama, mine loved me. As testimony of her love, and her fear for the fate of the manchild all slave mothers hold, she attempted to press, hide, push, capture me in the womb. The conflicts and contradictions that will follow me to the tomb started right there in the womb. The feeling of being captured . . . this slave can never adjust to it, it's a thing that I just don't favor then, now, never.[44]

It may be that black adults generally develop a greater ability to tolerate seemingly contradictory emotions than white Americans do. While this ability may develop, in part, reactively, as a defense against blocked opportunity and racial oppression, it has been argued that it may also reflect an intrinsic cultural element in black communities, a heritage of the feeling-oriented as opposed to concept-oriented African culture, which allows for the existence of opposites or contradictions without requiring an either/or resolution. This cultural tradition, which survives in black communities in America today, may foster a generally greater tolerance for stress, ambiguity, and ambivalence in black Americans than white Americans display.[45]

CHILDREN, FAMILY, AND COMMUNITY

Most of the children we knew in Harlem coped with a great deal of stress, ambiguity, and ambivalence without succumbing to continuous grief and despair. The children learned early that life is often unkind and that pain and suffering are a very real and unavoidable part of the human condition. They tended to develop the strength required to adjust to a life demanding early self-reliance, with minimal emotional support. They learned how to cope with a variety of people and situations on their own, with little protection from adults. They became increasingly hardened to physical punishment. All of these adaptations may be viewed as strengths, because they enhanced the children's chances for survival in a society that is hostile to them.

The uncertainty that often marked their family life pervaded their community as well. Children found it difficult to count on stability in their lives. Long-range planning seemed unrealistic to them, when day-to-day survival was itself problematic. Frustrations and disappointments were common experiences. There was little basis for building a sense of security for, in fact, insecurity marked the lives of most adults the children knew.

A minister who worked in the project observed by William Moore, Jr., commented on the predicament of the black underclass in the inner cities:

> People here aren't secure. I know that they go around with the façade of being callous, but few human beings are really like that. People need to be able to plan and dream. They can't just go along in this constant limbo of not knowing where they're going, what they are going to eat, wondering what new adversity will affect their lives each day, what new ingenuity will be necessary to make it through the day.[46]

Considering the relationship between inner-city black communities and the larger, white society, the black psychologist Kenneth B. Clark has observed: "The dark ghettos are social, political, educational, and—above all—economic colonies. Their inhabitants are subject peoples, victims of the greed, cruelty, insensitivity, guilt and fear of their masters."[47] The adaptations required of low-income urban black children traditionally fostered the development of characteristics needed for survival, for coping with severely restricted opportunities to exercise effective social, economic, or political power in the determination of their own lives.

To gain a greater appreciation of the developmental dilemmas of these children, we must distinguish between the condition of being adapted and the process by which it is achieved. Early adaptations to severe stress necessitate ways of perceiving and coping with life that are effective in reducing anxiety, avoiding danger, and obtaining scarce material and social rewards. However, in the process of adapting, children may forfeit much of the plasticity of mind and attitude necessary for continuing differentiation and expansion of the self. Early adaptations can rigidify. When they do, they may border on final solutions.

In their steadfast efforts to survive, the children forged life-styles that would enable them to make it, more or less, from day to day. But many children appeared to be growing older with mixed emotions concerning their success in functioning as "little adults," their adaptations to demands for early independence and self-reliance, in an atmosphere of uncertainty and danger. When he was feeling depressed, an older teenager in Harlem might reflect on his success in coming up fast in words similar to those used by Reno, in Claude Brown's *Manchild in the Promised Land:*

> Man, Sonny, they ain't got no kids in Harlem. I ain't never seen any. I've seen some real small people actin' like kids. They were too small to be grown, and they might've looked like kids but they don't have any kids in Harlem, because nobody has time for a childhood. Man, do you ever remember bein' a kid? Not me. Shit, kids are happy, kids laugh, kids are secure. They ain't scared-a nothin'. You ever been a kid Sonny? Damn, you lucky. I ain't never been a kid man. I don't ever remember bein' happy and not scared. I don't know what happened, man, but I think I missed out on that childhood thing, because I don't ever recall bein' a kid.[48]

We believe that Reno's statement is rather exaggerated. Most of the children we knew in Harlem had many moments of happiness. But most of them, as we have observed, also had a tendency toward rapid mood swings, from happiness to dejection. Children who were playing excitedly would rather quickly, in response to a variety of provocations, begin to pout or yell and scream with great agitation, often followed by sullen dejection. Not infrequently children would get into fights, and it was not unheard of for a child to have several fights in one day. Nevertheless, in spite of a great deal of conflict, for a good deal of the time, interspersed with periods of pouting or sullenness, the children appeared to be relatively happy.

They were most likely to be happy in the street, where the activities they engaged in with their peers provided many opportunities for fun, excitement, and companionship. The children experienced some happiness in school, but the accent of the school experience was frustration. So was home life for most of the children. Most of them did not seem eager to go home after school. Their comments indicated that they perceived home as a place where they were likely to be constrained, yelled at, and hit. This is not to say that the children were never happy at home. Nevertheless, the location in which the majority of low-income children in Harlem sought, and achieved, some happiness increasingly became the street.

But if the world of the street was filled with sound, humor, excitement, and activity, it was also filled with danger, and herein may lie Reno's truth. The children of Harlem had to develop a special alertness and perceptual sensitivity to enable them to size up another person quickly so as to assess his threat potential. This alertness to imminent danger could rarely be relaxed for long.[49] The children learned as they grew older that, unless one were on guard, he was likely to become a victim of manipulation, humiliation, or serious abuse. A great deal of energy was consumed in efforts to avoid becoming a victim. And while such an orientation to people is obviously adaptive for black people when relating to whites, a tragic irony of the children's lives is that, because they live in a black community and relate mostly to other blacks on a day-to-day basis, if they become victims it is most likely to be at the hands of a fellow black. In their relationships with each other, as well as with adults in the community, the children tended to maintain a high level of suspicion and distrust. They could play happily together, but they usually found it necessary to keep a wary eye open for potential insults and threats. Each child had to be prepared to hold his own at almost any time.

The development of a heightened fear of being used, abused, or victimized by others inhibited the ability of the children we knew to work cooperatively and interfered with their attempts to form long-lasting, mutually satisfying friendships and cohesive groups. Herein lies their developmental dilemma: The characteristics forged early in life as adaptations to a stressful existence may make it difficult for low-income urban blacks to develop in later life the group cohesiveness and organization necessary for long-range, cooperative group efforts. Further, these characteristics decrease, but do not preclude, the possibility of individual achievement in middle-class-controlled institutions, such as the public schools. We shall return to a consideration of the potential effect of black solidarity on child development at the community level in Chapter 11.

NOTES

1. See Jacob Riis, *How the Other Half Lives* (1890) (New York: Hill & Wang, 1957), and Jane Addams, *Twenty Years at Hull House* (1910) (New York: Signet, 1961).
2. Madeline Engel, George Marsden, and Sylvia W. Pollock, "Child Work and Social Class," *Psychiatry,* 34 (1971): 140–55.
3. Early assertion of independence from parental control is a phenomenon linked to urban poverty observed among the children of European immigrants to America more than eighty years ago. See Riis, *How the Other Half Lives.*
4. Suzanne Keller, "The Social World of the Urban Slum Child: Some Early Findings," *American Journal of Orthopsychiatry,* 33 (1963): 823–31.
5. Urie Bronfenbrenner, "The Split-Level American Family," *Saturday Review of Literature,* October 7, 1967, pp. 60–66.
6. Hylan Lewis, "Child Rearing Practices Among Low Income Families in the District of Columbia," paper presented at the National Conference

on Social Welfare, Minneapolis, May 16, 1961 (mimeographed), p. 3. Although most of the families Lewis observed were black, some white families were included in the sample. For similar observations, based upon a St. Louis sample, see Lee Rainwater, *Behind Ghetto Walls: Black Family Life in a Federal Slum* (Chicago: Aldine, 1970), pp. 211–34.

7. Eleanor Pavenstedt, *The Drifters: Children of Disorganized Lower-Class Families* (Boston: Little, Brown, 1967). Pavenstedt's subjects represent an extreme sample of the low-income population, much more psychologically incapacitated than most of the children we knew in Harlem.

8. Joyce A. Ladner, *Tomorrow's Tomorrow: The Black Woman* (New York: Doubleday, 1971), pp. 59–60.

9. *Ibid.*, pp. 61–62.

10. Hyman Meltzer, "Economic Security and Children's Attitudes to Parents," *American Journal of Orthopsychiatry,* 6 (1936): 590–608. See also L. Dolger and J. Ginandes, "Children's Attitudes Toward Discipline as Related to Socio-economic Status," *Journal of Experimental Education,* 15 (1946): 161–65.

11. E. Nuttall and R. Nuttall, "Effects of Size of Family on Parent-Child Relationships," Proceedings of American Psychological Association, 1971, p. 267.

12. James H. Bossard and Eleanor S. Boll, *The Sociology of Child Development,* 4th ed. (New York: Harper & Row, 1966), pp. 38–43.

13. Urie Bronfenbrenner, "Socialization and Social Class Through Time and Space," in Eleanor E. Maccoby, Theodore M. Newcomb, and Eugene L. Hartley, eds., *Readings in Social Psychology,* 3d ed. (New York: Holt, Rinehart & Winston, 1958), pp. 400–425.

14. Zena S. Blau, "Exposure to Child-rearing Experts: A Structural Interpretation of Class-Color Differences," *American Journal of Sociology,* 69 (1964): 596–608.

15. Melvin L. Kohn, "Social Class and Parent-Child Relationships: An Interpretation," *American Journal of Sociology,* 68 (1963): 471.

16. Constance K. Kamii and Norma L. Radin, "Class Differences in the Socialization Practices of Negro Mothers," *Journal of Marriage and the Family,* 29 (1967): 302–10.

17. Mary E. Garner and Barry Silverstein, "Childrearing Goals, Priorities, and Strategies: Assessing the World View of Low-Income Black Mothers," unpublished manuscript, William Paterson College, Wayne, New Jersey, 1972.

18. See Gerald Gurin, Joseph Veroff, and Sheila Feld, *Americans View Their Mental Health* (New York: Basic Books, 1960), pp. 134–36.

19. See Mirra Komarovsky, *Blue-Collar Marriage* (New York: Random House, 1964), pp. 75–81, and Lee Rainwater, Richard P. Coleman, and Gerald Handel, *Working Man's Wife: Her Personality, World and Life Style* (New York: Oceana, 1959).

20. Rainwater, *Behind Ghetto Walls* (n. 6 *supra*), p. 218.

21. For similar observations, see *ibid.*, and David A. Schulz, *Coming Up*

Black: Patterns of Ghetto Socialization (Englewood Cliffs, N.J.: Prentice-Hall, 1969).

22. Joint Commission on Mental Health of Children, *Crisis in Child Mental Health: Challenge for the 1970's* (New York: Harper & Row, 1970), p. 344.

23. Andrew Billingsley, "Family Functioning in the Low-Income Black Community," *Social Casework,* 50 (1969): 563–72.

24. William Moore, Jr., *The Vertical Ghetto* (New York: Random House, 1969), p. 62.

25. For similar observations in a similar context, see Helen C. Bee *et al.,* "Social Class Differences in Maternal Teaching Strategies and Speech Patterns," *Developmental Psychology,* 1 (1969): 726–34.

26. Camille Jeffers, *Living Poor* (Ann Arbor, Mich.: Ann Arbor Publishers, 1967), pp. 50–92.

27. Moore, *Vertical Ghetto,* p. 61.

28. A mixed pattern, combining withdrawal of love and physical punishment, appears to be used more often by working-class than by middle-class white parents. See Daniel R. Miller and Guy E. Swanson, *Inner Conflict and Defense* (New York: Henry Holt, 1960), p. 426.

29. Robert R. Sears, Eleanor E. Maccoby, and Harry Levin, *Patterns of Child Rearing* (New York: Harper & Row, 1957).

30. Black parents appear to become increasingly emotionally supportive of their children, and the children increasingly perceive their parents as playing an important role in shaping their future, as the family moves up from the working class into the middle class. See John H. Scanzoni, *The Black Family in Modern Society* (Boston: Allyn & Bacon, 1971), and Kamii and Radin, "Class Differences in Socialization Practices" (n. 16 *supra*).

31. See Andrew Billingsley, *Black Families in White America* (Englewood Cliffs, N.J.: Prentice-Hall, 1968), and Wade W. Nobles, "African Philosophy: Foundations for Black Psychology," in Reginald L. Jones, ed., *Black Psychology* (New York: Harper & Row, 1972), pp. 18–32.

32. See Rainwater, *Behind Ghetto Walls,* pp. 211–34, and Ulf Hannerz, *Soulside: Inquiries into Ghetto Culture and Community* (New York: Columbia University Press, 1969), pp. 88–104.

33. Hylan Lewis, "Culture, Class, and Family Life Among Low-Income Urban Negroes," in Arthur M. Ross and Herbert B. Hill, eds., *Employment, Race, and Poverty* (New York: Harcourt, Brace & World, 1967), p. 170.

34. Hannerz, *Soulside,* pp. 177–88. See also Rodman's concept of "value stretch," which holds that the poor, in general, accommodate their values to adapt to poverty. While sharing mainstream values, they also stretch them to suit their deprived circumstances. Hyman Rodman, "The Lower-Class Value Stretch," *Social Forces,* 42 (1966): 205–15.

35. Carol B. Stack, *All Our Kin: Strategies for Survival in a Black Community* (New York: Harper & Row, 1974), p. 123.

36. Hannerz, *Soulside,* pp. 34–58; St. Clair Drake and Horace R. Cayton,

Black Metropolis: A Study of Negro Life in a Northern City (New York: Harper Torchbooks, 1962); and William McCord, John Howard, Bernard Friedberg, and Edwin Harwood, *Life Styles in the Black Ghetto* (New York: W. W. Norton, 1969).

37. Rainwater, *Behind Ghetto Walls,* p. 219.

38. Robert Coles, *Children of Crisis* (Boston: Little, Brown, 1964), p. 66. Black parents in the South did not teach their children total, unconditional submission to whites. Even in slavery, black children were often taught to fight their masters when necessary to protect their relatives, and slave children might see their parents on many occasions disobey and sometimes fight their masters. Yet slave children often saw their parents behave in a contradictory manner, acquiescing to whites in public while, in the slave quarters, castigating whites for mistreatment. See John W. Blassingame, *The Slave Community: Plantation Life in the Ante-Bellum South* (London and New York: Oxford University Press, 1973), pp. 99–102.

39. E. Earl Baughman, *Black Americans: A Psychological Analysis* (New York: Academic Press, 1971), p. 87.

40. Florence Halpern, *Survival: Black/White* (Elmsford, N.Y.: Pergamon Press, 1973), p. 181.

41. See Robert L. Crain and Carol Sachs Weisman, *Discrimination, Personality, and Achievement: A Survey of Northern Blacks* (New York: Seminar Press, 1972), and David O. Sears and John B. McConahay, "Racial Socialization, Comparison Levels, and the Watts Riot," *Journal of Social Issues,* 26 (1970): 121–40. During the late 1950's Bertram Karon found that the need to deny aggressive feelings was more prevalent among a sample of Southern blacks than among a comparable sample of Northern blacks. In expressing aggressive impulses, blacks reared in the North resembled Northern whites more than they resembled Southern blacks, although the absence of a Southern white comparison group made it impossible to determine precisely whether the differences were racial, regional, or both. See Bertram P. Karon, *Negro Personality* (New York: Springer, 1958). In the early 1940's Charles Johnson, a black sociologist, also observed that migration northward offered blacks more opportunities for open displays of aggression than were possible in the South. Charles S. Johnson, *Patterns of Negro Segregation* (New York: Harper & Row, 1943).

42. William H. Grier and Price M. Cobbs, *Black Rage* (New York: Basic Books, 1968), p. 146.

43. Robert Staples, "The Myth of the Black Matriarch," *The Black Scholar,* January–February, 1970, pp. 8–16.

44. George Jackson, *Soledad Brother: The Prison Letters of George Jackson* (New York: Bantam Books, 1970), pp. 9–10.

45. See Vernon J. Dixon and Badi G. Foster, *Beyond Black or White: An Alternative America* (Boston: Little, Brown, 1971); James Haskins and Hugh F. Butts, *The Psychology of Black Language* (New York: Barnes & Noble, 1973); and Joseph White, "Toward a Black Psychology," in Jones, ed., *Black Psychology* (n. 31 *supra*), pp. 43–50. A

study that provides some empirical support for the proposition that tolerance for ambiguity increases significantly in blacks twenty to twenty-two years old while it decreases in whites in the same age bracket is J. D. Hampton, "Ambiguity Tolerance as a Function of Age, Sex, and Ethnicity," *Dissertation Abstracts,* vol. 27 (1967).

46. Moore, *Vertical Ghetto* (n. 24 *supra*), p. 65.
47. Kenneth B. Clark, *Dark Ghetto: Dilemmas of Social Power* (New York: Harper & Row, 1965), p. 11.
48. Claude Brown, *Manchild in the Promised Land* (New York: Macmillan, 1965), p. 285.
49. On the basis of an intensive study of twenty-five Harlem residents, Kardiner and Ovesey, in the early 1950's, reported that lower-class black adults tend to lack trust in other human beings and to be eternally vigilant, believing that the world is hostile. Their sample size, plus the fact that some of the subjects were patients in therapy, demand caution in generalizing these findings. The hostility of whites toward blacks also suggests that such characteristics may present good reality-testing. See Abram Kardiner and Lionel Ovesey, *The Mark of Oppression: Explorations in the Personality of the American Negro* (New York: W. W. Norton, 1951).

3 / EARLY SOCIALIZATION: MICRO VIEWS

The previous chapter considered some general trends in the socialization of low-income urban blacks and related them to the past and present political and socio-economic position of blacks in America. In this chapter we shall look more closely at some patterns of interaction between black parents and their children, with particular attention to the impact on the children's developing personalities.

AUTONOMY AND THE "MALEVOLENT TRANSFORMATION"

During the early years of childhood, children must learn to regulate their impulsive behaviors. A major task of parents is to push and press young children toward greater self-regulation in a manner congruent with the basic norms of their society. With increasing neuromuscular maturation, children gain a growing sense of autonomy, a sense of being able to regulate their own behavior, of being able to exercise will power. Autonomy implies independence, but it "does and can also mean defiance, stubbornness, self-insistence."[1] Underlying autonomous behavior is human will "in its variations of will power and willfulness."[2] The parents' task is to encourage enough self-willed behavior so that children become more able to direct their own impulses, building a sense of autonomy, while preventing the children from becoming so willful that they continue to behave in ways proscribed by the society.

The manner in which parents respond to assertions of will by young children is influenced by the norms and mores of their social groups and by their status within the groups. "For in the last analysis (as comparative studies in child training have convinced many of us) the kind and degree of a sense of autonomy which parents are able to grant their small children depend on the dignity and the sense of personal independence which they derive from their own lives."[3] A parent can foster the sense of autonomy that emerges in early childhood (and continues to develop thereafter) by handling children in a way that expresses the parent's own self-respect, pride, and independence, which receive societal affirmation and give the children the confident expectation that the autonomy enjoyed in childhood will not be frustrated later. "This, in turn, necessitates a relationship of parent to parent, of parent to employer, and of parent to government which reaffirms the parent's essential dignity within the hierarchy of social positions."[4]

Just as America has offered blacks relatively limited opportunities to exercise free choice and independent self-direction, so black adults, as parents, have tended to be similarly restrictive in relation to autonomous strivings in their young children, particularly self-assertive and aggressive responses directed toward whites. And although, as we have noted, black parents in the urban North encouraged more self-assertion and aggression with respect to whites than were traditionally allowed in the South, our observations suggest that even here it is often aggression directed toward fellow blacks rather than toward whites that is encouraged.

The general failure of adults to support the young child's strivings for self-regulation may lead to a significant erosion of trust, in relation both to the self and to others. If the child's environment generally does not back him up in his attempts to exercise choice and independent self-regulation he may be "overcome by that sense of having exposed himself prematurely and foolishly which we call shame, or that secondary mistrust, that 'double-take,' which we call doubt."[5]

Shame contributes to a sense of being small and powerless. Like doubt, it is a differentiated form of mistrust. While shame refers primarily to a sense of being exposed as inadequate or unacceptable because of some basic flaw that characterizes the self, doubt refers primarily to a lack of faith or trust in the "rightness" or "goodness" of what one does or can do, and a fear that others are trying to exercise control behind one's back.[6]

Parental restrictiveness and punitiveness combined with withdrawal of emotional support in the early years of childhood may also contribute to the developmental phenomenon that Sullivan has called the "malevolent transformation":

> For a variety of reasons, many children have the experience that when they need tenderness, when they do that which once brought tender cooperation, they are not only denied tenderness, but they are treated in

a fashion to provoke anxiety or even, in some cases, pain. A child may discover that manifesting the need for tenderness toward the potent figures around him leads frequently to his being disadvantaged, being made anxious, being made fun of, and so on, so that . . . he is hurt. . . . Under those circumstances, the developmental course changes to the point that the perceived need for tenderness brings a foresight of anxiety or pain. The child learns, you see, that it is highly disadvantageous to show any need for tender cooperation from the authoritative figures around him, in which case he shows something else; and that something else is the basic malevolent attitude, the attitude that one really lives among enemies —that is about what it amounts to.[7]

Even when parental restrictiveness is not motivated by an intention to be rejecting, the distinction is not likely to be clearly appreciated by young children. As Adler has pointed out, young children are excellent observers but poor interpreters.[8] Therefore, they may well feel cheated, resentful, and even unlovable as a result of parental punitiveness, regardless of the intent.

The persistence of the basic malevolent attitude into late childhood and early adolescence often leads to behavioral characteristics that make it difficult for others to feel or express tenderness toward the young person. Made anxious by his need for kindness and his expectation of rejection by others, he may beat them to it, so to speak, by a display of indifference or outright hostility. Eventually certain reaction tendencies may become characteristic of the self in interpersonal relationships; the uncaring, uncooperative, malevolent persona becomes habitually displayed whenever the person begins to feel desirous of giving or receiving tenderness, thus provoking the expected rejection by others and creating a self-fulfilling prophecy.

The malevolent attitude, shame, and doubt have in common a core element of mistrust; they are basic emotions centered in perceptions of features of the self as "bad" and of other people as rejecting. Children who hold these attitudes may become *submissive,* seeking to hide their "badness," accepting control to avoid rejection and punishment; they may become *precociously independent,* fighting against control by others while defiantly, shamelessly displaying a "bad self" and hiding any need for tenderness; or they may become highly *ambivalent,* fluctuating indecisively between attempts to gain tenderness and defiant displays of tenderness-rejecting "badness" or malevolence. All three patterns were observed frequently among schoolchildren in Central Harlem, the ambivalent pattern being by far the most common, and all represent distortions in autonomy.

We have commented on the apparent self-reliance of low-income black children compared with the more openly adult-dependent behavior and relationships of more affluent children of the same age. Harlem children generally appeared self-reliant at a very early age in that they displayed little inclination to turn to adults for security or instrumental aid. The children became adapted to surviving from day to day without much adult support and assistance, and they developed competence in competing for life's necessities and protecting themselves from aggression and manipulation from others. The children were able to wander throughout their neighborhood without adult supervision; they could negotiate their way through streets crowded with winos, junkies, and dangerous characters and thick with motor vehicles; they could go shopping on their own, and they often could carry out responsibilities at home such as cooking, child care, and housecleaning. They knew what to say—and what not to say—to welfare workers, policemen, and bill collectors. In all these areas, Harlem children generally depended relatively little upon adults, who, in fact often pushed the children to develop self-reliance so that adults could depend upon them to carry out chores or to be out of the way much of the time.

Because of their development of survival skills, Harlem children typically displayed greater maturity than is characteristic of more sheltered, protected, and nurtured children. By the upper elementary grades, most Harlem children seemed able to take care of themselves. Many of them seemed to be quite concerned about, and a few were even involved with, sex and violence; some seemed a bit jaded or demoralized by having come up fast.

Central to the apparent independence of these children, in our judgment, is a dependency conflict related to the development of feelings of shame and doubt, and to the malevolent transformation, representing a defense against anxiety associated with a child's desire to receive tenderness from (and express it to) others, particularly the powerful adults in his life. The malevolent attitude, present in varying degrees in a large proportion of the children we observed, seemed to us to be part of a larger pattern of mistrust, in which any impulse to be dependent upon an adult was a signal for anxiety fueled by expectations of frustration or punishment. Coming up fast in Harlem meant learning to be on your own, to expect to receive little from others while remaining alert to the manipulations and strategies used by others to take from you. Many children who showed some need for tenderness appeared to be unable to accept much tenderness without backing away. To continue to accept tenderness was to become dependent, which must lead to frustration, punishment, or manipulation. Other children would always remain aloof from adults, in either a submissive or a defiant mode. Much of the apparent self-reliance of these children represented a defense employed to block the tendency to seek emotional support or instrumental aid from an adult.

PARENT-CHILD INTERACTION AND PRESCHOOL BEHAVIOR

A variety of psychosocial qualities that contribute to future school achievement can be observed in the emerging behavior of preschool children, and these qualities can be related to particular types of parent-child interaction.

The constellation of curiosity, playfulness, independence, self-control, self-reliance, sociability, and outgoingness seems most likely to emerge in young children whose parents encourage and reward independent decision-making and responsible, self-reliant behavior.[9]

Parental nurturance and warmth appear to be key factors in young children's competence to meet new situations. Within a nurturant home context, parental control or firmness, in combination with pressures on the child to perform at a level of ability appropriate for his age, appears to promote generalized mastery and achievement strivings and independence. Competence in a variety of situations and independence in young children are not encouraged by authoritarian discipline, high punitiveness, and high restrictiveness.[10]

Research data suggest that low parental restrictiveness fosters strivings for mastery, achievement, and self-directed behavior in boys more than in girls. Perhaps this is because girls in our society traditionally have been encouraged to be more dependent and passive than boys.[11] Black girls, of course, are exceptions to this rule, and this point will be discussed below. At any rate, it is important to note that the low parental restrictiveness so highly associated with general competence and independent behavior in boys is not of the indifferent or neglectful variety but, rather, appears to be imbedded in a context of parental expectations, guidance, and standard-setting for independent achievement.

Black women in America have had far more need to be independent and self-assertive than white women, and this is reflected in somewhat different socialization practices. Baumrind, for example, suggested that nonsupportive, authoritarian parental practices may have a different impact on daughters in black families than in white families because of the over-all differences in the contexts in which these parental practices are experienced.[12] The study compared the socialization experiences of nine black preschool girls and sixty white girls. Since the black sample is very small, the findings are only tentative. All the children studied came from intact, relatively advantaged homes, though the black families on the average had lower (predominantly lower-middle-class) social status. Five of the black families were classified as "Authoritarian-Rejecting," while only eight of the sixty white girls had parents who were so classified. The parents of the black girls tended, by comparison with those of white girls, not to encourage independence and individuality; they very much discouraged infantile behavior; fathers were authoritarian in their practices and did not tolerate nonconformity; mothers practiced firm enforcement, were not passive-acceptant, and were somewhat rejecting. The child-rearing practices designated as authoritarian appeared to affect black and white girls quite differently. Black daughters of authoritarian parents were significantly more independent than their white counterparts in the sense that they were more dominant with peers and somewhat more resistant to adult direction.

Black families in this study scored higher than white families on indices of discouraging infantile dependency and lower on paternal rejection. It would appear, therefore, that the black parents were not so much rejecting their daughters as training them to take care of themselves from an early age. However, it is important to note that the black daughters of authoritarian parents, while competent in the sense that they were independent, displayed certain patterns in interpersonal relationships that encouraged discord rather than cooperation. Nor were authoritarian childrearing practices associated with intellectual achievement in young children, either black or white.

Measures of interaction between black mothers (of varying social classes) and their children have been found to be as useful as, or better than, IQ scores or social-class indices for predicting young children's behavior in schoollike, problem-solving situations.[13] Imperative demands for performance from children, without much explanation, from mothers who appeared to be cold and punitive were negatively related to the children's intellectual performance. Such maternal behaviors were observed far more among very low-income urban black mothers than among middle-class black mothers.

Certain other important relationships were found by Hess and Shipman. Lower-class black mothers tended to rate higher on measures of feelings of "powerlessness" than middle-class or working-class black mothers. Basic to scoring high on "powerlessness" were expressions of frustration and futility in trying to change either the unruliness of children or the forces that determine one's life ("the system"). The children of mothers who rated high in feelings of powerlessness were not likely to engage in initiatory behavior in a testing situation (the Stanford Binet), to respond quickly in a testing situation, or to be socially confident and comfortable with an adult examiner.

As we have noted, because their emphasis is so often on socialization for survival, low-income black mothers, by severely discouraging dependency behaviors in young children and often restricting and punishing them, inhibit or frustrate the children's curiosity and strivings for autonomous mastery. The results are evident in the play behavior of many children in preschool centers. In a study of black four-year-olds in a Head

Start program in Philadelphia, for example, Minuchin observed that these children commonly expressed less curiosity and displayed less exploratory behavior in the school setting than middle-class children (black or white) of the same age.[14] About one third of this group was described as extremely deficient in curiosity and constructive exploratory behavior.

Studies of the play behavior of black preschool children in Chicago have found a considerable range of individual differences in the organization and content of the children's play and in their modes of establishing interpersonal relationships with adults.[15] This finding is especially significant because it runs counter to the tendency in the literature to categorize all lower-class black children simply as "disadvantaged." The observers found that they could be most effective in planning preschool programs if they first divided the children into groups of high, middle, and low "competence" on the basis of observer ratings of the organization and content of play behavior and ways of relating to adults. About one third of the children displayed quite adequate, age-appropriate competence in these areas. The rest were described as presenting developmental problems in one or more areas.

Meers observed a sample of low-income black first-graders in Washington, D.C., who had been judged by school officials to be unable to follow a normal first-grade curriculum.[16] Depression was the most dramatic and pervasive emotional attitude in evidence among this group. Many of the children were described as "hopelessly, passively indifferent." Whether these depressive emotions reflected individual psychodynamic factors or were direct reactions to stresses in the children's lives, or some interaction between the two, could not be determined. Of course, the school itself was one more source of tension, and the children's depressive emotions may have been a reaction to their inability to cope with schoolwork or to a lack of positive attention from school personnel, who apparently regarded these children as "failures" even in grade one. In some cases, nutritional deficiencies may have been responsible for apathy and listlessness.

Camille Jeffers, reporting upon participant-observation research in a low-income public-housing project in Washington, D.C., noted two features of the play behavior of urban low-income black children: "the need to learn to hold one's own, and the delayed development of play skills." The importance of fighting back against other children, protecting one's person and one's possessions, was learned very early by these children. Mothers seemed to deny their young children much protection from other children, pushing them to fight back and take care of themselves.

> The intent of the mothers seemed to be on teaching their children some of the harsh lessons of survival. In this sense, the court, the playground and the streets are frequently grim, informal, and effective educational settings for low-income populations. The fact that children have to learn

to hold their own was nothing new to me. What was new was that they were learning to do so at the ages of two and three.[17]

Jeffers's observations suggested that many of the children had not had a great deal of encouragement and opportunity for sustained imaginative play. Not only was there a lack of developed play skills among the few children who were not supplied with toys, but Jeffers observed a similar unresponsiveness to imaginative play in the children who were well supplied with toys but whose mothers were low on nurturance and protection and high on punitive restrictiveness. This is not to argue that these children had no areas of competence. Comparing her own four-year-old son with his playmates in the project, Jeffers concluded:

> While he had been learning play skills in the nursery school, the children he came to know during these fifteen months had been learning to hold their own. He was learning the ABC's of cooperative play while many of his playmates-to-be were learning the ABC's of survival in conflict.[18]

Prekindergarten children we observed often seemed timid and even reluctant in handling simple play materials, unable to experiment with or explore toys and puzzles. Many of these children sat at a table and handled the pieces tentatively but would not put them together. When they tried to do so, after much encouragement, they usually wanted to abandon the activity quickly, especially if they encountered difficulty. Many seemed reluctant to ask a teacher for help or otherwise reveal their need for aid in solving problems.

DEPENDENCY CONFLICT AND PRESCHOOL BEHAVIOR

While dependency implies helplessness or immaturity, humans, as social animals, require contact with other humans, and all are basically interdependent; developing maturity implies not only greater independence and autonomy but also greater competence in seeking interpersonal contact, recognition, and help in ways that are not infantile or destructive. Studies at the Harvard Preschool Project have found that intellectual and problem-solving competence is associated with competence in expressing dependency or human interdependence.[19] The three-year-olds judged to be the most generally competent were not clinging but knew when to turn to adults for help, and they were successful in getting and holding the attention of adults, using adults as sources of information and help, and expressing affection under appropriate conditions. In relation to peers, the most competent three-year-olds were able to be either leaders or followers as circumstances warranted. They could show affection to peers or ignore them, and they could use peers to get help.

Beller found dependency conflicts to be an important factor in inhibiting autonomous striving and achievement-oriented behavior among a population of low-income black children in a Head Start program in Philadelphia.[20] Dependency conflict refers to a young child's difficulty in accepting and openly expressing his desire to relate dependently to adults —that is, to permit himself to ask adults for help or for attention and emotional support. The children in the program were divided into three groups on the basis of changes in IQ test scores since the beginning of the program. Those who had gained in IQ points seemed to experience much less dependency conflict than the other children; that is, they were more able to make realistic demands for help from the teacher. These children also received more positive reactions from the teacher and coped more effectively and constructively (nondefensively and nonregressively) with the teacher's attention to them.

The results of Beller's study also suggest that low dependency conflict is more important for boys than for girls in improved performance on IQ tests. Boy IQ gainers made at least twice as many realistic requests for help from the teacher than boys in the other two groups. Of all the dependency requests made by the boy gainers, twice as many were for realistically needed aid as for emotional support alone. In the other groups, dependency requests were less frequent and were equally divided between requests for instrumental aid and requests for attention or emotional support. Girls who lost IQ points made, on the average, less than half as many realistic requests for aid as the other two groups of girls. Girls who gained in IQ made less than half as many attempts to gain teacher attention through negativistic behaviors as the other two groups of girls.

PARENTAL REACTIONS TO ACHIEVEMENT EFFORTS

Many of the children we knew had not received much praise or reward for their play activities, questions, or comments before they came to school. Because the children were obviously incompetent compared with adults, their mothers typically appeared to see no significance or praiseworthy qualities in their drawings, dramatic play, block constructions, or remarks. With the increasing involvement of black mothers and children in various day-care programs since the late 1960's, the encouragement of children's play and recognition of its significance for future development has been on the rise in poor black communities. Over the last few years a number of black mothers who worked as paraprofessionals in day-care centers have attended our developmental-psychology classes. They reported to us an increasing interest in providing play opportunities for the children and concern for their intellectual development on the part of low-income black mothers. An increasing interest in children's development appears to be associated with the movement for race pride and solidarity in black communities. The growing number of blacks attending college as well as black personnel in the schools appears to have increased the expectations of many black mothers that their children can and should succeed in school and in life.

Numerous conversations with low-income black mothers convinced us that many of them saw their children as incompetent, or at least unlikely to achieve in school. They often said that they hoped the children would do "good work," and some mothers even hoped for professional careers for their children. However, these desires and aspirations quickly evaporated when they recognized that the children were not achieving in school —as most of them were not. The mothers (as well as many teachers) tended to accept the children's lack of school achievement rather passively, as though it were inevitable. They seemed unable to think of any way of influencing the children to do better work or to behave differently except by beating them—a method that, as they had already come to know, brought little desired change.

In so readily accepting their children's failure to achieve in school, black mothers may have been projecting their own self-image of powerlessness. Without the dependable aid of a husband and with little comfort or security, it is small wonder that many mothers expressed or manifested despair and depression. To the extent that the mothers saw their children as extensions of themselves, they seemed fatalistic about the children's chances for achievement in school or in later life. In a racist society, such pessimism had a strong element of realism.

Many of the mothers we knew in Harlem were not simply uncertain about their children's futures; they were despairing. Although the mothers wanted their children to achieve in school, many of them did not believe that the children could do so. One mother, for example, commented to the teacher that she had noticed some written work displayed on a bulletin board outside the room and was amazed to find that the name on the papers was the same as her daughter's. When told that the work she saw had in fact been done by her own daughter she refused to believe it.

Often unwittingly, parents begin to communicate their doubt or despair to their children when the children are quite young, in part through their responses to the children's achievement efforts. Crystal, a four-year-old black child, produced a collage one morning in a Harlem Head Start center. At noon, when her mother arrived, Crystal ran toward her excitedly with her artwork. Her mother looked at it and said, "I don't believe you made this, Crystal, put it away." After Crystal had gone home, we found her collage crumpled up on the floor.

We saw many other children who were inhibited from autonomous achievement strivings in preschool centers by their mothers' discouraging responses. For example, four-year-old John, painting at an easel in his pre-K classroom, accidently spilled some paint on his shirt. When he noticed the paint he became extremely upset, although the teacher tried to assure him that it could be removed. She thereupon took off John's shirt and washed it, gave him a clean shirt to wear, and put the shirt she had washed into a plastic bag. When his mother came to call for John the teacher explained what had happened, making it clear that John had soiled his shirt *accidentally* while making a beautiful painting. As John and his mother left, the mother shook her fist at the boy in a threatening manner. The next day, John told a teacher-aide that his mother had given him a beating for getting paint on his shirt. After that, John refused to paint.

In fact, John did not have many shirts, and his mother's action may have reflected the difficulty she experienced in obtaining clothing for him with little money to spend. But whatever his mother's motivation, John's autonomy suffered.

We often saw mothers in Harlem hitting their children when displeased by their behavior. A prekindergarten teacher we observed routinely informed each parent how her child had behaved that day. On one occasion, a mother asked the teacher, "How did Mary do today?" When the teacher replied, "Well, she was a little wild today," the mother immediately slapped the child across the mouth. "I'll beat you when we get home," she exclaimed.

As the children grew older, some appeared to become inured to physical punishment. Nevertheless, the frequency and harshness of punishment experienced remained a source of fear and resentment for many children. It was not uncommon for older children to tell us that they did not want to go home after school because they knew they would receive a beating. One Harlem fifth-grader we knew who had been remanded to Youth House temporarily for a minor offense actually expressed distress upon his release when he considered the prospect of returning home. He told a former teacher that he would have preferred to continue living in Youth House.

Arthur, another Harlem fifth-grader, expressed a similar aversion to returning home, in this case clearly motivated by fear of punishment. Arthur usually followed his mother's instructions to report to the school lunchroom every day at one o'clock. At that time, the workers in the kitchen would give him leftover food, and he would bring it home to his mother. One day, Arthur was asked by his friends to accompany them during the lunch period while they went to fight with a group of boys from another school. Unable to refuse without "losing face," and wishing to be with his friends, the boy went off to the "wars" and arrived back at school after the lunchroom staff had completed their cleanup routines. No food was available. The boy never came to class that afternoon, and he never went home that night. Although it was midwinter, he slept on a bench in the courtyard of a local housing project. The following afternoon, his mother came to school to ask if his teacher knew where her son was. Toward the end of that day, the boy came to see his teacher, explained his story, and then insisted that he could not go home because his mother would "really kill him" this time. She would "beat me with a coat hanger and I ain't gonna let her do it no more."

Although our sympathy immediately goes out to Arthur, his mother's behavior becomes more understandable if we see it in the context of her life. This mother had several young children and hardly any money. Her husband worked infrequently and earned very little. Without the food that Arthur brought home, some of her children would miss a meal.

The socialization techniques employed by many Harlem parents are basically status-oriented; children are expected to obey adults without question or argument. The typical abrupt commands and physical punishment tend to narrow the child's choices of response to conforming passivity or rebellion, covert or overt. They teach him that "might makes right" while instilling shame, doubt, anxiety, and resentment. These emotions, in turn, affect the child's willingness and ability to strive to please adults, at home and in school, and foster the development of mistrustful attitudes and behaviors.

A study of thirty-six black fifth- and sixth-grade boys in Detroit documents this pattern.[21] Among these boys, a pattern of low achievement, high anxiety, and a propensity for self-devaluation was commonly found and was typically related to the boys' perceptions of their parents as uninterested in the boys, rejecting, and highly punitive. Girls were not evaluated extensively in this study because preliminary testing found little difference in the self-evaluations of high- and low-achieving girls.

Alfred Adler, discussing demoralized children in Europe in 1920, made some observations that seem applicable to many of the children we knew in Central Harlem about fifty years later:

I have asked children among the proletariat of what they were most in fear and practically all answered—*of being struck*—in other words, of occurrences taking place in their own family. Children who grow up in fear of a strong father, stepfather, or mother retain this feeling of fear till puberty. . . . This is the most venomous kind of poison for developing *pessimism* in children, for they retain this perspective throughout life, have no self-confidence, and are indecisive.[22]

In a study of first-graders in a Central Harlem school, Vosk found that fear and demoralization were related to early learning and behavior problems in the classroom.[23] One fifth of the first-grade pupils in the school were studied. These were children who had been referred to a school psychologist by their classroom teacher because of some classroom learning or behavior problem. Although the children's scores on standardized tests of intelligence were quite low, it was the judgment of the tester that these scores were not accurate indicators of the children's intelligence. The very low scores appeared to be largely a function of the children's fear and demoralization, which were manifested in the testing situation by their rigid, restricted modes of responding to questions. These children typically seemed afraid that if they responded incorrectly they would be punished, so they frequently hid behind a façade of not knowing, not caring, or not being accessible. To many of the children, it seemed better to do nothing than to risk punishment for being wrong or "bad."

Our observations in schools indicated that the proportion of children who manifested learning or behavior problems in school was likely to increase as the children moved through the second and third grades. In part, this phenomenon is due to the school's practice of favoring certain types of children, separating them from the rest, and sorting children out into groups from which achievement is expected and not expected. It also has to do with the fact that, for many of the children, life grew more difficult during the early elementary school years. Often families were under increased stress because of a growing number of children. For several reasons, adult influence over children declined considerably during the early elementary school years while peer influence, often anti-adult and antischool in orientation, gained considerably. (These issues are discussed at length in later chapters, when we focus on older children.)

COMMUNICATION PATTERNS

As we have noted, a striking feature of the communication pattern we observed between low-income black mothers and children was the inhibiting nature of maternal reactions toward children. When a parent spoke to a child, it was frequently with the intent of stopping the child from continuing with an activity. Communication flowed from the parent to the child; the child was not encouraged to speak up or to answer. The inhibiting signals were frequently quite sharp if not rejecting in tone and were restricted to a small number of key words carrying maximum restrictive impact: Stop that! Come here! Don't touch that! Children were often ridiculed and shamed. We heard relatively few exchanges between mothers and children in which the children were encouraged to ask questions or to verbalize their personal concerns.

One study of parent-children interaction in Harlem found distinct social-class differences in patterns of mother-child interaction as well as a relationship between these patterns and the child's reading readiness in grade one.[24] A composite score from a number of reading-readiness tests was highly correlated with social class; that is, dividing the children into high and low groups on the basis of reading-readiness scores resulted in about the same two groups as when they were divided into higher and lower social-class groupings. Interviews with the children and their mothers revealed a number of differences in parent-child interaction. The children who scored higher on reading-readiness tests (the higher socio-economic class group) enjoyed a richer verbal interaction with their mothers, experienced more opportunities for conversation with their mothers at meals and other times, and were read to more often. The lower-income (lower-scoring) children had less opportunity for recipro-cal verbal exchanges with mothers. For example, mothers of low scorers indicated more frequently that as a rule they did not eat breakfast or supper with their children or talk to them during these meals. Low scorers were also subjected to physical punishment much more often than higher scorers.

The low-income parent-child relationship in Harlem seemed to be based substantially on a set of status-role expectations emphasizing the power position of the parent and the instant obedience required of the child. The child was expected to comply with parental dictates. The par-ent did not have to justify his requests or consider the child's point of view. Within this system of social relationships, children learn the role of the regulated: They learn how to behave in the presence of others who control their behavior, and they learn to expect force to be used as an appropriate means of controlling others. Frequently, young children in Harlem schools expressed amazement when their teachers responded to disruptive behavior with psychological techniques such as appeals to the child's conscience. Young pupils commonly asked their teachers, "Why don't you hit him?" When a teacher failed to hit a misbehaving child, during the early grades, pupils might call out, "Go get Mrs. X [a teacher known for her use of physical punishment]. She don't take no jive!"

Parental restrictions and reproof can have a variety of consequences for children. Attempts to change a child's behavior by appealing to his need for affection and self-esteem appear likely to foster a more inter-nalized moral orientation, whereas physical coercion and shaming lead to more externally controlled and authority-regulated orientations and behaviors. Parental communication is as important for the development of an internalized moral orientation as emotional appeals; parental com-munication can direct the child's attention to the consequences of his actions for others.[25] When parents give reasons for punishment in terms of the consequences of the child's actions for others, children are more likely to adopt these reasons for themselves and use them in regulating their own conduct when no adult is present than is the case when parents punish without giving reasons and use shaming techniques. But children are more likely to internalize critical communications from adults if they perceive the adults as warm and nurturant than if the adults are cold or rejecting.[26] When controlling adults are warm and nurturant, the with-drawal of affection leads to anxiety since the child has something to lose if he displeases such an adult. This anxiety becomes associated with the reasons for the punishment given by adults concerning the child's motives and the consequences of his behavior. The result is that the child internalizes the reasons as his own rules. The internalized rules (reasons) represent a cognitive basis for guilt, while anxiety associated with rule violation (hurting others) represents an emotional basis.

Although both shame and guilt are negative or painful emotions, they differ in that in the experience of shame the cognitive focus is on some defect in the self that ought not to show, whereas the cognitive focus in the experience of guilt is on the consequences of one's actions for other people. In the experience of shame, the self is perceived as deserving of scorn, contempt, and ridicule; the view of other people, or the individual's perception of others' views, is the source of such judgments. Thus the self is essentially passive; the self is "bad" because of what one is. In the experience of guilt, the self is the source of rule-violating behavior, and others are perceived as the injured parties. The self is "bad" because of what one did. Shame as well as guilt may be internalized; that is, one may feel shameful ("bad," inadequate) before an imaginary audience, just as one may feel guilty (wrong) even though one was not observed committing an act that caused another person loss or harm.

In our judgment, the socialization techniques typically employed by low-income black parents foster the development and internalization of shame, a consciousness of the self as intrinsically "bad," small, contemptible, and ridiculous, with attendant anxiety and defensive and compensatory behaviors, much more than internalized guilt. We believe that shame played a more central role than guilt in shaping the developing personalities of the children we knew in Central Harlem.

THE IMPORTANCE OF A FATHER

Because of job discrimination, black fathers often find it difficult to play a continuing central role in the lives of their growing children. Nevertheless, a considerable number of low-income black fathers do successfully maintain an influence in their children's lives. We came to know a few such fathers, and we had to admire their tenacity in trying, amid much stress, to protect their children. In a few families, the fathers were employed irregularly but continued to play significant roles in their homes. We knew other fathers who were no longer living with their children and the children's mother but nevertheless continued to see the children fairly regularly. But a very large proportion of the children we knew in Central Harlem did not have any continuing or consistent relationship with their fathers. Discussions (sometimes arguments) over who one's father was or where he was were very common among the boys in our classes. Many of the boys seemed to be especially eager for attention from men in the schools, although they usually were ambivalent about these feelings and often defensive about expressing them openly. In the preschool and kindergarten rooms, by contrast, one could usually see a few little boys who, not yet having become guarded in approaching adults, would trample one another in the race to grab hold—quite literally—of any adult male who came into the room.

Children whose fathers were not living in their homes sometimes had other adult males in residence who might play a supportive role in relation to the mother and the children. Mothers' boyfriends sometimes played quasi-paternal roles for children and could be quite supportive. Such mother-boyfriend relationships could be quite transitory, however, providing children with a succession of foster fathers, or "uncles."[27]

Mothers who were rearing their children without the aid of husbands often appeared to be uncertain of their ability to direct and discipline them, especially if the children were boys. It was when they perceived street and environmental influences to be detrimental to their children that husbandless mothers seemed most likely to try to restrict the children's freedom of movement outside their apartments.[28] Such mothers warned and scolded children a great deal, hoping, often against hope, in this way to protect the children from a dangerous outside world.

The influence of male support on the mother's childrearing priorities and expectations was documented in in-depth personal interviews with fifty black mothers in a Northern city, conducted by Mary Garner, herself a black mother from the community.[29] Twenty-eight of the mothers had husbands living in the home; the remaining twenty-two had no husband or permanent boyfriend living in the home and were the heads of their households. Most of the mothers were working poor, with only a few in the working-nonpoor, or nonworking-poor (welfare) categories.

Certain significant differences emerged between the husband-present and husband-absent mothers. Although virtually all of the mothers stressed the importance of obtaining quality education for their children, each group saw education as related to a different priority. The husband-absent mothers saw education primarily as a means for individuals to achieve above-poverty-level incomes. Significantly more husband-present mothers stressed the view that quality education was vital as a means to ensure black survival (economic and psychological) in America. The husband-present mothers, more economically and socially stable, appeared to be able to extend their awareness beyond their families' immediate physical needs to their psychological needs and to relate these needs to current movements for racial pride and solidarity. The husband-absent mothers seemed less able to afford this luxury. Finally, with respect to their children's futures, significantly more husband-present mothers expressed optimism, while husbandless mothers tended to express uncertainty.

The overwhelming majority of Garner's subjects said they believed that it was important and desirable to have a male share in childrearing. However, there was a significant difference in the principal reasons expressed for wanting a male in the home by mothers whose husbands were present and those who had no male living steadily in the home. The mothers with husbands present stressed the importance of the husband's sharing childrearing as a responsibility he has toward the family and the male role as an effective disciplinarian for children. The husbandless mothers stressed the importance of bringing a male into the home to provide a positive male image for their children.

The mothers we worked with in Harlem were generally poorer than those interviewed by Garner; many were on welfare, and many were heads of husbandless households. These facts, it seems safe to conclude, contributed significantly to lowered maternal morale, which is communicated to children in a variety of ways.

On the basis of his study of black families, Herbert Hill argues that, contrary to the widespread belief in a matriarchy among blacks, most black families, whether low-income or not, are characterized by an egalitarian pattern in which neither spouse dominates, but decision-making and tasks are shared.[30] Hill's position may have general validity with respect to the husband-wife relationship. Concerning childrearing, however, it was our observation that whether or not they had husbands, low-income black mothers bore the brunt of the responsibility, as do most mothers, and that their treatment of children was authoritarian in manner and spirit. A study of 555 families in Newark found that, as one goes down the social-class ladder, among two-parent families mothers are more likely to be the sole disciplinarians for young children; but black mothers are about twice as likely as white mothers to be the sole disciplinarians of young children.[31] The classic picture of the dominating black matriarch appears to be exaggerated in that low-income black mothers clearly want males to share childrearing responsibilities. Nevertheless, low-income black mothers rear young children with less assistance from husbands than they would like, even when husbands are present, in contrast to white families of similar social-class status. The burden of being the sole disciplinarian may increase the tendency of low-income black mothers to rely on authoritarian methods, because they appear most immediately efficient in controlling young children.

POWER AND INTERPERSONAL RELATIONS

Low-income children in Central Harlem, generally accustomed to power-oriented discipline utilizing restricted verbal cues, were encouraged to order their social world substantially on the basis of power relationships. In the classroom, many Harlem children had great difficulty exercising self-control, but they often accepted the exercise of control by an adult if they perceived him as having superior power or force at his disposal to back up his demands.

Harlem children frequently sized up their relationships with one another in terms of who could beat whom. The implication was: "If I can beat you, I don't have to do what you want, but if I can't beat you, perhaps I had better." Although these tendencies sometimes made it difficult for the children to form close, trusting relationships, they offered some security in that a child who ordered his relationships on a power-status basis knew just how to relate to his inferiors and superiors. However, the frequency with which children changed residence and the changing membership of classroom groups often left the process of establishing the pecking order within a peer group unfinished, and this process generated a good deal of conflict among the children.

The nature of parent-child relations encouraged an underlying passivity in many children. Some sought to form relationships with strong individuals or groups for the purpose of being protected, told what to do, and taken care of. Being taken care of often required that a child give up much initiative and that he refrain from challenging the status arrangements by always complying with the requests of the superior person. By following a strong leader or a defiant child who challenged adult authority, a relatively passive child might remain essentially dependent and yet appear to be self-reliant and independent because much of his behavior appeared to be self-assertive.

AMBIVALENCE

The most common interpersonal pattern we observed among Central Harlem schoolchildren was ambivalence, particularly toward adults. Many children appeared to be torn between the desire to relate to adults as dependents and the desire to remain aloof. They wanted to trust adults, but they could not do so for long. They wanted adult help but were afraid to be dependent. They wanted to be friendly to adults, but at any minor frustration they would quickly switch from friendliness to sullenness, uncooperativeness, antagonism, or defiance.

Ambivalent children were quick to change moods. They were learning how to live with conflicting emotions, how to develop stoic-resistant or passive-defeated life-style accommodations to the contradictions inherent in being black and American. But their adaptations involved sustaining severe restrictions upon the exercise of their autonomous will, at first in the family, later in school, heightening shame and doubt and causing a continuing, at times debilitating, condition of ambivalence.

Shame contributes to ambivalence by creating anxiety over exposure. Heightened shame leads to approach-avoidance conflicts in which children experience severe difficulties in resolving their conflicting desires to be open and friendly, on the one hand, and to avoid looking foolish, or inadequate or being duped or rejected, on the other.

Doubt contributes to ambivalence by creating anxiety over possible failure. Children may wish to strive for achievement or to cooperate with others and yet be torn between approach and avoidance because approach risks frustration or rejection for inadequacy, weakness, or "badness." Doubt also contributes to ambivalence by heightening suspicion of the motives of others. Children may wish to approach and be friendly but must be on guard lest someone "mess with" them or put them in a "trick-bag."

The stratagems and defenses employed for coping with shame, doubt, and ambivalence become the foundations of character development. The inadequate, "bad," shameful me can become the basis for one type of negative identity, a restricted, impoverished "good self" rigidly maintained and presented to the world. The malevolent, defiant, shameless, "bad" me can become the basis for another type of negative identity, the "bad self." Vacillation between rather limited but rigidified elements representing a "good self" and a "bad self" can become the basis for a type of identity confusion marked by a crushing self-consciousness and a weak sense of will and purpose.

These identity patterns may represent adaptations to the contradictions inherent in being both black and American and to the day-to-day stresses of life in black inner-city communities. They do not absolutely preclude conventional achievement; nevertheless, they represent functionally maladaptive behavior patterns for achievement in most middle-class-controlled institutions, such as schools and most business establishments.

NOTES

1. Erik H. Erikson, *Young Man Luther* (New York: W. W. Norton, 1958), p. 122.
2. *Ibid.*, p. 225.
3. Erik H. Erikson, "Identity and the Life Cycle," *Psychological Issues*, 1, Monograph 1 (1959): 72.
4. *Ibid.*, p. 73.
5. *Ibid.*, p. 68.
6. Erik H. Erikson, *Childhood and Society*, 2d ed. (New York: W. W. Norton, 1963), pp. 253–54.
7. Harry Stack Sullivan, *The Interpersonal Theory of Psychiatry* (New York: W. W. Norton, 1953), p. 214.
8. Alfred Adler, *The Individual Psychology of Alfred Adler*, ed. by Heinz L. Ansbacher and Rowena R. Ansbacher (New York: Harper Torchbooks, 1956), p. 386.
9. Diana Baumrind, "Child Care Practices Anteceding Three Patterns of Preschool Behavior," *Genetic Psychology Monographs*, No. 75, 1967, pp. 43–88, and Alfred L. Baldwin, "The Effect of Home Environment

on Nursery School Behavior," *Child Development,* 20 (1949): 49–62.

10. See Diana Baumrind and A. E. Black, "Socialization Practices Associated with Dimensions of Competence in Preschool Boys and Girls," *Child Development,* 38 (1967): 291–328, and Eleanor E. Maccoby and John C. Masters, "Attachment and Dependency," in Paul H. Mussen, ed., *Carmichael's Manual of Child Psychology,* 3d ed. (New York: John Wiley & Sons, 1970), pp. 73–157.

11. The question is open, but Bayley and Schaeffer suggest, on the basis of data from the Berkeley Growth Study, that the intellectual performance of boys is more responsive to environmental events, while that of girls has a larger element of genetic control. See Nancy Bayley and Earl S. Schaeffer, "Correlation of Maternal and Child Behavior with the Development of Mental Abilities: Data from the Berkeley Growth Study," *Social Research in Child Development,* vol. 29, Monograph No. 6, 1964. For further evidence that the mental abilities of males are more strongly related, both positively and negatively, to emotional aspects of the environment, see Nancy Bayley, "Development of Mental Abilities," in Mussen, ed., *Carmichael's Manual,* pp. 1163–1209.

12. Diana Baumrind, "An Exploratory Study of Socialization Effects on Black Children: Some Black-White Comparisons," *Child Development,* 43 (1972): 261–67.

13. Robert D. Hess and Virginia C. Shipman, "Maternal Influences Upon Early Learning," in Robert D. Hess and Roberta M. Baer, eds., *Early Education* (Chicago: Aldine, 1968), pp. 91–103. See also Robert D. Hess and Virginia C. Shipman, "Maternal Attitudes Toward the School and the Role of the Pupil: Some Social Class Comparisons," in A. Harry Passow, ed., *Developing Programs for the Educationally Disadvantaged* (New York: Teachers College Press, 1968), pp. 109–29.

14. Patricia Minuchin, "Processes of Curiosity and Exploration in Preschool Disadvantaged Children," final report, Contract OEO-2403, Bank Street College of Education, 1968. See also *idem,* "Correlates of Curiosity and Exploratory Behavior in Preschool Disadvantaged Children," *Child Development,* 42 (1971): 939–50.

15. Gene H. Borowitz and Jay Hirsch, "A Developmental Typology of Disadvantaged Four-Year-Olds," Research Report No. 5 (1), Institute for Juvenile Research, Chicago, 1968. See also Jay Hirsch, Gene H. Borowitz, and Joan Costello, "Individual Differences in Ghetto Four-Year-Olds," *Archives of General Psychiatry,* 22 (1970): 268–76.

16. Dale R. Meers, "Contributions of a Ghetto Culture to Symptom Formation," in Ruth S. Eissler, ed., *The Psychoanalytic Study of the Child,* 25 (New York: International Universities Press, 1970): 209–30.

17. Camille Jeffers, *Living Poor* (Ann Arbor, Mich.: Ann Arbor Publishers, 1967), p. 102.

18. *Ibid.,* p. 104.

19. Daniel M. Ogilvie, "Distinguishing Social Behaviors of Competent and Incompetent Three- to Six-Year-Old Children," paper presented at Society for Research in Child Development meeting, Santa Monica, Calif., March 27, 1969.

20. E. Kuno Beller, "The Evaluation of Effects of Early Educational Intervention on Intellectual and Social Development of Lower-Class Disadvantaged Children," in Edith H. Grotberg, ed., *Critical Issues in Research Related to Disadvantaged Children* (Princeton, N.J.: Educational Testing Service, 1969), unpaged.

21. Irwin Katz, "The Socialization of Academic Motivation in Minority Group Children," in David Levine, ed., *Nebraska Symposium on Motivation* (Lincoln: University of Nebraska Press, 1967), 15: 133–91.

22. Alfred Adler, *The Practice and Theory of Individual Psychology* (Paterson, N.J.: Littlefield, Adams, 1959), pp. 341–42. Emphasis in original.

23. Janet S. Vosk, "Study of Negro Children with Learning Difficulties at the Outset of Their School Careers," *American Journal of Orthopsychiatry,* 36 (1966): 32–40.

24. Esther Milner, "A Study of the Relationship Between Reading Readiness in Grade One School Children and Patterns of Parent-Child Interaction," *Child Development,* 22 (1951): 95–122.

25. See Justin Aronfreed, *Conduct and Conscience: The Socialization of Internalized Control over Behavior* (New York: Academic Press, 1968), and Martin L. Hoffman and Herbert D. Saltzstein, "Parent Discipline and the Child's Moral Development," *Journal of Personality and Social Psychology,* 5 (1967): 45–57.

26. See Joan Grusec, "Some Antecedents of Self-Criticism," *Journal of Personality and Social Psychology,* 4 (1966): 211–15, and Richard H. Walters and Ross D. Parke, "The Influence of Punishment and Related Disciplinary Techniques on the Social Behavior of Children: Theory and Empirical Findings," in Brendan A. Maher, ed., *Progress in Experimental Personality Research* (New York: Academic Press, 1967), 4: 179–228.

27. For more detailed discussions of the role of the father, and of the boy-friend as father, in the ghetto, see David A. Schulz, *Coming Up Black: Patterns of Ghetto Socialization* (Englewood Cliffs, N.J.: Prentice-Hall, 1969); Ulf Hannerz, *Soulside: Inquiries into Ghetto Culture and Community* (New York: Columbia University Press, 1969); and Elliot Liebow, *Tally's Corner: A Study of Negro Streetcorner Men* (Boston: Little, Brown, 1967).

28. For similar observations, see Louis Kriesberg, *Mothers in Poverty: A Study of Fatherless Families* (Chicago: Aldine, 1970).

29. Mary E. Garner and Barry Silverstein, "Childrearing Goals, Priorities, and Strategies: Assessing the World View of Low-Income Black Mothers," unpublished manuscript, William Paterson College, Wayne, New Jersey, 1972.

30. Herbert B. Hill, *The Strengths of Black Families* (New York: Emerson Hall, 1972).

31. Ludwig L. Geismar, *555 Families: A Social Psychological Study of Young Families in Transition* (New Brunswick, N.J.: Transaction Books, 1973).

4 / IDENTIFICATION AND IDENTITY

In the summer of 1970 we witnessed a poignant incident in a preschool center on New York's Lower East Side. Five four-year-old boys, four of them light-skinned Puerto Ricans and one a dark-skinned black, were playing together. The game consisted of piling their hands one on top of another. The boys were quite excited, laughing wildly while exclaiming that no one could tell whose hand was whose. One of the Puerto Rican boys called out rather innocently, with the enthusiasm that comes from discovery: "Hey, I know whose this is—this hand is yours—because it's black!" "No, it's not!" the black child cried out. "No, it's not!"

COLOR CONNOTATIONS

In a multiracial society, sooner or later all children discover that there are people whose skin is a different color from theirs. This discovery initially may be the source of some anxiety. Even as early as eight months of age, infants are easily frightened by a strange adult's face or by a person wearing a mask.[1] Infants seem most likely to show signs of fear when they encounter a person, object, or situation that is slightly different from what they are accustomed to. Older infants generally may be frightened at first by an encounter with people of a different color. Preschool children in integrated nursery schools often seem concerned and even a bit anxious over the perception of skin-color differences.[2] Mastering skin-color anxiety and learning to value people of various skin colors are important interrelated developmental tasks of children in a racially mixed society.

In a society that is basically antiblack, the prevailing mode of coping with skin-color anxiety has been for white children to learn to devalue or reject blackness. For generations many black children have internalized some of the prevailing antiblack attitudes and become ashamed of their own pigmentation, hair texture, facial features, and African origins.[3] This is not to say that black children had no self-esteem or that they saw themselves in a totally negative light; rather, many black children unwittingly adopted white standards of physical beauty and thus came to see their own features as a source of shame rather than pride.

Euro-American languages and folklore have contributed to the antiblack orientation that affects many American children. Traditionally, in Euro-American culture, whiteness has had positive symbolic connotations (e.g., Snow White, white as snow), while blackness has had negative connotations (e.g., blackball, black-hearted, blackmail, black sheep, black magic, and things look black). Studies have found a general trend among both white and black preschool children to assign more positive adjectives to pictures of animals painted light gray and more negative adjectives to duplicate pictures in which the animal was painted black.[4] Another series of studies found a general trend for young white children to assign objects of high value to a white box and objects of low value to a black box; young black children responded similarly, although they associated white with good and black with bad less consistently than the white children did.[5] Further studies by the same researcher had preschool children sit between a white box and a black box containing tape-recorder speakers. The children heard statements broadcast simultaneously from both boxes with equal intensity. Asked to guess which box the sounds were coming from, the children more often chose the white box as the source of positive statements than they did the black box. However, this difference was significant only among white children. Black children heard more negative statements from the white box than white children did.[6]

Since the mid-1960's with the rise of the black-power movement and various black-nationalist ideologies, black children and youth generally have moved in the direction of decreasing positive evaluations of whiteness and increasing positive evaluations of blackness.[7] We shall discuss such changes in later chapters. Here, however, we wish to discuss some of the difficulties faced by black children in accepting and evaluating positively their own blackness, a developmental dilemma of deep significance.

Through the mid-1960's, most of the children we knew in Central Harlem appeared to see their color as a stigma, and they definitely did not want to be identified in many contexts as "black." Many fights broke out because one child called another child "black." Black was a term of insult. Black was ugly. Black was laughable. Black was shameful. Black was bad. Children made fun of each other's "nappy heads" and "thick lips." They hesitated or refused to use brown or black crayons to color pictures of people they drew. They laughed when teachers held up pictures of black people taken from books or magazines. And they giggled anxiously when teachers talked about Africa.

EARLY DOLL STUDIES

From 1939 to 1941, in a now-classic study, Kenneth and Mamie Clark investigated the racial attitudes and preferences of samples of black children, aged three through seven, some living in the South and some in the North.[8] Each of the children was asked to choose between two dolls, one with dark brown skin and the other "white," in response to the following requests:

1. Give me the doll that you like to play with—[or] like best.
2. Give me the doll that is a nice doll.
3. Give me the doll that looks bad.
4. Give me the doll that is a nice color.
5. Give me the doll that looks like a white child.
6. Give me the doll that looks like a colored child.
7. Give me the doll that looks like a Negro child.
8. Give me the doll that looks like you.

The Clarks assumed that the children's responses to the first four requests would reveal racial preferences; to requests 5 through 7, awareness of racial differences; and to request 8, self-identification. The results can be summarized as follows: Fifty per cent or more of the black children at every age level preferred the white doll. White-doll preference reached a peak at five years, when this doll was selected 75 per cent of the time.

Racial awareness increased with age; 93 per cent of the seven-year-olds made correct race choices, while only 61 per cent of the three-year-olds did so.

Light-skinned children showed more white-doll preference than darker-skinned children (70 per cent versus 59 per cent).

Children attending integrated schools in the North displayed greater white-doll preference than did children from segregated Southern schools.

The dark-skinned doll was identified as the "Negro doll" about equally by Northern and Southern children.

Light-skinned black children identified the white doll as "looking like them" more frequently than did medium- or dark-skinned children (80, 26, and 19 per cent, respectively).

Psychologists generally have interpreted the Clarks' results as follows:

The consistency with which black children chose white dolls in response to the "play with," "nice doll," and "nice color" requests and switched to the black doll for the "looks bad" request indicated that the majority of black children had negative feelings about black skin and appeared to prefer white skin.

The fact that many black children (about one third) selected the white doll as "looking like them" suggests that they themselves may have wished to be white or had a confused sense of racial identity, although this interpretation is more controversial than the preference interpretation.

During the 1940's and 1950's, the essential elements of the Clarks' study were replicated many times, and the results rather consistently indicated that black children tended to select white over black dolls. Clark summarized many of these studies in his book *Prejudice and Your Child*.[9] Similar studies carried out during the middle and late 1960's[10] yielded very similar results.

Concerning the Clarks' second major conclusion—that the black children's selection of the white doll as "looking like them" indicated a possible racial misidentification, not just a color preference—a study conducted in 1961 pointed to possible methodological flaws in the Clarks' original procedure.[11] Greenwald and Oppenheim noted that the Clarks' sample had included no white children as a control group and that therefore one could not determine from their data whether racial "misidentification" was any more or less pronounced among black children than among whites. In addition, they questioned the Clarks' finding that "misidentification" was much greater for light-skinned black children than for medium- and dark-skinned children. To determine whether variations in black skin tone were responsible for the "misidentification," Greenwald and Oppenheim used a dark brown, a "white," and a light brown doll, all three with dark hair. They found that 78 per cent of the light-skinned, 69 per cent of the medium-skinned, and 93 per cent of the dark-skinned black children chose either the light brown or the dark brown doll when asked, "Which one looks like you?" The percentage of dark-skinned children "misidentifying" themselves with the white doll was reduced from 19 per cent, as in the Clarks' study, to zero; only 13 per cent of the total black sample "misidentified," compared to 39 per cent of the Clarks' Northern black children. It is most interesting to note, however, that the dark-skinned black children chose the mulatto doll as looking like them 50 per cent of the time while the medium- and light-skinned children selected the white doll at rates of 25 per cent and 11 per cent, respectively. The heavy selection of the mulatto doll for self-identification by dark-skinned children and the greater "misidentification" of medium- than light-skinned children suggest that underlying psychodynamic factors may have played some role in the doll choices of black children who "misidentified" in the direction of seeing themselves as lighter than they were. On the other hand, since only 47 per cent of the white children sampled chose the white doll as "looking like themselves" (25 per cent selected the mulatto doll and 19 per cent the dark brown doll, the same percentage as that of dark brown children choosing the white doll in the original Clark study), the precise meaning of "misidentification" with dolls was left open to debate.

Although Greenwald and Oppenheim found less racial "misidentification" among black children in 1961 than did the Clarks, all the children in their sample, both black and white, displayed a disproportionate preference for the white doll and a corresponding rejection of the darker dolls. These results were essentially consistent with the Clarks' results obtained twenty years earlier.

In 1968 a further refinement on the Clarks' procedure was carried out by Gitter, Mostofsky, and Satow.[12] Their subjects were eighty white and black children between four and six years of age, all enrolled in Head Start centers in Boston. Each child was individually shown six 35-mm. slide presentations. Each slide depicted three of a set of nine dolls photographed in color. The dolls in the set differed not only in degree of color but also in aspects of physiognomy, from Caucasian (thin lips, thin nose, straight hair) to mulatto (thicker lips, wider nose, and wavy hair) and Negroid (thick lips, wide nose, kinky hair). After each slide presentation, the child was asked, "Which doll looks most like you?" Finally, the child was asked "Are you white, or are you Negro, colored, or black?" Each child was also photographed in color, and the photographs were used by four judges to rate the child's color and physiognomy according to the same criteria used to rate the slides.

Black children "misidentified" significantly more than white children in terms of color, physiognomy, and verbal misidentification. The extent to which black children perceived their skin color to be lighter than it was judged to be was greater than the extent to which white children perceived their skin to be darker than it was. The extent to which black children perceived their lips and noses to be thinner and their hair straighter than they were judged to be was greater than the extent to which white children perceived their lips and noses thicker and their hair kinkier than they were. Finally, fifteen of the forty black children "misidentified" themselves by answering that they were "white"; none of the white children answered that he was "black," "colored," or "Negro." The extent to which boys perceived their skin as lighter than it was judged to be was significantly greater than was the case for girls. Sex differences were not significant in "misidentification" based upon physiognomy or verbal replies.

Further, darker-skinned black children "misidentified" significantly more than those with lighter skin. The former greatly misperceived their skin color to be lighter than it was, their lips and noses thinner, and their hair straighter.

The data from this study support the Clarks' hypothesis that black children, at least up to 1968, were more likely than white children to identify themselves with dolls that had racial features different from their own. They also suggest that physiognomy and verbal labels may be as important as skin color in influencing racial "misidentification." Racial-preference studies to date have generally been heavily weighted on the feature of color; other physiognomic qualities have not been sufficiently studied as variables contributing to children's racial preferences.

If the black-power and black-nationalist movements (and perhaps rising expectations) have had any significant impact upon black children's feelings about color and race, more recent doll studies might reflect a change in the children's racial preferences. We shall examine some of these recent doll studies later in this chapter.

CLASS, PERSONAL IDENTITY, AND GROUP IDENTITY

Among most of the children we knew, the initial development of racial identity generally had little to do with specific experiences with whites. Poor black children in Northern cities, often living in neighborhoods populated mostly by blacks, apparently first develop an awareness of the invidious as well as the positive connotations of "black" and "nigger" during their early years within their families and neighborhood groups; they are unlikely to encounter whites using these terms until they are at least of school age, and even then they are unlikely to be the target of white racial insults very often. Ghettoization often blocks, at least temporarily, a clear recognition of the specific role of whites and white institutions as oppressors of blacks.

We have discussed in Chapter 3 the tendency for the socialization experiences of many urban black children to encourage shame, doubt, and even malevolence. On the basis of his studies of low-income black families of St. Louis, Lee Rainwater has observed:

> In most societies, as children grow up and are formed by their elders into suitable members of the society they gain a sense of competence to master the behavioral environment the world presents. In Negro slum culture, growing up involves instead an ever-increasing appreciation of one's shortcomings, of the impossibility of finding a self-sufficient and gratifying way of life. It is in the family first and most devastatingly that one learns these lessons. As the child's sense of frustration builds, he too can strike out and unmask the pretensions of others. The result is a peculiar strength and a pervasive weakness. The strength involves an ability to tolerate and defend one's self against degrading aggressions from others and not to give up completely. The weakness involves a reluctance to embark hopefully on any course of action that might make things better, and particularly any action that involves cooperation with and trusting attitudes toward others.[13]

In our observation, children from families that were relatively secure economically, usually families with fewer children, tended to be more

supervised and protected by adults than was generally the case fo
lower-income peers. Most working-class and working-poor fan
seemed to have greater stability and more "togetherness" than fam.
on public assistance. The working-poor families seemed to have mo.
involvement with community institutions, such as church groups, and
more ethnic or racial pride than their nonworking counterparts. Among
the working poor, there were families who, although they used harsh
methods in socializing children, instilled in them some positive sense of
black ethnicity, of appreciation and enjoyment of the black ethos and
black togetherness. Among the families that were least well off economically, not only did the socialization of children foster shame, doubt, and
malevolence, but these attitudes and emotions were linked with racial
identity more than they were in the working-poor families. The children
learned in their families not only that they were black, but that black was
ugly, powerless, evil. They learned not only to be ashamed of themselves
but to be ashamed of being black, to doubt the goodness or worth of that
which was black, and to be on guard against other black people. For
many very poor urban black children during the 1960's, and for some
even now,

> . . . in the heart of a ghetto, *black* comes to mean not only deprivation
> and frustration but also membership in a community of persons who think
> poorly of each other, who give each other small comfort in a desperate
> world. Black comes to stand for an identity as no better than these destruc-
> tive others. The individual feels that he must embrace an unattractive self
> to function at all.[14]

Porter has suggested the importance of differentiating between group
and personal identity when interpreting data on the self-concepts of black
children.[15] Group identity refers to a person's attitudes about being identified with a particular group—that is, being a black person. Personal
identity refers to attitudes concerning oneself as an individual. On the
basis of doll-choice and self-concept studies of 400 black and white children, ages three to five, in Boston (1965), Porter concluded that these
dual components of identity, although *interrelated,* also varied *independently* within the black community, as did attitudes toward whites—
generally along social-class lines. We interpret her results as suggesting
the following pattern of relationships:

(1) Black children from the lowest social stratum displayed generally
negative personal identity, negative group identity, and negative attitudes
toward whites.

(2) Black children from working-class families, which tend to be
somewhat more secure economically and interpersonally than the welfare families, also displayed negative personal identity and negative at-

titudes toward whites. However, they generally expressed more positive group identity than welfare children.

(3) Black children from middle-class families tended to display more positive personal identity—more positive attitudes toward themselves as persons—than children from either lower-class group. The "old middle-class" black children also expressed more positive attitudes toward whites. However, these children tended to express dislike or ambivalence toward membership in the black community, a rather negative group identity. Although the milieu in which they had been socialized apparently encouraged the development of self-respect and a sense of personal worth, it also encouraged identification with white standards and referents and a tendency to dissociate from many aspects of the black community, which were viewed negatively.

(4) A fourth group of children came from upwardly mobile families, the "new middle class." Children of this group tended to express more positive personal identity than children from the lower classes. In this respect, the two groups of middle-class black children were similar. But, unlike the "old middle class," children of the "new middle class" tended to express *both* negative and positive attitudes toward whites, being more openly hostile to whites. Children from the "new middle class" also tended to express more positive attitudes toward blackness than children from the "old middle class," although they were still somewhat ambivalent in these attitudes.

Porter's data suggest that social class was an important determinant of attitudes toward self and toward blackness (as well as toward whites) among black children in 1965. On the eve of a sharp rise in and elaboration of black consciousness in America, Porter found a movement toward more positive group identity and increasing hostility toward whites among children from upwardly mobile families. In retrospect, it would appear that during the mid-1960's black ethnic pride and negative attitudes toward whites' attitudes, which had been quite moderately expressed in the working class, began to take on more militant overtones among children and youth from upwardly mobile families who had more positive personal identities than were typical of their working-class counterparts.

Some evidence that differences in racial and individual identity are beginning to become less dependent on the class position of black children is provided by a 1971 study of the relationship between self-esteem and racial preference in black girls and boys aged seven and eight.[16] A significant relationship was found between racial preference and self-esteem. The median self-concept score was higher for those children who showed stronger black preferences. Yet no significant difference was found between lower- and middle-class children. These two findings lend themselves to speculations that a facilitative relationship exists between increasing racial pride and increasing self-acceptance, although racial identity may change more easily and quickly in response to social movements; that this mutuality is becoming less dependent on a child's class position; and that the black movement has been the most visible social-psychological motivator of most of these identity-related qualities.

Today, increasingly positive group identity as well as more militant antiwhite attitudes or assertive postures appear to be developing among the most economically disadvantaged black children in the nation's cities.

Positive black group identity is likely to be further enhanced by supportive and cooperative interaction among blacks. However, such negative personal-identity elements as shame, doubt, inferiority, and a malevolent orientation have led to personal behaviors and characteristics that have inhibited this interaction. Although blacks call one another "brother" and "sister," their interrelationships have been marked by "sibling rivalry" rather than brotherly love. This situation, though shaped by socialization, has its roots in long-standing economic exploitation and political oppression based upon race:

> The constricted opportunities and the racially determined limits of the rewards available to the ghetto tend to intensify petty status competitiveness and suspiciousness in the ghetto, particularly against those who break through the barriers of the invisible wall. It stimulates, too, a capricious flirtation between a superficial hostility and an equally superficial and exaggerated admiration for even minor achievements of a fellow ghetto dweller.[17]

The requirements for survival in urban black communities perhaps leave many individuals unwilling to make any personal sacrifice for group cohesion, organization, and united action, because individual survival has already required many involuntary sacrifices. The call for nationalist consciousness and the submergence of individual interests to group goals, less "me" and more "we," has been a main element in the rhetoric of various groups that have tried to create a more positive group identity for many young black people. But the critical question remains, given that many young blacks now feel and express more pride in being black than ever before: Have they really internalized positive group-identity elements sufficiently to promote cooperative black social, economic, and political action, or is the rhetoric of positive group identity—e.g., "soul"—too often invoked superficially in defensive efforts to cope with individual shame and doubt or for shameful malevolent manipulation of others? We shall return to this issue when we discuss identity development of older black children and youth in later chapters. Here let us return to our consideration of the development of racial identification and preference among young black children.

MORE RECENT DOLL STUDIES

The first undeniable evidence that some changes in group identity were occurring among black children came in the late 1960's. The use of the word "black" as a term of insult began to decline quite noticeably. We heard increasing numbers of children respond to being called black by saying, "I'm proud to be black!"—something we hardly ever heard during the early and middle 1960's. As "proud to be black" responses became more common, fewer children appeared to use the word "black" as a pejorative.

This transformation seemed to be influenced by a number of events, such as the urban riots and the attendant riot ideology of the mid-1960's; the increasing media coverage given to black-power and black-nationalist spokesmen; the appearance in the Harlem community of increasing numbers of young blacks wearing African-style clothing and preaching black nationalism; and the arrival in the schools of increasing numbers of young black teachers and supervisors, who usually made very deliberate efforts to be models of black pride. Some parents, particularly young parents, began to wear their hair Afro-style and to try consciously to encourage their children to have positive feelings about blackness and to act more assertively in relation to whites. Community-control experiments within the public schools, largely spearheaded by young militant teachers, became focal points for black consciousness-raising. The murder of Dr. Martin Luther King was a particularly traumatizing event that sent shock waves throughout the Harlem community and thrust many people into an unavoidable confrontation with their blackness and a sense of common destiny for all black people in America. From the mid-1960's on, some blacks openly speculated about the possibility that whites might be planning to use military force against black communities and put all blacks in concentration camps or on reservations, or devise other forms of genocide.[18]

Evidence of a decline in negative attitudes toward blackness among black children began to appear in doll studies about 1969. Spurlock asked a group of Southern black children aged four to nine to (1) identify the "prettier" of two dolls, one black and one white, and to explain their choice; and (2) to draw and color a picture of "a person" and of themselves. All the children from relatively high socio-economic groups gave clear indications of awareness of racial differences, but none overtly expressed negative feelings about their own color. But there was a class difference: Several children from lower socio-economic homes also indicated racial awareness in their drawings, but, even though they mouthed the phrase "black is beautiful," the rest of their verbalizations about blackness were essentially negative.[19] This finding, taken together with the findings that their doll preferences and use of brown crayons to color "a person" was somewhat inconsistent from one interview to another, may suggest that ambivalent feelings about race were present among these Southern lower socio-economic children.

Dansby reports a number of studies in the South during the 1970's that document an increase in black pride but also point up the persistence of ambivalent racial attitudes.[20] She cites a study carried out by Carolyn Bright in 1970 using a modification of the Clarks' technique, investigating social class differences in the racial identification of Southern black children. Black kindergarten children were shown three dolls, two of them black (one with an Afro, one with short straight hair); all the dolls had Caucasian features, and they were dressed exactly alike. Female children were asked to give the interviewer "(1) the doll that is the prettiest, (2) the doll that you would rather play with, (3) the doll that you will look like when you get big, (4) the doll that you want to look like when you get big." Males were asked only the first question. In response to the request for the prettiest doll, the majority of males chose the white doll, while the majority of females chose one of the black dolls (without appreciable difference in preference for the Afro or straight-hair style). Of the males who chose a black doll, the lower-class boys tended to select the one with the Afro while more of the middle-class males chose the black doll with the straight hair. In response to "the doll you would rather play with," more lower-class females chose the Afro doll and more middle-class females chose the black doll with straight hair. As the "doll you will look like when you get big," most females chose the black doll; however, black identification was stronger in lower-class than in middle-class females. Although more females also chose the black doll in response to "the doll you want to look like when you get big," the preference was not nearly so marked; lower-class females chose the black doll more than middle-class girls.

Not enough social-class data were provided in the 1969 Spurlock study to permit an adequate comparison with the 1970 Bright study. The later study, which controlled better for class, indicates that by 1970 lower-class Southern girls' racial identity had begun to incorporate more positive images of black features, such as natural hair styles. Lower-class Southern black girls appeared to feel less ambivalent about black hair and skin than middle-class Southern black girls or boys of either social class.

Dansby also presents data collected by Brown in 1970 in an attempt to determine whether there were behavioral indices on the part of Southern male black college students to correspond with verbalizations of "black is beautiful." The men were asked to name the three prettiest girls in a particular dormitory. A sociometric device was employed on two floors of the same dormitory, the key question being, "Which girl gets the most dates?" Finally, the number of times girls in that dormitory were asked to dance at a social was recorded. When girls were rated as to skin color, those with lighter skin tones tended to be chosen more often in all three situations.

Although these results indicate that black pride was not fully developed or internalized by many Southern black children and youth in 1970, Dansby cites further evidence to indicate that black pride is on the increase. For example, a survey of the label preferred by black college students (Negro, black, Afro-American, etc.) at Tennessee State University indicated a shift in preference toward "black" from 68 per cent in 1970 to 78 per cent in 1972. Similarly, Dansby found an increase in the percentage of female black students preferring an Afro hair style from 30 per cent in 1970 to 38 per cent in 1971. While Afros and other ethnic badges may no longer be of critical cultural and personal significance today (the "corncrib" hairdo has come into fashion more recently), we may safely assume that, until recent years, they represented a turning point for the black masses.

Moving outside the South, Hraba and Grant carried out a replication of the Clarks' doll study with black children of ages three to eight from integrated school settings in Lincoln, Nebraska, in 1969.[21] A majority of their sample at all ages showed preference for the black doll, and this preference increased with age. Hraba and Grant reported no data on the socio-economic class backgrounds of the children.

In an earlier cited study, conducted about two years after Hraba's and Grant's, Ward and Braun found additional evidence of increasing positive group identity among black children in Pennsylvania.[22] The subjects were sixty black girls and boys of ages seven and eight. Thirty were from a middle-class interracial suburban school, and thirty were from a lower-class interracial inner-city school. Self-esteem was assessed from the children's responses to an eighty-item "yes-no" questionnaire read aloud to them (the Piers-Harris Children's Self-Concept Test). Racial preference was assessed through an adaptation of the Clarks' doll-choice test. Instead of dolls, two puppets were presented to the children, one of medium-brown color with black hair, the other with light skin and hair. The majority of the children displayed a clear preference for the black puppet: 70 per cent chose the black puppet as "nice" and 82 per cent chose it as a "nice color." In addition, 70 per cent of the black children identified the white puppet as the one that "looks bad." No significant sex or social-class differences were found. Finally, a relationship between self-concept and racial preference was found: Those children who indicated more black color preferences had higher self-concept scores than those who indicated fewer black color preferences. As we suggested earlier, in this instance, perhaps, there was a positive interaction occurring between group and personal elements of identity, and it cut across social-class boundaries.

In 1970, David J. Fox and Valerie Barnes carried out a large-scale replication of the Clarks' doll study with 1,374 children aged five to seven in New York City.[23] The study sampled black, white, and Chinese American children. In one phase of the study, black and white children responded to the same questions asked by the Clarks by choosing among four dolls, identical except for skin color. In a second phase of the study, Chinese and white children responded to the Clarks' questions by choosing among color photographs of Chinese and white children who were dressed identically and closely matched for general appearance and facial expression. All children were then individually interviewed by an examiner of the same racial group.

On all four racial-preference questions, significantly higher proportions of children in the 1970 black sample made racially self-accepting choices than did the Northern black children in the Clark study. Moreover, on each of the four preferences, at least half and as many as three fifths of the black children made a racially self-accepting choice.

In response to "give me the doll that looks like a Negro child," fewer black children in the 1970 sample were able to identify the "Negro" doll; they did not select the wrong (white) doll, but they could not or would not make a choice. This may be indicative of the fact that, as the term "black" has acquired more positive connotations, the label "Negro" has acquired more negative connotations among blacks. Higher proportions of black children in the 1970 sample selected the black doll as the one that "looks like" themselves.

Significantly more white children made racially self-accepting choices. On all racial-preference questions, the lowest percentage of white children making a racially self-accepting choice was 68 per cent ("nice color"), whereas the *highest* percentage of black children making a racially self-accepting choice was 62 per cent (same question). The Chinese children were more self-rejecting than the black children in the 1970 sample and close to the Northern black children in the Clark study.

In summary, Fox and Barnes found black children in 1970 to be less racially self-accepting than white children, but significantly more accepting than their counterparts thirty years earlier. Moreover, black children showed a significant increment in racial group identification, selecting the appropriately colored doll as looking like themselves as often as white children did. This may reflect an increased desire on the part of the black children to identify with their own racial group. Although the black children in 1970 made more black racial-preference choices than Northern black children thirty years ago, the fact that they did not make racially self-accepting choices as often as whites indicates that black children have not yet fully overcome ambivalence stemming from the negative connotations of a black group identity despite their search for positive black referents.

The Fox and Barnes study found certain sex differences in responses.

Black females demonstrated greater own-group preferences on the "nice" question than did black males. White girls more often selected the black doll as "nice" and the one they "liked best" and less frequently chose the black doll as "bad" than did white boys.

In the early 1970's, the Clark study was replicated with preschool children in Harlem as part of a research evaluation of a community-control experiment.[24] No differences in racial identification were found between the IS-201 preschool children and those in a comparison district not involved in the community-control experiment. But on racial preference, the IS-201 girls showed a stronger preference for own-race dolls. The same was true of boys, though it was not so pronounced as for girls. This result suggests that the special social climate of the community-controlled schools had penetrated even to the *preschool* level, where girls, as usual, showed the greatest responsiveness to positive group-identity inputs.

Studies of the human-figure drawings of black children and youth have also revealed a trend toward increasing black preference over the past decade. In the early 1960's, black children typically avoided coloring pictures of people they drew brown or black.[25] Since the mid-1960's, *older* black children and youth have increasingly drawn people with dark skin color and black facial characteristics.[26]

In spite of the evidence of increasing black pride, many low-income black children may continue in some degree to associate negative connotations with blackness, in part because of their perceptions of the relative inability of many black adults to provide *economic security* for their families. Low-income black boys may be especially sensitive to the low status of the jobs held by many black men. One study, conducted in 1970, showed seventy fourth-grade black boys from a large Midwestern city a set of twelve cards, each containing three pictures of adult black males, one with light skin, the others with medium and dark skin.[27] The subjects were comparable in age, expression, dress, and general appearance. The boys were asked to select one man per card in response to twelve questions concerning which of the three men they thought represented a particular occupational group. Six high-status and six low-status occupations were presented. The black boys significantly assigned high-status occupations (doctor, minister, teacher, movie actor) to men with light skin and low-status occupations (dishwasher, janitor, porter) to men with dark coloring. Since dark-skinned black men often did experience more job discrimination than their lighter-skinned peers, the boys' judgments apparently indicate a good grasp of reality. However, the recognition of the low class and caste status and low power positions of many dark-skinned black men may create heightened ambivalence in the boys concerning identification with such men as adult models.

Adolescence and young adulthood may represent a time when, because of major psychological changes, racial identity may be enhanced as cultural conditioning regarding blackness changes. In a 1970 study of preference for black skin, twenty-four Omaha black males of various ages were asked to choose a real and ideal face from eleven faces differing in skin color.[28] They were also required to attribute desirable and undesirable behavioral characteristics to ten black and ten white figures. There was no significant preference among all the subjects for dark skin colors, nor any increasing tendency for older subjects to prefer *light* skin. On the second task as well, across all age groups there was no preference for *dark* skin. However, the youngest males, fifteen to twenty-five years of age, assigned significantly more positive behavioral qualities to black skin than did males aged thirty-five to forty-five and fifty-five to sixty-five.

On the other hand, as recently as 1972, white suburban Detroit lower-middle-class early adolescents had a predominantly negative view of a picture of a black male and preponderantly favorable view of a white male figure, as measured by a verbal checklist.[29]

RACISM AND PARENTAL IDENTIFICATION

The negative impact of racism upon the developing personal and group identities of black children may be substantially neutralized by close, supportive relationships with trusted adults during the early years. The black family, particularly when buttressed by a supportive black community, may serve as a buffer between the antiblack attitudes of the larger society and the developing personality of the black child. In the remainder of this chapter, we focus on children's identifications with adults, particularly parents. First, we review some theory and research related to the process of identification with adults in general. With this information as background, we consider identification with adults among low-income urban black children.

Identification with Parental Models. The years from age three to age six are characterized by the identification of children with their parents and their internalization of parental standards of behavior. During this period, children generally admire the power and competence of their parents and typically desire to be like them. Identification with parents in part indicates the child's belief that he possesses some of the attributes of a parent (strength, skills, etc.).[30] In addition, identification leads children to feel as if they, not their parents, had experienced success or misfortune. Children of this age take joy and pride in their parents' accomplishments and feel shame in response to the parents' misfortunes and defeats. Through identification with a parent, children begin to adopt as their own the behaviors, attitudes, and values that they perceive to be characteristic of the chosen model.

During the elementary school years, children increasingly orient their actions and motives away from parents and family and toward peers and peer-group-related events and relationships. When children have identified strongly with parental models at ages three to six, however, the parents will continue to exert a strong influence over behavior during the elementary school years. Elementary school children who have identified with their parents in effect carry the parents with them into their peer world, even in the absence of the parents.

Generally speaking, elementary-school-age children have not completely overcome their desires and needs to be trustingly dependent upon their families. Preschool identifications with parents are reinforced in children if the parents continue to be nurturant, competent, and powerful models.

The Roots of Identification. Children's identification with their parents is rooted in the infant's development of an attachment to a caretaker. The traditional view of attachment stressed nursing or feeding as the basis for the establishment of a close emotional bond between infant and mother: Because the mother reduced pain and produced pleasure she herself became valued by the infant, a source of comfort and security. In recent years, developmental psychologists have come to recognize that the formation of a bond between an infant and his mother is more complex than simply a sequence of conditioned responses; it involves, in addition, a dynamic process of mutual mother-infant attachment built into the species as a result of a long evolutionary heritage. This process of mutual attachment has to be seen as a behavior system that is part of the basic nature of the human species, one aspect of an inherent need for relatedness to people, not merely a by-product of the nursing experience.[31]

The human brain is potentially capable of a great deal of learning because of the large association areas within the cortex. These cortical areas in the brain are largely unorganized or unprogramed at birth. The fact that the human cortex is programed primarily through experience rather than through genetically determined organization allows man to learn more and to be more flexibly adaptive to his environment than any other animal. The relatively long period of time necessary to build programs into the human cortex is reflected in the slow acquisition of adult behavior patterns in humans as compared to other animals. For at least the first five or six years of life, parental (usually maternal) nurturance and protection are crucial needs of human children if development is to proceed normally. The attachment process, the forming of emotional bonds between infant and mother, with a reciprocal pattern of influence, seems to have evolved to ensure the proximity of mothers to infants and young children and, therefore, the creation of a protective environment within which the human potential for intellectual development can become actualized.

Human mothers serve as both a psychological and a physical "home base" for their infants and young children. By protecting the children from quantities or qualities of stimulation, from within and without, with which they could not cope effectively, mothers help to keep the child attentive to the environment. By representing a continuing source of stability in an ever changing world, the mother helps the child to overcome his fear of new stimuli and situations and to give vent to his curiosity about an expanding environment.[32]

The formation of an emotional attachment to a caretaker is an important prerequisite for the development of dependency. This dependency is expressed during the first and second years of life in the baby's attempts to remain physically close to the caretaker and, when separated, to return at least periodically. When two-year-olds play in a room in which their mothers are present, they frequently glance at their mothers to maintain some form of contact, even while they are occupied in play activities. This dependency leads to desires to win the parent's acceptance and to avoid her punishment and rejection, desires that are of critical significance in the socialization process during the second and third years of life.[33]

Facilitating Identification with Parental Models. Socialization during the second and third years may facilitate the child's development of autonomy, but he will still acquire behaviors desired by the parent and gradually inhibit behaviors considered undesirable, provided that (1) there is a nurturant relationship between parent and child so that the child's anxiety over the possible loss of nurturance can motivate him to learn and to behave in other ways so as to please the parent; (2) the child receives verbal instructions concerning the responses desired or not desired by the parents, with some reasons for these behaviors; and (3) the child is sufficiently mature to comprehend and carry out the behaviors required of him. As these circumstances unfold, the child acquires and is functionally aided by the development of mental symbols (images, words) representing behaviors that have been approved or disapproved. Thinking about behaviors disapproved by parents becomes associated with anxiety concerning the consequences of the expression of such behaviors. These mental representations of behavior, combined with the motivational push of anxiety, facilitate self-regulation according to parental standards.[34]

During the years from age three to age six, as the child extends the range of his behavior, the processes of identification add a new motivational force to the internalization of standards of behavior, supplementing the goals of maintaining parental affection and avoiding parental punishment and rejection. On the basis, in part, of attachment and dependency, children select and identify with adult models, thus internalizing their standards for self-regulation of behavior.

There appears to be little disagreement that children between the ages of three and six adopt a great deal of the behavior of available adult models, even when the adults are not directly rewarding or punishing children for their imitative behaviors. There is considerable disagreement, however, concerning the reasons children imitate the behavior they observe in adults and strive to become similar to adults. According to Mowrer, a child's imitation of a model is influenced by the nature of his relationship with the model. Adults who have provided nurturance and to whom children have learned to relate dependently are likely to be imitated because children value such adults and hence value behaviors associated with them.[35]

A number of studies have obtained results that support the assertion that children, especially preschool children, will imitate a model who has been nurturant, warm, and affectionate more than a neutral model.[36] The adoption of conventionally masculine interests by kindergarten boys has been associated with paternal warmth; boys who displayed the highest degree of sex-typed masculine interests told stories that contained more evidence of the boys' perception of the father as nurturant and rewarding than did stories of the less masculine boys.[37] Boys' perception of fathers as nurturant appears to facilitate their adoption of the attributes of the fathers.

The nurturance and warmth of a model have also been found to be significant in determining that model's effectiveness in reinforcing and modifying children's behavior. Experimental studies have demonstrated that positive interaction with an adult prior to attempting a task desired by the adult leads to greater effort and persistence by children at that task in response to verbal reinforcement from the adult than is the case if the children had no prior contact or only neutral contact with the adult.[38] In addition, field studies consistently have found that parents rated high in warmth are the most effective in shaping their children's behavior.[39]

Another view of identification stresses frequency of exposure to the model and the degree to which the model commands power as two important determinants of the child's imitation of behavior.[40] Experimental evidence suggests that young children are likely to imitate a model with visible power (e.g., one who dispenses gifts to others) more frequently than they will imitate a model with less power (the one who receives the gifts).[41] However, males in the power position are imitated more frequently than females in the same power role. This might suggest that children generally regard power and the control of resources as more appropriate characteristics of males than females. Studies of the development of gender stereotypes in American children indicate that, by age five or six, children generally associate greater power, strength, and competence and, consequently, higher status with the male.[42] Furthermore, boys who observed a female in the power position while an adult male was present but ignored by the female imitated the ignored male rather than the female. The remarks of the children suggested that they felt sorry for the man, but the boys imitated him anyway. Boys' imitation of low-power males implies that, in addition to nurturance, warmth, observability, and power, the child's perceived similarity to the adult model influences his imitation of a model and may override the other factors.[43] By age six, even though boys have usually had much more exposure to the behavior of women than of men, they are still more likely to imitate men. Perception of similarity to a model is an important basis for the emergence of vicarious emotional experiences appropriate to the model.

The majority of the children we knew in Central Harlem appeared to be highly ambivalent concerning identifications with their parents during the elementary school years. Although they imitated parental behavior, the children often appeared to view the parents as unattractive adult models. Most of the children did not appear to internalize their parents' expressed standards for children's behavior; if they did internalize parental standards, the children often seemed unable or unwilling to regulate their behavior in a manner that would please their parents very much. By the time the children had reached the third grade, the parents had commonly lost effective directing influence over the children's behavior.

The early withdrawal of nurturance experienced by many of the children of Central Harlem weakened but did not destroy their attachment to caretakers in the first few years of their lives. But, as we have noted, because the children generally received little nurturance, positive attention, or emotional support from their caretakers, during the preschool years they tended to lose much of their desire to please adults. Because they give the children little support, the caretakers cannot motivate compliance from the children by threatening to withdraw these parental attributes. In part for this reason, they tend to rely increasingly on physical punishment and verbal commands and abuse to exact compliant behavior from the children. This process typically led to a cycle of children's noncompliance with parental desires, followed by escalation of parental attempts at coercion, followed by increasing noncompliance, and so on.

The parents' tendency to concentrate on stopping unwanted behavior quickly, through coercive force, also inhibited their children's development of mental representations (symbols) of parental standards for behavior. The demand that the child become functionally independent while very young, performing various tasks to assist adults, at the same time receiving little nurturance and support, requires considerable concentration of energy and attention on the part of the child. This markedly saps his curiosity, playfulness, and sense of joy in living. In these circumstances, many children tend to view their caretakers as infrequent dispensers of a narrow variety of rewards for the behaviors that the caretakers appear to desire. The children sense that they have relatively little to lose in failing to regulate their own behavior by adult demands. Further, some of the children develop a stoic resistance to physical punishment and verbal abuse, so that these techniques become less effective in exacting obedience.

Many children find their parents to be relatively unattractive models. The caretaker models generally available to the children we knew were characterized by stinginess or inconsistency in dispensing nurturance and positive attention, and by defensiveness, quarrelsomeness, and punitiveness. These traits tend to inhibit emotionally close relationships between parents and children. But this trend is partially adaptive in preparing children early to "go for themselves"—an important means of survival in poor black communities, where individual competition for meager material and emotional resources is a potent reality. "Going for yourself" means learning to defend against one's impulses to rely on others, to become stingy in giving emotional support and praise to others, to resist impulses to cooperate with others, and, instead, to seek individual advantage by manipulating others. Children learn to become willing to hurt others to get what they want. These qualities prepare the children to survive in the street culture.

It is the street culture, however, that badly frightens many of the parents. Even though the parents may be quite proud of their children's ability to take care of themselves, they generally do not want their children to become immersed in the street culture. They sense that the children will become lost to them if they are swallowed up by the ghetto street culture, that involvement in this culture will lead the children into failure in school and "trouble" of one sort of another. However, the parents usually cannot prevent children from becoming deeply involved. Involvement in the street culture and trouble in school become issues around which much futile, exhausting conflict between parents and children revolves during the elementary school years. The children's ability to "go for themselves" makes it almost impossible for the parents to keep many of them effectively under control.

On the basis of their early attachments to adults, their actual condition of dependency upon adults, and the sparse rations of nurturance and attention that they receive from adults, many Harlem children continue to desire, although with increasing ambivalence, attention from adult caretakers. The context in which caretakers reinforce children's behavior, however, teaches the children that the most reliable way to get attention from others is often by displaying traits or behaviors that the others regard as "bad." By making their attention (even though often negative) contingent upon the children's behaving in a manner that the parents regard as "bad," many parents unwittingly encourage the very traits that distress them. This leads to a cycle of more punishment, more incitement by children of parents to react to their "bad" behaviors, more punishment, etc.—in short, more conflict between parents and children.

One factor that decreased the attractiveness of parental models was the low power position of the black parents in America. The first indication the children had of the parents' relative powerlessness was personal —the inability of the parents to provide resources for the children. Gradually, however, the children became aware that powerlessness was related to blackness in America; that blacks controlled few resources in the society or even in their own community. The children could not, however, avoid recognizing their own similarity to powerless models around them, a factor that contributed to their later development of negative attitudes toward the self and toward their racial group.

Boys in Harlem, whether or not they had the father present in the home, frequently sought male models to identify with. Their correct gender categorization of themselves usually led to their imitation of male models more than female models from age five on. For those boys with fathers or father-substitutes present in the home, the crucial variables that determined the strength of the boys' identification with fathers appeared to be essentially the same variables that determine the strength of boys' identifications with fathers in other communities. These variables are the father's nurturance toward the boy, the father's power in the home, and the father's power in the society. When black boys had fathers who were nurturant toward them, who were relatively dominant figures in their homes, and who supported their families, the boys were most likely to identify with their fathers with some pride, and their fathers were most likely to maintain some controlling influence over the boys' development. If, however, the father or father-substitute in the home was not very nurturant toward the boy, if the father used force—even to the point of brutality—to maintain authority in the home, then the boy was likely to be more ambivalent regarding identification with him.

A cold and dominant father may represent an unattractive model for a growing boy, particularly if the boy comes to recognize a severe discrepancy between his father's economic, social, and political power in the larger society, as manifested by his inability to provide for his family, and his tendency to dominate coercively the members of his family at home. If, in addition, the coercive force is severe in the home, some young boys may not be able to perceive sufficient similarity between their powerless selves and their unapproachably powerful fathers to imitate the father's aggressiveness very much. The poignant irony in such a situation is that it may perpetuate feelings of impotence. A father who feels socially powerless to carry out paternal roles, even if he does not regard himself as personally inadequate, may brutalize his children in an attempt to maintain some control over them and in the process may instill feelings of personal powerlessness in his sons. If the mother is warm and nurturant while the father is cold and dominant, weakened identification with the father may be combined with continuing imitation of the mother, resulting in adoption of the victim role. This role may be perpetuated if the boys develop heightened anxiety over the expression of their impulses toward self-assertive, aggressive behavior, and they may use various defenses to stifle these impulses excessively.

If, on the other hand, both parents are low in warmth and nurturance and if there is conflict in the home with the father powerfully dominant, the boy is likely to imitate the father's behavior (identification with the aggressor role), even though he may regard the father, hence the self, as unattractive.[44] Such boys experience little anxiety related to the expression of highly self-assertive, aggressive behaviors and may become, at times, even brutal (brutalized).

Many Harlem mothers expected their children to learn at a very young age to cope with the aggression of other children. The mothers typically punished their children's defiance of parents and stressed obedience to adults in general, but at the same time they stressed the importance of holding one's own in conflict with other children. They often refused to protect their young from the attacks of other children and punished them for turning to mother instead of fighting back. For this reason, the lack of aggressiveness often found in samples of fatherless boys from other communities is not so characteristic of fatherless boys from urban black communities.[45] Early peer pressure to defend against the attacks of others in the ghetto also contributes to this outcome, as does the availability of aggressive adult models.

Through the years, black families have been forced to make certain adaptations because black men have been denied stable employment. Unemployed and underemployed men are not necessarily rejected by their wives, and many of them maintain relationships with their families. In a study carried out in Detroit, exactly half of 130 black male adolescents from families on welfare, all of whom had fathers who were unemployed and living in the home, reportedly perceived their fathers as "the boss" in their families, for reasons varying from "When we eat, he gets his first, then we get ours," to "He tells us what to do, and if we don't do it, he kicks hell out of us."[46] The fathers played a significant role in compelling obedience from their adolescent sons even when the boys perceived the mothers as running their families. As one boy explained: "When my mother tells me to do something and I don't, nothing usually happens. But when my dad tells me to do something and I don't, I can't set down for a week 'cause my behind is sore. He don't take no stuff off us." Ghetto homes in which fathers are present, particularly those in which fathers are somewhat dominant and nurturant, are most likely to maintain some controlling influence over the behavior of growing boys, even if the father is not working and has been unemployed over a long period of time.

In general, the sons of unemployed fathers did not perceive an open opportunity structure in the larger society. They tended to feel socially powerless, but they did not necessarily feel normless: For example, luck —"hit a number" or "find some money"—was perceived by most boys in the study as the only means of escaping poverty. In response to the question, "How could you get enough money to live on if you can't get a job?" a not atypical response was, "I guess I could get me a good hustle—hit a number—something."

The writer James Baldwin, commenting upon his childhood in Harlem, recalls: "The boys, it was clear, would rise no higher than their fathers. School began to reveal itself, therefore, as a child's game that one could not win, and boys dropped out of school and went to work. . . . I no longer had any illusions about what an education could do for me; I had already encountered too many college-graduate handy men."[47]

Similarly, Malcolm X recalls his youth in Harlem: "Almost everyone in Harlem needed some kind of hustle to survive and needed to stay high in some way to forget what they had to do to survive. . . . Right now, in every big-city ghetto, tens of thousands of yesterday's and today's school dropouts are keeping body and soul together by some form of hustling in the same way I did."[48] Although deplored by many black people, contemporary films such as *Super Fly* provide a glorified model of a black hustler (drug seller) who exploits his people. Many black children find Super Fly exciting; they fantasize being like him when they grow up. Even though the opportunity structure is opening for blacks who achieve college degrees, among black youth who do not attend college, particularly those who drop out of school, unemployment and underemployment remain extremely high, and illegal money-making activities are consequently attractive.[49]

David Schulz, who has studied low-income urban black families in which fathers are present, has found that black fathers in such homes do not tend to be simple passive figures controlled by their wives.[50] His data suggest that the father's status depends not only upon his capacity to support his family but also upon the degree to which he adheres to the norms of monogamous marriage, copes with ghetto street life, and is attentive and supportive to his children. According to Schulz, the family that seems best able to survive as a unit in a situation where there is little hope of upward mobility by legitimate means is one that adapts to the coexistence of conventional and street-culture values in the ghetto environment. Such a family is typically headed by a type of father that Schulz calls "the discreet free man," a man who manages to be involved in a variety of interests outside the home, such as gambling, relationships with other women, or pimping, without making these activities so highly visible that they impair his relationships with his wife and children. Such a father is generally supportive of his children, and what goes on in his family is a central concern for him, which leads him to use discretion in handling his outside and street-culture activities. The father's somewhat successful coping with ghetto realities increases his attractiveness as a model for his sons.

"Indiscreet free men"—fathers whose outside interests are highly visible and who display less loyalty to their wives and children—may continue to head their households, but their homes are more likely to be full of strife. Children are likely to take their mother's part in disputes with such a father, whom they do not see as sufficiently supportive of or interested in them. Sons may come into frequent conflict with the father and instigate him to violent reactions against them.

Many Harlem mothers we knew carried a great deal of responsibility in caring for many children, and yet those husbandless mothers who found it necessary to seek welfare relief were forced by the system to surrender much of their status as adults in exchange for minimal economic assistance. Caseworkers visited the homes and made inquiries concerning how the mothers spent their money, implying that the mothers were not mature or responsible enough to spend it properly. The mothers were questioned as to their relationships with men, with the implication that they must not continue or establish any mature relationship with a male. The mothers' homes were inspected for indications that they were not taking proper care of their children. The children often witnessed this process and not infrequently were warned by their mothers to be silent when the caseworker came by. Many children began to perceive their mother's powerlessness during their early years. Thus, the mother became less attractive as an adult model, even though contempt was felt toward "welfare."

Boys in every community who do not have fathers or other male models (e.g., older brothers) in the home will seek out male models wherever they can find them. For many fatherless boys in the ghetto the most available male models are enmeshed in the culture of the streets. Sometimes these models are older brothers or cousins; sometimes they are simply men "on the corner." To many young ghetto boys, these male models seem very exciting and powerful. Displays of hip, cool, "tough" aspects of masculine power may amuse the mother when the boy is quite young. She may even take pride in her little "man" who is going to be "real bad" when he grows up. During the elementary school years, however, many low-income black mothers, including some who were amused by early signs of ghetto-specific aspects of masculinity in their sons, begin to despair over the deepening involvement of the boys in street-culture activities.

But in recent years, children in black communities have begun to see some adult models who represent—thereby increasing the number of—alternatives to conventional powerless roles or roles of power in which ghetto dwellers exploit one another. Movement spokesmen have inspired some young black youth to join organizations that provide support, discipline, and direction and produce communally oriented self-assertion and achievement. This trend is positive but not yet sufficiently widespread to help the masses of very poor ghetto dwellers to "get it together" in their own communities.

NOTES

1. Sandra Scarr-Salapatek and Philip Scarr-Salapatek, "Patterns of Fear Development During Infancy," *Merrill-Palmer Quarterly,* 16 (1970): 53–90.
2. See Marjorie McDonald, *Not by the Color of Their Skin: The Impact of Racial Differences on the Child's Development* (New York: International Universities Press, 1971).
3. See James A. Banks, "Racial Prejudice and the Black Self-Concept," in James A. Banks and Jean D. Grambs, eds., *Black Self-Concept* (New York: McGraw-Hill, 1972), pp. 5–35.
4. John E. Williams and John R. Stabler, "If White Means Good, then Black—" *Psychology Today,* July, 1973, pp. 50–54. See also John E. Williams and Cynthia A. Rousseau, "Evaluation and Identification Responses of Negro Preschoolers to the Colors Black and White," *Perceptual and Motor Skills,* 33 (1971): 587–99.
5. Williams and Stabler, "If White Means Good."
6. John R. Stabler, Edward E. Johnson, and Susan E. Jordan, "The Measurement of Children's Self-Concepts as Related to Racial Membership," *Child Development,* 42 (1971): 2094–97.
7. John E. Williams, R. Tucker, and F. Y. Dunham, "Changes in the Connotations of Color Names Among Negroes and Caucasians: 1963–1969," *Journal of Personality and Social Psychology,* 19 (1971): 222–28. See also Jean D. Grambs, "Negro Self-Concept Reappraised," in Banks and Grambs, eds., *Black Self-Concept,* pp. 171–222.
8. Kenneth B. Clark and Mamie P. Clark, "Racial Identification and Preference in Negro Children," in Theodore M. Newcomb and Eugene L. Hartley, eds., *Readings in Social Psychology,* 1st ed. (New York: Henry Holt, 1947), pp. 169–78.
9. Kenneth B. Clark, *Prejudice and Your Child* (Boston: Beacon Press, 1955).
10. Steven R. Asher and Vernon L. Allen, "Racial Preferences and Social Comparison Processes," *Journal of Social Issues,* 25 (1969): 157–66, and Judith D. Porter, *Black Child, White Child: The Development of Racial Attitudes* (Cambridge, Mass.: Harvard University Press, 1971).
11. Harold J. Greenwald and Don B. Oppenheim, "Reported Magnitude of Self-Misidentification Among Negro Children—Artifact?" *Journal of Personality and Social Psychology,* 8 (1968): 49–52.
12. A. George Gitter, David I. Mostofsky, and Yoichi Satow, "The Effect of Skin Color and Physiognomy on Racial Misidentification," *Journal of Social Psychology,* 88 (1972): 139–43.

13. Lee Rainwater, *Behind Ghetto Walls: Black Family Life in a Federal Slum* (Chicago: Aldine, 1970), pp. 385–86.

14. *Ibid.*, p. 387.

15. Porter, *Black Child, White Child.*

16. Susan H. Ward and John R. Braun, "Self-Esteem and Racial Preference in Black Children," *American Journal of Orthopsychiatry,* 42 (1972): 644–47.

17. Kenneth B. Clark, *Dark Ghetto: Dilemmas of Social Power* (New York: Harper & Row, 1965), p. 196.

18. Some blacks anticipated starvation and forced birth control as genocidal measures. See Samuel F. Yette, *The Choice: The Issue of Black Survival in America* (New York: G. P. Putnam's Sons, 1971).

19. Jeanne D. Spurlock, "Problems of Identification in Young Black Children—Static or Changing?" *Journal of the National Medical Association,* 61 (1969): 504–7.

20. Pearl G. Dansby, "Black Pride in the Seventies: Fact or Fancy?" in Reginald L. Jones, ed., *Black Psychology* (New York: Harper & Row, 1972), pp. 145–55.

21. Joseph Hraba and Geoffrey Grant, "Black Is Beautiful: A Reexamination of Racial Preference and Identification," *Journal of Personality and Social Psychology,* 16 (1970): 398–402.

22. Ward and Braun, "Self-Esteem and Racial Preference."

23. David J. Fox and Valerie B. Barnes, "Racial Preferences and Identification of Black, Chinese and White Children," paper presented at American Educational Research Association Convention, New York, February, 1971; see also *idem,* "Racial Preference and Identification of Black, American Chinese, and White Children," *Genetic Psychology Monographs,* 88 (1973): 229–86.

24. Marcia Guttentag, "Children in Harlem's Community-controlled Schools," *Journal of Social Issues,* 28 (1972): 1–20.

25. See Robert Coles, *Children of Crisis* (Boston: Little, Brown, 1967).

26. See Wayne Dennis, "Racial Change in Negro Drawings," *Journal of Psychology,* 69 (1968): 129–30. See also James H. Wise, "Self-Reports by Negro and White Adolescents to the Draw-a-Person," *Perceptual and Motor Skills,* 28 (1969): 193–94; Earl Ogletree, "Skin Color Preference of the Negro Child," *Journal of Psychology,* 79 (1969): 143–44; and Jeanne E. Fish and Charlotte J. Larr, "A Decade of Change in Drawings by Black Children," *American Journal of Psychiatry,* 129 (1972): 81–86.

27. Frank Sciara, "A Study of the Acceptance of Blackness Among Negro Boys," *Journal of Negro Education* (Spring, 1972): 151–55.

28. N. H. Hamm, D. O. Williams, and A. D. Dalhouse, "Preference for Black Skin Among Negro Adults," *Psychological Reports,* 32 (1973): 1171–75.

29. R. M. Lerner and M. Karson, "Racial Stereotypes of Early Adolescent White Children," *Psychological Reports,* 32 (1973): 381–82.

30. For elaboration of this concept, see Jerome Kagan, *Personality Development* (New York: Harcourt Brace Jovanovich, 1971), pp. 56–71.

31. See John Bowlby, *Attachment,* vol. 1 of *Attachment and Loss* (New York: Basic Books, 1969); Harry F. Harlow, *Learning to Love* (San Francisco: Albion, 1971); and H. Rudolph Schaffer, *The Growth of Sociability* (Baltimore: Penguin Books, 1971).

32. See Harriet L. Rheingold, "The Effect of a Strange Environment on the Behavior of Infants," in Brian M. Foss, ed., *Determinants of Infant Behavior* (New York: John Wiley & Sons, 1969), pp. 137–66, and Mary D. Ainsworth and Silvia M. Bell, "Attachment, Exploration, and Separation, Illustrated by the Behavior of One-Year-Olds in a Strange Situation," *Child Development,* 41 (1970): 49–67.

33. For a more extended discussion of these issues, see Kagan, *Personality Development,* pp. 40–54.

34. See Martin L. Hoffman, "Moral Development," in Paul H. Mussen, ed., *Carmichael's Manual of Child Development,* 3d ed. (New York: John Wiley & Sons, 1970), 2: 261–359.

35. Orval Hobart Mowrer, "Identification: A Link Between Learning Theory and Psychotherapy," in *idem, Learning Theory and Personality Dynamics: Selected Papers* (New York: Ronald Press, 1950), pp. 573–616.

36. See, for example, Albert Bandura and Aletha C. Huston, "Identification as a Process of Incidental Learning," *Journal of Abnormal and Social Psychology,* 63 (1961): 311–18, and Paul H. Mussen and Ann L. Parker, "Mother Nurturance and Girls' Incidental Imitative Learning," *Journal of Personality and Social Psychology,* 2 (1965): 94–97.

37. Paul H. Mussen and Luther Distler, "Masculinity, Identification, and Father-Son Relationships," *Journal of Abnormal and Social Psychology,* 59 (1959): 350–56.

38. See, for example, Norma McCay and Edward Zigler, "Social Reinforcer Effectiveness as a Function of the Relationship Between Child and Adult," *Journal of Personality and Social Psychology,* 1 (1965): 604–12.

39. See, for example, Robert R. Sears, Eleanor E. Maccoby, and Harry Levin, *Patterns of Child Rearing* (New York: Harper & Row, 1957).

40. Eleanor E. Maccoby, "Role Taking in Childhood and Its Consequences for Social Learning," *Child Development,* 30 (1959): 239–52.

41. Albert Bandura, Dorothea Ross, and Sheila A. Ross, "A Comparative Test of the Status Envy, Social Power, and Secondary Reinforcement Theories of Identification Learning," *Journal of Abnormal and Social Psychology,* 67 (1963): 527–34.

42. Lawrence Kohlberg, "A Cognitive-Development Analysis of Children's Sex-Role Concepts and Attitudes," in Eleanor E. Maccoby, ed., *The Development of Sex Differences* (Stanford, Calif.: Stanford University Press, 1966), pp. 82–173.

43. *Ibid.,* and Kagan, *Personality Development* (n. 29 *supra*), pp. 56–71.

44. For a discussion of conditions associated with identification with an aggressor, see Irving Sarnoff, "Identification with the Aggressor: Some Personality Correlates of Antisemitism Among Jews," *Journal of Personality,* 20 (1951): 199–218. For evidence that children are likely to

identify with the dominant parent under conditions of high conflict when both parents are low in warmth, see E. Mavis Hetherington and Gary Frankie, "Effects of Parental Dominance, Warmth, and Conflict on Imitation in Children," *Journal of Personality and Social Psychology,* 6 (1967): 119–25.

45. See, for example, E. Mavis Hetherington, "Effects of Parental Absence on Sex-typed Behaviors in Negro and White Preadolescent Males," *Journal of Personality and Social Psychology,* 4 (1966): 87–91.

46. Michael Schwartz and George Henderson, "The Culture of Unemployment: Some Notes on Negro Children," in Arthur B. Shostak and William Gomberg, eds., *Blue-Collar World* (Englewood Cliffs, N.J.: Prentice-Hall, 1964), pp. 459–68.

47. James Baldwin, "Letter from a Region of My Mind, *The New York Times Magazine,* November 17, 1962, p. 59.

48. Malcolm X, *The Autobiography of Malcolm X,* ed. by Alex Haley (New York: Grove Press, 1965), pp. 92, 109.

49. Twentieth Century Fund Task Force on Employment Problems for Black Youth, *The Job Crisis for Black Youth* (New York: Praeger, 1971).

50. David A. Schulz, "Variations in the Father Role in Complete Families of the Negro Lower Class," *Social Science Quarterly,* 49 (1968): 651–59. See also *idem, Coming Up Black: Patterns of Ghetto Socialization* (Englewood Cliffs, N.J.: Prentice-Hall, 1969).

5 / PEER RELATIONS: THE STREET

THE LURE OF THE STREET

In part because relationships with adults in the home often led to pain without sufficient compensation in warmth, direction, or emotional support, many Harlem children we knew, especially boys, spent a great deal of time "in the street" as early as their elementary school years. Often their apparent freedom from parental control had not been granted but wrested from begrudging parents or parental substitutes; black mothers frequently indicated that they tried very hard to keep their young children at home and away from the street.[1] They sometimes seemed to make the children virtual prisoners in the home. However, as the children grew older and went to school, most of them joined a peer group and took part in its activities. At this point, many mothers gradually appeared to give up the attempt to control their children, apparently feeling that, once the children had been lost to the pernicious outside world, little could be done to direct their development.

Whether their freedom was due to a lack of parental involvement or had been won from reluctant parents, many elementary school children could be seen roaming the Harlem streets virtually every night, well into the late evening. Because there were so many children with similar needs out on the streets, a child in Harlem had available to him at a relatively young age a peer group to which he could attempt to shift some of the dependency needs that were not being met at home.[2] The street peer group thus took over much of the socialization function of the family. In fact, it soon emerged as the greatest influence on the behavior of most elementary school children in Harlem.

The attraction of the streets, we suggest, stemmed from a combination of the various "push" factors that created in the child the wish to remove himself from his home, plus the "pull" factors—the inherent lure of street life. The "push" phenomena included the diminution or loss of adult support, direction, and attention on the arrival of new infants; parental inconsistency in the routines of daily life and in meeting the child's emotional needs; the extensive restrictions placed upon the children, together with harsh punishment for misdeeds; and the children's heavy responsibilities (e.g., caring for younger siblings).

Many Harlem parents, like most parents everywhere, were largely insensitive to the relationship between the problems they were having with their children and their treatment of the children: Although they disapproved of the direction their children seemed to be taking, they often were fatalistic with regard to the children's future. They expressed little confidence that their beatings and warnings would help the children to avoid trouble, and they had very few positive guidelines to offer.

Parental inconsistency in meeting various needs of the child and in day-to-day events at home predisposed some Harlem children to turn to the streets. For some children, even the meeting of basic physical needs was sometimes problematic. They ate breakfast and sometimes dinner on a catch-as-catch-can basis, because the food staples had already been consumed and there was no money to buy more, or because nothing had been provided for them to eat. The children often tried to make do with soda, candy, potato chips, cookies, pretzels, and the like, which they foraged for or bought. Some children came to school often without having eaten anything.

Many children were forced to play "musical beds," giving up, sharing, or alternating their place in bed with siblings or other family members to make room for the various visitors who often came for indefinite stays with the family, for a variety of reasons. Hours for waking and going to sleep varied considerably in some homes. Homework often had to be done at different times and places each day.

For many children, parental attention, direction, support, rules, rewards, punishments, and responses in general had an erratic quality that left the children confused and aimless, unable to develop the organized life-style they needed to cope effectively in rule-oriented school contexts or a wide variety of learning situations. The children were often inhibited or impulsive in school situations that demanded concentrated, self-directed behavior. Strong external controls, harshly and sometimes randomly enforced, constricted and frightened some children, slowed them down, and discouraged them from many learning or achievement-oriented behaviors in school and in life in general. Many children were slow to develop independently governed inquisitive behaviors. The highly impulsive quality of many of their communications and actions in turn slowed their continuing development of differentiated language and perception as well as internalized personality controls. The many unexplained "don'ts" they received from parents, caretakers, and teachers and the rarely understood "dos" left many of the children confused and mistrustful, a few of them so seriously that they appeared intellectually and socially ineffectual—unable to gain a foothold in life. Of relevance to our discussion are the research findings that, although middle-class first-grade children normally perform better than lower-class first-graders on problem-solving tasks in a laboratory, when the middle-class children have to cope with high levels of random reinforcement their performance becomes much less effective and resembles the behavior of their lower-class peers.[3]

Since many of the children had to learn to regulate their behavior on the basis of cognitively threadbare instructions, which seemed sometimes to be based solely on the power of an adult to produce pain, they learned to stay alert to sudden mood changes in others and especially to cues that indicated how they were to act in a given situation. The result was sometimes a high degree of perceptual acuity for people, but at the cost of drained energy and reduced attentiveness to other aspects of the environment.

We have noted that many children had multiple nurturing figures—mothers, grandmothers, aunts, and older siblings often alternated in caring for the younger children. No doubt this "system" (whatever its limitations) at its best provides the children with emotional warmth, rich stimulation, and feelings of security. But at its worst, with inconsistent handling, emotional attitudes, demands, and amounts of stimulation, multiple care may cause delays in the child's progress from diffuse, impulsive, and egocentric cognitive and emotional behaviors to a more differentiated, articulated, focused sense of inner life and outer world.

The children's experience with possible loss of continuity through death, illness, desertion, and separation of many kinds—including their own possible removal from their homes to live with another relative—convinced some of them of the capriciousness, unpredictability, and instability of life in general and confirmed their feelings of mistrust, malevolence, or apathy.

For many children the most general result of this socialization process was the intuitive feeling that they might not be able to hold their world together. It seemed difficult to plan anything. Life seemed unclear; the children often were not heard or understood unless their actions were extreme, intense, noisy, full of impact and drama. Their intentions usually did not count for much. Their actions frequently led to frustration and punishment. They experienced much shame and doubt.

All these features of life in Central Harlem weakened children's ties to their homes very early in life. Some became ambivalent; others turned away altogether, no longer placing any further hope in home or adults. Since street life in Central Harlem was in many ways quite exciting (albeit sometimes frightening), it was the street that attracted the children who were thus alienated from their homes. Particularly during the warmer months, much of Central Harlem life was lived out on the streets. The streets were full of people, on the steps of brownstones and on street corners, who passed the time in lively and animated conversation. Older men would bring crates and folding chairs onto the sidewalk and set up games of checkers, often watched by a small crowd of people who kept up a running commentary on the players and their skills. Transistor radios filled the block with soul music, which sometimes led to spontaneous singing and dancing in the street. Vendors came around selling ices and sweets. Girls jumped rope while boys played scully, tag, and makeshift forms of basketball and stickball.

On some blocks one might find groups of teenagers, with boys rapping to girls to achieve sexual conquests or playing a variety of verbal games involving boasts and artfully insulting repartee ("sounding"). The fast-talking, hip, slick teenagers and young men and women on the street were highly stimulating and fascinating to the younger children. The children often heard exciting arguments, funny jiving, joking, and exchanges of mock (and real) insults. They saw such interesting, exciting, and sometimes dangerous people as hustlers, con men, pimps, prostitutes, winos, and junkies. Many children went for frequent walks along 125th Street, where there were stores and theaters, and where they might see and hear speeches and protests by a variety of black-nationalist and religious spokesmen.

The street world thus offered its own pleasures as well as relief from problems in the home. In some cases the streets *became* the home. Thus Claude Brown recalls his boyhood in Harlem:

> I always thought of Harlem as home, but I never thought of Harlem as being in the house. To me, home was the streets. I suppose there were many people who felt that. If home was so miserable, the street was the place to be. I wonder if mine was really so miserable, or if it was that there was so much happening out in the street that it made home seem such a dull and dismal place.[4]

PEERS AND SOCIALIZATION

For many middle-class children today, the late elementary and junior high school years are a time of transition when children tentatively begin to move away from their parents and look increasingly to their peers for opinions, support, advice, and company in various activities. For these children, the movement toward peers and away from parents may be occurring at earlier ages and may be more pronounced than in recent generations.[5] Middle-class American children today probably spend less time in the company of family members and other familiar adults than was the case years ago, in part as a result of increasing urbanization and the economic and social pressures on middle-class fathers, which force them to spend much time away from their homes and children. More and more, fathers, mothers, and school-age children live in three separate worlds. Thus the guidance of children's lives has shifted away from the family setting and toward other institutions—the school, summer camp, television, music, other media, and their own peer groups. The peer groups of many middle-class children have become rather autonomous congregations, resistant to adult control and highly ambivalent concerning some of the values and conduct of their elders. Nevertheless, the majority of middle-class children still appear to accept substantially their parents' values, attitudes, and goals, particularly as regards school achievement.[6]

This trend toward earlier separation from adults and turning to peers for support and direction is far more pronounced among low-income urban black children, who are forced to turn to one another for solace and direction much sooner than children in other communities.

C. V. Brittain tested a group of adolescent girls on a questionnaire that described hypothetical parent-peer cross-pressure situations.[7] He found that, in the situations involving status norms and age-related identity issues, a shift toward peer-endorsed norms took place, but when future aspirations or achievement in school were involved, shifts toward adult-endorsed alternatives occurred. In the 1950's, Henry Maas reported that surveillance of and interest in children declined earlier among lower-class parents than among parents of the "core culture."[8] George Psathas later found that lower-class families were more permissive than middle-class families as regards outside-the-home activities and age-related activities for adolescents.[9] According to Psathas, this reflected a relaxation of parental controls more than deliberate training for independence.

Suzanne Keller, reporting on the after-school and home activities of inner-city children in New York City in the early 1960's, observed a pattern of little sustained contact with adults at both the first- and the fifth-grade levels, with few organized conversations with family members and little shared activity.[10] And, as is noted above, this is corroborated by our own observations in Central Harlem throughout the 1960's, as well as by the reports of observers in other low-income black communities.

Street gangs of children and adolescents, relatively free of adult controls, are a phenomenon traditionally associated with urban poverty. New York City tenements of the nineteenth and early twentieth centuries, for example, were typically so crowded that the children of large families were rarely at home except to eat and sleep. They were driven out to the street to play from an early age, with little adult supervision, and many children spent little time in school.[11] Yet, lacking formal schooling and despite the power of street-based peer groups, these children for the most part grew up, found jobs, and were acculturated into the economy with the real possibility of some economic advancement. Then as now, society was much more open to the offspring of European immigrants than it has ever been for blacks who have been here for hundreds of years.

In some societies, adults encourage early peer-group affiliation among children and use children's groups as socializing agents while playing down the role of individual families as socializers of children.[12] Adults usually supervise children's groups rather closely, and the group experience is utilized as a vehicle to pressure the children into accepting the values of their adult caretakers and the behaviors desired by adults. Peer influence does not have to oppose parental influence, as happens so often in the American middle class, and even more among low-income blacks.

THE DEVELOPMENT OF PEER INFLUENCE

The observations of Anna Freud and Dann on very young children rescued from Nazi concentration camps demonstrate clearly that it is social conditions more than any inherent factor that determine the age at which the peer group becomes more important to a child than adults.[13] These children were separated from their parents in infancy and were passed along in the concentration camp from one adult caretaker to another. Until their arrival in England at three or four years of age, the most stable factor in their environment was the presence of one another. When they were first observed, in England, the children were extremely attached to one another. They reacted with strong, uncontrolled aggression toward adults and were hypersensitive and restless. The disappearance of any member of the group for even a short time deeply upset all the other children. Because the children had had no opportunity to form strong parental attachments, they became, in effect, one another's first real love objects. When some of the children began to develop attachments to adults in their English nursery, however, their relations with other group members became conflictful; close friends began to treat each other as rivals for adult attention.

✳ The experiences of these children from concentration camps and of ghetto children are similar in their lack of opportunities to form or maintain lasting, positively reinforcing emotional attachments to adults. Because of this common problem, children in both groups were predisposed to become more dependent on one another than on adults to satisfy needs for attachment, dependency, and belongingness. The early timing and extensiveness of peer contact, in combination with difficulties in relations with adults, influenced the early development of strong peer-group affiliations and orientations.

Although it has long been acknowledged that adults serve as models for imitation or identification by preschool children, it is only since the

1960's that the role of peers as models for younger children has received widespread attention.[14] Studies have found that nursery-school children reproduce the aggressive actions of other children whose behavior they have witnessed in a movie;[15] that young children exposed to a peer model who displayed an unusually high level of "sharing behavior" subsequently shared more of their materials than children who had no opportunity to observe such a model;[16] and that a variety of preschoolers' social behaviors, including aggression, cooperation, and speech, could be somewhat controlled by social-reinforcement contingencies established by peers.[17] Thus it has been established that, even in the nursery-school years, peers can serve as models for various pro-social and antisocial behaviors, as sources of "contagious" influence, and as social reinforcers for other young children.

According to Piaget,[18] children pass through three major stages in responsiveness to peers. During the first stage, they relate to one another in an egocentric manner with a rather casual and indifferent attitude toward peer-group rules or norms. At this stage children are responsive to social pressures, but these are usually pressures of an absolutistic sort, such as those that come from adults. The second stage, corresponding to the elementary school years, is marked by extreme responsiveness and conformity to peer influences, in part as a result of the child's tendency to see social rules as coercive and binding. The third stage usually begins during preadolescence or early adolescence, when children comprehend that rules develop from group consensus. At this stage there is a marked decrease in the widespread conformity to peer influences that characterizes middle childhood. In essence, then, Piaget's theory suggests that conformity to peer influence rises slowly during the preschool years, showing a marked increase around the age of five or six; conformity to peer influence is maximal from this point to the late elementary school years (age eleven or twelve), then slowly declines.

Research has generally confirmed Piaget's hypothesis regarding conformity to peer influences. Berenda reported that seven- to ten-year-olds readily yielded to group norms in agreeing with false judgments concerning the length of a line shown on a card, but that children aged ten to thirteen agreed somewhat less frequently, although the difference was not very substantial.[19] By contrast, studies of the influence of group pressures on the judgments of preschool and kindergarten children reared in nuclear families have reported very little evidence of conformity to peer norms.[20] In one of the most comprehensive studies of age differences in yielding to peer pressures, Costanzo and Shaw found that conformity was relatively low among children aged seven to nine; it was highest among children between eleven and thirteen; and it was low again for subjects between nineteen and twenty-one years of age.[21] McConnell found that conformity to false judgments was relatively high between ages six and thirteen and progressively declined from age fourteen to eighteen.[22]

Various situational factors, such as the nature of the task and the status of the peers involved, undoubtedly influence the extent of conformity to peers found in any study. Nevertheless, the findings present a rather clear pattern, even though the results from study to study were not identical: For Western, nuclear-family-reared children, conformity to peer norms increases during middle childhood and peaks during preadolescence. For our purposes it is important to note that the period of maximal sensitivity to normative influence from peers encompasses the later elementary school years.

In this connection, it is worth noting the findings of a series of studies carried out in Texas by Iscoe, Williams, and Harvey.[23] These researchers studied conformity to false peer judgments in a click-counting situation. Their subjects were urban children aged seven, nine, twelve, and fifteen years, including equal numbers of males and females and equal numbers of whites and blacks (each group attending racially segregated schools) for each age group. A significant interaction between age and race was found. Peer conformity among the white children increased between nine and twelve years and then decreased, while peer conformity among the black children increased between seven and nine years and decreased continuously from then on. As a group, the white children were more conforming than the black children, but the peak in peer conformity occurred three years later than among the black children. White girls were the most conforming group and black girls the least. Black and white boys were similar in their conformity behavior.

If the socialization experience of the urban black children in this study was roughly similar to the socialization we observed in Central Harlem, then these children may have had earlier, more intense, and more extensive peer contacts than the white children. This might help to explain their earlier peak in peer conformity. The earlier decline in conformity among black children might be due to the greater ambivalence or conflict in their peer relations and also (during the early 1960's) to their perception of their black peers as having less status and power—making peer judgments seem to be worth less—than was the case for the white children. Mock and Tuddenham found that in the late 1960's in Berkeley, California, both black and white children, aged ten and eleven, appeared to hold the judgments of white children in much higher regard than the judgments of black children.[24] When the children were placed in same-sex, racially mixed groups and asked to make perceptual judgments, the results showed that, the more white children there were in the group, the more both black and white children conformed to what they thought was the group's opinion.

The expectation of future family responsibilities for black girls and the toughness and competitiveness needed by black females to keep their families together may have led many black mothers to stress the development of early instrumental independence in their daughters. This independence training may be reflected in the relatively great resistance of black females to peer pressures. Iscoe and his colleagues reported that working mothers and absent fathers were "common features" among their black sample. The mean family income of the black subjects in their study was well below that of the white subjects, a factor that may also have contributed to the results they reported.

Bowerman and Kinch studied a sample of several hundred children from the fourth to the tenth grade in an investigation of age trends in the tendency of children to turn to peers rather than parents for opinions, advice, and company in various activities.[25] In general, they found a turning point around the seventh grade: 87 per cent of the fourth-graders were family-oriented, about 50 per cent of the eighth-graders, and 32 per cent of the tenth-graders. The shift from adult to peer orientation was not monolithic. By the tenth grade, only 15 per cent of the subjects indicated a preference for the company of family. On the other hand, 52 per cent of the tenth-graders still identified more closely with parents than with peers, indicating that they thought their family understood them better and that when they grew up they would rather be the type of person their parents were than the type they thought their friends would be.

EARLY PEER ORIENTATION

From the Bowerman and Kinch data, a number of factors emerged that distinguished those children who made the earliest shift away from a predominant family orientation. From the seventh grade on, children from large families (more than four children) shifted their orientation away from the family more abruptly and more extensively than did children from small families. In addition, children who shifted early to a predominant peer-group orientation were likely to be experiencing the greatest difficulty in relationships with their families. Children whose relationships with their families were primarily positive remained close to their families even while their peer groups were becoming more significant.

Devereaux has reported similar findings from cross-cultural research.[26] He found that orientation toward adults as opposed to peers was positively related to family warmth and supportiveness. Both English and American children who "swarmed in gangs" were likely to come from homes rated high on punitive controls or on permissiveness (interpreted by the children as neglect). Compared to children who were more strongly attached to their families, gang children displayed less guilt. High punitiveness in the home was associated with anxiety and low guilt. None of the boys who reported high association with gangs, often gangs with high "misconduct" rates, came from homes with high nurturance and moderate discipline. Children who came from moderately controlling homes spent relatively more time with parents, stayed close to home, and preferred the company of one or two friends to the company of gangs.

In a further series of cross-cultural studies, Bronfenbrenner and a group of Cornell researchers found that English six-graders were more peer-oriented than American or German sixth-graders; Russian sixth-grade children were the most resistant to peer pressures to deviate from adult-supported norms.[27] In all these cultures, boys were less conforming to adult norms than girls. The timing and extensiveness of peer contact appeared to play a crucial role in producing these differences. Compared to the American children, the English children spent less time with their parents, less time alone, and more time with their peers. And, as mentioned above, in England, Germany, and the United States, there was a negative correlation between time spent with peers and with gangs in particular and the level of adult orientation. Although the education of the Russian children was conducted in a group-related manner, the children's groups were closely supervised by adults and used to support adult-endorsed norms.

For boys, the father's absence (if no other male is present in the home) may be an important factor leading to an early predisposition for dependent peer-group relationships. Hetherington found that both black and white boys who came from fatherless homes were significantly more dependent upon their peers than were father-present boys. This was particularly true of boys who had not had a father present during the first four years of their lives.[28] Barclay and Cusumano have reported significant differences in the cognitive orientations of adolescent males (black and white) depending upon whether their fathers were present or absent: The father-absent males displayed a higher level of passive, field-dependent orientation than father-present boys.[29] This preference may easily translate into an orientation to go along with the gang.

The earlier peer orientations of lower-class children, made possible by the early availability of peer contact, would appear, then, to function in part in a compensatory way, as an attempt to secure the nurturance and belongingness that are relatively unavailable at home. Maas described differences in the interpersonal patterns of ten- to fifteen-year-old boys and girls from lower-class and "core culture" groups.[30] He reported a much less dependent relationship among siblings and peers in "core culture" peer groups. In contrast, the interpersonal relationships of lower-class preadolescents and adolescents were marked by two types of security-seeking relationships: one in which the child identified with power and needed peers to establish his high status in relation to his agemates, and another in which the child seemed to be desperately dependent upon the physical presence of peers for mutual succor and direction.

In some ghetto families where many children are present, children learn to depend a great deal upon one another. This is most likely to be true when maternal responsibilities are shifted to siblings, when maternal nurturance is available only inconsistently, or when mothers fail to treat their children as distinct individuals (for example, expressing anger at all children present rather than at the one child who actually did something "wrong"). In such situations, alliances are sometimes formed among the siblings. The shift in dependency from parents to siblings predisposes children to seek need satisfaction from peers rather than adults at an earlier age than children more extensively nurtured by adults. An intense need for affiliation with a street-based peer group sometimes derives from partial displacement of dependency from adults to children within the home.

Children in large families often had to compete for the little adult attention available to them. Often we observed that the delegation of parental authority to older children led to conflict between these children and their charges. For these reasons, sibling relationships in large Harlem families often appeared to be highly competitive and full of conflict, even though the children often were forced to be dependent upon one another and would often defend each other against non-family people.

Bronfenbrenner and his colleagues at Cornell have compared the characteristics of predominantly peer-oriented and adult-oriented American children. Bronfenbrenner sums up their findings this way:

> In general, the peer-oriented children held rather negative views of themselves and the peer group. They also expressed a dim view of their own future. Their parents were rated as lower than those of the adult-oriented children both in the expression of affection and support and in the exercise of discipline and control. Finally, in contrast to the adult-oriented group, the peer-oriented children report engaging in more antisocial behavior such as "doing something illegal," "playing hooky," "lying, teasing other children," etc. In summary, it would seem that the peer-oriented child is more a product of parental disregard than of the attractiveness of the peer-group—that he turns to his agemates less by choice than by default. The vacuum left by the withdrawal of parents and adults from the lives of children is filled with an undesired—and possibly undesirable—substitute of an age-segregated peer-group.[31]

Somewhat similar findings emerged from a study by Larson of seventh-, ninth-, and twelfth-grade boys and girls.[32] Not surprisingly, Larson found that parental influence was greatest where "parent-adolescent affect" was highest. In addition, adolescents with high parent-adolescent affect were significantly less likely to differentiate between the influence of their parents and that of their best friends.

PEERS AND FRIENDS

Although for many Central Harlem children, as we have noted, dependence upon peers grows very rapidly during the elementary school years, and children's peer groups become increasingly autonomous and anti-adult, the children's feelings about themselves and their peer groups are often ambivalent. Nor do relations with peers supply enough security or self-esteem to compensate for the children's negative self- and group feelings.

Because of their ambivalence toward adults, their lack of trust in others, their tendency to organize their relationships on the basis of status as defined by power, their tendency to respond aggressively to frustration and anger, and their frequent preoccupation with personal needs, many children failed to develop strong loyalties to one another throughout the elementary school years. The children continued to spend a great deal of time together and were often easily affected by others' feelings and needs; however, because their personal needs and concerns usually predominated, many children unwittingly asked a great deal of one another while they could give only very little. Thus, children's peer groups in the ghetto often become spawning grounds for new frustrations and conflicts as the children become increasingly dependent upon the company of others and yet continue to hurt each other, intensifying the pain resulting from earlier wounds.

✗ Relatively few children of either sex in our classes developed a lasting "best friend" relationship with any of their peers. Friendship patterns seemed to change frequently. Throughout the elementary school grades, children's peer groups were highly fragmented, with shifting, loosely formed cliques on the one hand and large numbers of unattached children seeking to be accepted into a clique on the other.

Such a pattern is not unique to school-age children in Central Harlem, but it was particularly striking there because of the desperate, intense longing of many of the children for attention, recognition, acceptance, and belongingness and their deep mistrust and fear of being hurt, shamed, used, and abused. Alliances formed frequently but could be broken at the slightest disagreement, frustration, or provocation. The children were on guard much of the time lest their friends turn on them, make fools of them, or in some other way benefit at their expense. Children who played together appeared to bicker a great deal of the time.

Particularly among the boys, games of basketball, tag, scully, or marbles were punctuated by frequent shouting, complaining, and challenging remarks. Not infrequently, the exchange included fanciful boasting about the speakers' prowess and insulting remarks about other players' skill, appearance, or background. These exchanges could be part of the fun of being with the group and did not necessarily stop a game or lead to a physical fight; however, it was quite common for such repartee to escalate into fights among the children.

It is possible that the stresses associated with inner-city living, such as crowding and noise, overstimulate children, keep them "on edge," and make cooperative interaction with peers extremely difficult. Support for this hypothesis can be found in the results of a comparative study of co-operative and competitive behaviors of samples of urban Afro-American, Anglo-American, and Mexican American children, on the one hand, and Mexican urban and village children, on the other, all aged seven to nine years.[33] On tasks that required cooperative effort, the urban children, whether American subgroups or Mexican, displayed higher degrees of nonadaptive competitiveness than the Mexican village children. The urban American children commonly engaged in wild, aggressive shouting matches when it was necessary to work together to achieve a desired goal. Urban Mexican children behaved like the urban American children. The slower, quieter, more deliberately cooperative behavior of the Mexican village children, therefore, apparently represents a subcultural characteristic associated with village life rather than a broad national characteristic associated with Mexican ethnicity. Similarly, children from Israeli kibbutzim have been observed to be more cooperative than urban, middle-class Israeli children (the magnitude of the difference in cooperative behavior being greater for boys than for girls).[34]

COMING UP MALE

In spite of the often conflictful nature of peer relations, loose, general peer-group attachments continued to predominate over strong individual or family attachments for many individuals in Harlem even when they became adult, married, and had children. This was particularly evident among males, although we knew a number of young teenage girls who had babies, gave the babies to their mothers to raise, and continued to function as part of an adolescent street group. The tendency of some adults to remain peer-oriented rather than family-oriented is not unique to Central Harlem. Among white males from blue-collar or stable working-class communities Komarovsky has observed an orientation toward continuing all-male peer-group involvements after marriage to predominate over an orientation for a husband and wife to spend time together.[35] For a variety of reasons, including economic instability and the related inability of many black males to play the husband-breadwinner-father roles, the pattern of loose male attachments to families, wives, children (and friends) is seen more commonly in black ghettos than in other communities.[36] White blue-collar males may be more interested in staying out with the boys than staying home with their wives, but they are generally more able than black males to support their families and tend to maintain primary loyalties to "wife and kids" in areas other than preferred association and shared activity patterns. One aspect of coming up male in the ghetto for many young blacks is the acquisition of orientations and life-styles that will enable them to survive frequent unemployment or underemployment by making and breaking relationships somewhat opportunistically and manipulatively. In this pattern, the relationship of a black male to the woman and children in his life becomes unstable or without continuing commitment.

Some observers argue that the "battle of the sexes" is a key element in the social structures of lower-class black ghetto residents. According to Charles Keil, this phrase is no mere figure of speech in the ghetto but describes a view of men and women as separate and antagonistic species that overrides other distinctions, such as creed, class, or color. Many ghetto residents, he claims, believe this:

> Men are "by nature" primarily interested in sexual satisfaction and independence (money will get you both); they are "strong" sexually, and will take favors from anyone who will grant them. Women are said to be primarily interested in emotional support and their families (money is needed to keep the household intact); they are "weak" sexually, and tend to become attached to one or two men at a time. Men call women self-righteous, money-grabbing, treacherous, and domineering. Women simply say that all men are no good. Relationships between the sexes are usually governed by variations of the "finance-romance" equation that appears in so many blues lyrics.[37]

Keil may be exaggerating this orientation to male-female relationships among lower-income urban blacks; however, it surely does exist, and whether it is a reaction to economic discrimination against black males in America or simply a ghetto-specific cultural element or both, the orientation and ideology are learned as an integral part of coming up male in the ghetto, and to a greater degree than in other communities. Support for this proposition can be found in the responses to a questionnaire on heterosexual relations obtained from a predominantly working-class sample of 341 black and 921 white ten- to seventeen-year-olds living in a Northern city.[38] To the question, "Would you like to get married some day?" the number of black males answering "yes" dropped from 71 per cent at ages ten and eleven to 58 per cent at ages sixteen and seventeen; the "yes" responses for white males, on the other hand, rose from 57 per cent at ages ten and eleven to 77 per cent at ages sixteen and seventeen. The percentage-point difference in affirmative responses between black and white males aged sixteen and seventeen was statistically significant— i.e., not likely to be simply a chance occurrence. Although more white females aged sixteen and seventeen expressed a desire to marry someday than white males of the same age (90 per cent as opposed to 77 per cent) or than black females of the same age (84 per cent), these differences were not as large as the 19-point gap between white and black males. Thus, by their mid-teens, black males appeared much more likely to view marriage negatively than either black females, white males, or white females, and black males deviated from mainstream cultural orientations to a far greater extent than black females.

One aspect of the experience of black ghetto residents is their awareness of both street-culture and mainstream-culture values and ideology,
which exist alongside each other. The "battle of the sexes" values and
ideology are most strongly embraced by children who are most absorbed
in peer activities and are an important part of indoctrination into the
male peer group of the streets. Those children who did not become
deeply involved in street culture and street-based peer-group activities,
who represented a larger percentage of girls than boys, adhered less to
"battle of the sexes" values and ideology as they grew up and were likely
to give allegiance to mainstream values, particularly in relation to school.
(We shall discuss the coexistence of ghetto street culture and mainstream
culture more fully in Chapter 10.)

For Harlem boys, as for all boys reared primarily by their mothers in
the early years, the formation of all-male peer groups early in the elementary school years appears to be a crucial step toward learning many
socially defined and normative aspects of the male role in their particular
community and in the larger society. Lower-class black mothers, through
their relatively harsh treatment of their sons and sometimes open preference for their daughters, frequently appeared to convey certain messages
to boys coming up in the ghetto, knowingly or not, even before the boys
became part of a peer group. For example, the boys were often aware of
their mothers' expectations that they should become tough, cunning,
and able to protect and fend for themselves. Many mothers also, though
often unwittingly, conveyed the expectation that their sons were not
likely to behave responsibly but rather would almost inevitably get into
one kind of trouble or another (lying, playing hooky from school, drinking, drugs, stealing, etc.).

Within their male peer groups, during the elementary school years,
many Harlem boys continued to develop and elaborate such personal
traits as skill in fighting, physical bravery and daring, the ability to outwit others, and adroitness in the exchange of verbal insults. As they
neared preadolescence boys learned the art of "sounding" or "playing the
dozens," the exchange of rather ritualized verbal insults, often involving
abusive comments about opponents' mothers (sometimes with suggestions of promiscuous or perverted sexual practices). Through the exchange of such insults, boys help one another to break any residual,
though ambivalent, dependency upon their mothers. By ridiculing and
tearing down one another's mothers as sexual objects, they simultaneously affirm their power to capitalize on a woman's presumed sexual
weakness and, in the process, to direct sexual drives away from their own
families. Arguing against a psychoanalytic interpretation of the dozens,
which sees these ritualized insults directed at mothers as a defense against
incestuous sexual desires, Joseph White criticizes white psychologists and
linguists and offers an alternative explanation:

Assuming the dozens to be part of our matriarchal bag, they literally think we want to have destructive sexual encounters with our mamas. An alternate historical explanation from the black experience might be that the brothers and sisters use the dozens as a game to teach them how to keep cool and think fast under pressure, without saying what was really on their minds.[39]

Without negating the possibility that the dozens might sometimes serve as a safety valve for the expression of forbidden sexual desires and hostility, particularly for boys without fathers who have young mothers entertaining boyfriends in crowded apartments, it is our judgment that the dozens is a cultural device that has served principally to train black males in America to tolerate high levels of shame, based upon powerlessness, without exploding into possibly suicidal open aggression against their tormentors and oppressors. In a similar vein, Grier and Cobbs argue:

> In the deepest sense, the essence of the dozens lies not in the insults but in the response of the victim. To take umbrage is considered an infantile response. Maturity and sophistication bring the capability to suffer the vile talk with aplomb at least, and hopefully, with grace and wit . . . it is possible that the most important effect of the dozens is a pronounced degradation of the spirit. It may be more than chance that the introduction of the black boy to manhood is made via insult and that manhood is proven by an ability to stand by while those whom he holds dearest are vilified.[40]

Although Northern socialization has allowed for more direct expressions of aggression than Southern socialization, Northern black male aggression has been expressed predominantly within black communities and has been directed against fellow blacks.[41] According to Labov, who studied the linguistic behavior of preadolescent and adolescent male members of street gangs in Harlem, the ideal member of such a group

> . . . is a dangerous and effective fighter; he pays no attention to rules of a fair fight; he is a daring and successful thief; he pays no attention to any taboos on language, even in front of older women, and he has a good command of invective; he can handle large amounts of whiskey and will drink anything in sight, including port; he gets high on reefers, heroin and cocaine; gets all the women he wants by a bold and direct approach, but has no personal regard for women at all.[42]

In recent years, some politically conscious and nationalist-minded young men and women have influenced a small minority of Harlem youth who might otherwise have fitted into the gang pattern described above to refrain from drugs and in-group fighting and to channel their energies into trying to organize and rebuild their community. This influence remains overshadowed, however, by the divisive in-group and intra-group relationships of many Harlem children and adolescents and the resistance of peer-group members to direction and control by adults.

Although the characteristics described above were found most often in boys, it is not uncommon for ghetto girls to show similar traits to a degree that sets them apart from their female counterparts in most other American communities. Girls frequently compete successfully with boys in exchanges of insults and even in physical combat. In elementary and junior high school groups in Harlem, we have seen girls challenge boys and hold their own in boxing.

In our fifth- and sixth-grade classes, we saw a number of boys who were struggling hard to free themselves from what they considered to be female domination. These boys would refuse to stay in a classroom with a female teacher, insisting on accompanying their male teachers whenever the classroom was left in the charge of a woman, complaining bitterly that they didn't like women telling them what to do. When left with women teachers, the boys frequently created disturbances in the classroom that forced their male teachers to come back and take them out of the room.

The peer group early became the principal institution in which many Harlem children, especially boys, strove to develop feelings of "belongingness" and self-esteem. Because many of the children belonged essentially only to one another, they had strong tendencies to affiliate and congregate and to seek succor and direction from one another. Many of the children, however, spent a great deal of energy attempting to enhance their self-esteem by establishing a power relationship to their contemporaries. This often led to recurring contests in which children tried to gain social recognition by getting the best of others physically, through verbal abuse, or through shrewdness and cunning.

Thus, we observed the development of a competitive system in which children in the early elementary school grades were initiated in techniques for gaining status at the expense of others. Although such a system has been found to be more or less typical of lower-class groups in general, Harlem children frequently went to extremes in attempting to establish identity on the basis of success in the continuing contest.[43] The children strove to develop and present those aspects of themselves that would make them seem exciting and worthy of attention and that would help them obtain satisfaction of their needs. For boys, fighting ability, bravery, and the ability to outwit others, to be "one up" on an opponent, were stressed. For older boys and girls, skill in arousing or exploiting the opposite sex often developed as a means of gaining acceptance and proving personal adequacy or superiority.

VERBAL CONTESTS

The street-based peer group is the context within which many Harlem children learn to develop and express a variety of forms of linguistic-cognitive competence. The "good talker," one who is skilled in the ghetto idiom and style, especially in verbal repartee, gains attention, high status, and esteem. Some children developed great ingenuity in inventing squelching remarks. For example, two nine-year-old girls were engaged in an argument about whose family was the poorer. The argument was finally terminated when one child said, "Honey, your mother's drawers got so many holes in them, she don't know which ones to put her feet in!"

Children enjoyed listening to their peers exchange insults and were highly appreciative of especially creative examples, to which they responded by laughing, shouting "whoooowee" or "woof," or slapping each other across the palm.

In the early elementary grades, the insults were essentially attempts at funny name-calling. By the upper elementary grades, they had become more elaborate, sometimes involving one-line gags or mimicry. Certain topics and one-liners were used rather routinely and often became the basis for rather malicious teasing. The precarious economic position of the children's families was a prime area.

Parental drinking was another topic that often came in for brutal comment. In a number of elementary schoolrooms we saw boys mimicking the mother of a classmate by staggering around the room and announcing: "This be John's mother when she be drinkin that Gypsy Rose wine. . . . Oh, yeah . . . this John's mother." A typical response was: "At least I got a mother!!" This last remark often led to physical combat among elementary-school-age boys.

As noted earlier, until about 1967–68, skin color and other physical features were often used as the basis of personal insults. Children would call each other "big head," "nappy head," "big lips," "black African," "black ass," "black nigger," and the like in an effort to shame others. But blackness and obviously negroid physical features have become less and less appropriate as a basis for insults. During the late 1960's we started to hear the children perform little rhymes and songs indicating a change to a more positive orientation toward blackness. For example:

> Black is beautiful,
> brown is hip,
> yellow is makin' it—
> white is shit!

Some street songs the children sang in the late 1960's began to incorporate political phrases that were becoming popular at that time in the community:

> Oh, foxy mama,
> what you gonna do?
> Bosco bugaloo.

> What you say is best?
> Hit em in the chest.
> Umgawa!
> Black Power!

Among teenage urban black males the exchange of insults becomes more elaborate and more ritualized. The following excerpt is from an exchange among Chicago ghetto youth during the mid-1960's:

FRANK: Hey, Leroy your mama . . . calling you, man . . .
CUNNY: Leroy, you stupid bastard, you let Frank make a fool of you. He said that 'bout your mama.
PRETTY BLACK: Aw, Fat asshead "Cunny" shut up.
CUNNY: Ain't that some shit. This black slick head motor flicker got nerve 'nough to call somebody "fat head." Boy, you so black, you sweat Permalube oil.

(This eased the tension of the group as they burst into loud laughter.)

PRETTY BLACK: What you laughing 'bout, Nap, with your funky mouth smelling like dog shit!

(Even Leroy laughed at this.)

NAP: Your mama motherfucker.
PRETTY BLACK: Your funky mama too.
NAP: (strongly) It takes twelve barrels of water to make a steamboat run; it takes an elephant's dick to make your grandmammy come; she been elephant-fucked, camel-fucked, and hit side the head with your grandpappy's nuts.
REESE: Godorr-damn; go on and rap motherfucker.

(Reese began slapping each boy in his hand, giving his positive approval of Nap's comment.)

PRETTY BLACK: (in an effort not to be outdone, but directing his verbal play elsewhere) Reese, what you laughing 'bout? You so square, you shit bricked shit.
FRANK: Whoooowee![44]

As we noted earlier, the most common targets in any exchange of insults among Harlem children were the children's mothers. Young children frequently complained to their teacher that their classmates were passing remarks about their mothers—"He always talkin' 'bout my mother!" they would say vehemently or in exasperation. Although this happened more often with boys, it was true of both sexes.

In many arguments, regardless of their nature, the word "mother" would be heard—the intent was always to be insulting or unnerving. Children would commonly retort, "Your mother!" in the way of a final insult to those with whom they were in conflict. Any insult or criticism, mild or severe, received by a child could be answered with "your mother!" A child pointing out to his neighbor that his schoolwork was "wrong" would hear "your mother's wrong." A child would call another stupid and instantly hear "your mother" ringing in his ears. "Your coat's too big" would be followed by "your mother's hole too big." Again, these diatribes were typical among the boys, but it was not uncommon to hear girls engage in them, too.

By the late elementary school and early junior high school grades the insults concerning mothers tended to become more frequent, more stylized, and more ritualized among the boys. The value placed on verbal ability by the peer group became clearer, and some boys began to develop a repertoire of "sounding" or "woofing" one-liners about mothers and families. For example:

"I went up Clarence house and ask his mother for a drink of water. She say, 'Wait till the tide comes in.' "

"I went to sleep in your house and yo mama say I had to sleep in a pissy bed."

"I went to your house and ask your mother could I go to the bathroom. She say, 'The submarine just left.' "

"I went to your house and saw roaches walkin' round in combat boots."

The following one-liners, collected from fifth- and sixth-grade black boys in Chicago, are similar to the insults we heard in Central Harlem:

Yo mama is so bowlegged, she looks like the bit out of a donut.

Yo mama sent her picture to the lonely hearts club and they sent it back and said, "We ain't that lonely!"

Your family is so poor the rats and roaches eat lunch out.

Your house is so small the roaches walk single file.

I walked in your house and your family was running around the table. I said, "Why you doin' that?" Your mama say, "First one drops, we eat."[45]

During the elementary school years, insults about mothers frequently led to fights, but as the children grew older they learned how to tolerate shame and yet strive for status among peers by playing the dozens, answering back, sometimes with rhymed insults. Usually the game started when one boy said something about another boy's mother. Another peer would say, "Are you going to let him say that 'bout your mama?" This instigating role is known as "signifying." The exchange of insults then began with one-liners and built up to ritualized rhymed retorts. The following example comes from a collection of black narrative and folklore made on the streets of Philadelphia. After mentioning the name of one boy's mother in conversation—say, "Constance"—a fourteen- or fifteen-year-old would remark, "Yeah, Constance was real good to me last Thursday." Then Constance's son would have to reply in kind: "I heard Virginia [the other boy's mother] lost her titty in a poker game." "Least my mother ain't no cake, everybody get a piece." The other might reply:

> I hate to talk about your mother,
> She's a good old soul.
> She's got a ten-ton pussy
> And a rubber asshole.
> She got hair on her pussy
> That sweep the floor.
> She got knobs on her titties
> That open the door.

The response might be:

> I fucked your mother on
> an electric wire.
> I made her pussy go
> higher and higher.

> I fucked your mother
> between two cans.
> Up jumped a baby
> and hollered, "Superman."[46]

Missing fathers also were fair game. A group of fifth-grade boys in Harlem held the following conversation while they were working in their classroom:

"I'm goin' with my father—he come to see me every Sunday."
"He don't come to see you."
"He do, man!"
"You lyin'."
"NO, he DO. He gonna take me for a ride in his Bonneville."
"Your father ain't got no Bonneville."
"He do!"
"You lyin'; you never see your father."
"Look, man, at least I know who my father is!"

On another occasion we heard a boy of about twelve say to a group of boys that his mother was suing his father for not paying to support the kids. After he left the group, another boy commented, "At least he knows where his father lives. That's better than my father. He wouldn't recognize me if he saw me in the street."

In the early training that many black mothers give their children to enable them to fight back and be self-reliant, in the bickering and challenging that so frequently accompany the play of ghetto children, and in the continuing socialization of verbal skills for competence in the context of a continuing peer-group contest system, we saw the same element: the need to learn how to hold one's own in the competition for material goods and esteem. The emphasis on "holding one's own" made much of the children's play highly competitive and aggressive and their social relations highly manipulative. In the process, many children developed skills in both controlling and expressing aggression and in manipulating others that would enable them to survive in the world of the streets as they grew older.

Within the street-based peer groups in Harlem, the prestige norms that had the greatest influence on the speech of the children as they came up were those that led to success in manipulating and controlling people and situations. The function of much of the language used in these peer groups was to project the speakers as worthy of attention, to assert themselves in competition, or to arouse emotion in others, frequently with the intent of getting others to give up or do something that would be of some benefit to the speaker. This central orientation to the use of language reinforced the children's tendency to view the social situations in which they moved as a series of transactions requiring them to be ready always to take advantage of a person or situation or to defend themselves against being shamed or victimized.

In their street peer groups, Harlem children elaborated their defensive strategies for dealing with the power aspects of human relationships. Children supported one another in finding ways to circumvent the limited power of parents to control their behavior. Peers also supported one another in defensive or assertive behaviors for dealing with whites, particularly teachers, school administrators, and police. When faced with adult power or white power, the children could display loyalty to one another and support one another. When faced with rival peer groups from other parts of the community, the children also were able to band together for defense or for exploitation of "outsiders." But in relationships within their own groups, competitiveness and manipulation appeared to outweigh cooperation and support much of the time.

Competitiveness and divisiveness can of course be found in the peer relations of white middle-class children as well, but it appeared to be highly exaggerated among the children of Harlem.

Verbal skills and quick wits, developed early in the competitive peer-group games, might be employed later in a career as a street hustler, living by one's wits and ability to outmaneuver others. Malcolm X has described the hustler mentality as follows:

> Full-time hustlers never can relax to appraise what they are doing and where they are bound. As is the case in any jungle, the hustler's every waking hour is lived with both the practical and subconscious knowledge

that if he ever relaxes, if he ever slows down, the other hungry, restless foxes, ferrets, wolves, and vultures out there with him won't hesitate to make him their prey.[47]

Many psychologists who have focused upon the low IQs and poor school performance of urban black children have failed to appreciate the verbal creativity, the mental toughness and cunning of some of the children, which is used to achieve high status in ghetto peer groups. They have failed to recognize the role of the peer group in developing mental and verbal survival skills in those whose lives are marked by blocked opportunities in the larger society. They have ignored the cognitive agility needed by black children to "shuck" and "jive" white teachers and school administrators or "work their game" on other children or adults and the mental concentration required for the presentation of an exciting and dynamic personality style, which children develop to gain attention, prestige, and status in their groups. Schools generally have not recognized these skills and abilities as strengths, and they generally have not been able to capitalize on the particular coping styles that the children put so much energy into perfecting.

Some linguists, psychologists, and educational reformers have recognized the verbal creativity and mental agility ghetto children display in their street peer world, but they have tended to romanticize it. They have not paid sufficient attention to the manipulative or defensive context in which they are frequently employed or sufficiently appreciated the divisive elements in the children's peer relations. The competencies developed within street peer groups are decided strengths: These strengths are often employed, however, in ways that inhibit the development of the mutual trust and group solidarity blacks need to "get it together" in their own communities.

OTHER STATUS-SEEKING BEHAVIOR

Not all members of street peer groups are verbally and mentally creative. Many children continually sought acceptance by their peers only to be made the victims of "sounds" or "woofs" by the more adroit. A large number of children seemed to be in a perpetual state of confusion or ambivalence: They kept seeking anchorage with their peers, experienced frequent frustration, withdrew for a time into detached, sullen isolation, and repeated the cycle by trying to gain peer attention and acceptance.

The most verbally skillful could gain status in ways other than "sounding" or putting someone down cleverly. A Harlem youth could gain high status among his peers if he was able to recite with skill and feeling a variety of long narrative poems and stories which form a part of the oral-aural culture of American blacks and derive from the oral traditions of Africa. These poems, called toasts, often are recited from memory, with additional dialogue sometimes supplied by the speaker as he goes along. For example, this excerpt is from a version of a classic toast, "The Signifying Monkey and the Lion":

> Deep down in the jungle so they say
> There's a signifying motherfucker down the way.
> There hadn't been no disturbin in the jungle for quite a
>   bit,
> For up jumped the monkey in the tree one day and
>   laughed,
> "I guess I'll start some shit."
> Now the lion come through the jungle one peaceful day,
> When the signifying monkey stopped him and this what
>   he started to say.
> He said, "Mr. Lion," he said, "a bad-assed motherfucker
>   down your way."
> He said, "Yeah! The way he talks about your folks is a
>   certain shame."[48]

A speaker might also offer a long narrative parody such as the following recital by a thirteen-year-old verbal leader of a Harlem street group:

> It was the night before Christmas and all through
>   the pad
> Reefers and cocaine was all we had,
> The nod in the corner, coppin' a nod,
> One more scratch he saw he was God.
> As I went to the phone to dial with care
> Wishing the reefers man soon would be there.
> And all of a something I heard the clatter.
> I ran to the door to see what was the matter.
> As I opened the door, in my surprise
> Five shiny badges was shinin' in my eyes.

The poem goes on to describe how the hero is caught by the police, escapes from jail, and eventually, after more troubles, comes to a bar:

> As I slipped and slid through the mud,
> I came to this place called "The Bucket of Blood."
> I asked this man for a bit to eat.
> He gave me some dirty water and a fucked-up piece of
>   meat.
> I say . . . *"Man,* do you realize who I am?"
> He say, "I don't give a damn."
> I pulled out my forty-four.
> I shot him *all* in his head.

> This bitch ran out there, said, "Is he dead?
> Is he dead?"
> I say, "If you don't think he's dead count the bullets
> in his head."[49]

Dancing was a very important activity for both boys and girls in Harlem. Even at the elementary school level, the child who was proficient in the latest steps could use his expressive ability to call attention to himself. Dancing did not have a feminine connotation among black children as it often does among whites. Boys would take pride in their dancing ability, and some practiced certain steps diligently until they perfected them. Young boys would try to imitate performers, such as James Brown. Dancing provided both a good time and a vehicle for self-expression. Although young black children were restricted in various areas during socialization, they were encouraged by adults and peers to express themselves freely through dancing.

In order to be noticed and respected by their peers, many boys in Harlem tried to perfect and manifest certain expressive traits, such as ways of walking and talking, that would show that they were wise to the ways of the street, that they were not "lame," could take care of themselves, and were not to be "messed with." Boys in Harlem who did not develop the "correct" style of walking and talking often became targets of aggression or exploitation. Similar pressures are faced by boys in many other American communities, but the ghetto is a particularly brutal arena in which boys often meet physical abuse and ridicule to an extent unheard of in most middle-class communities. For this reason, in part, some Harlem boys became highly sensitive in assessing the potential toughness or cunning of their peers through quick appraisals of their physical mannerisms.

James, a third-grade boy, offered an example of this special sensitivity. During the school lunch period, he came up to the classroom with another boy from his class who was crying bitterly. James explained that some other boys had been "hittin" on Donald. Later he privately explained to the teacher why the boys always bothered Donald: "It's because he don't walk right. That's why people hit him and pick on him. He walks like this [demonstrating by walking slowly and stiffly with his head down]. If he walked like this [bouncing up and down, thrusting his right shoulder forward, with his eyes straight ahead and his arms hanging very loosely], then no one would hurt him."

Harlem boys often tried to gain prestige by displays of daring or lack of concern for personal safety. A boy who never backed away from a fight, no matter what the odds, was recognized as someone who had "heart." Thus Claude Brown recalls a lesson learned from peers during his boyhood in Harlem:

Throughout my childhood in Harlem nothing was more strongly impressed upon me than the fact that you had to fight and that you should fight. Everybody would accept it if a person was scared to fight, but not if he was so scared that he didn't fight.[50]

Piri Thomas also recalls his boyhood in East Harlem; he had just been accepted as a member of a street group after he had displayed "heart" by not "punking out" on a fight with one of the members:

My heart pumped out, *you've established your rep. Move over, 104th Street. Lift your wings, I'm one of your baby chicks now*. . . . Not that I could relax. In Harlem you always lived on the edge of losing rep. All it takes is a one-time loss of heart.[51]

Expressive language is employed frequently as boys try to display "heart" through acts of courage or defiance. A teacher might find himself up against a dramatic display of defiance as he tries to exercise his authority: Often older boys (and girls) challenge a teacher who tries to control them. For example, in a school lunchroom in Harlem, sixth-graders were on line to be served. A male teacher who was in charge at one point asked some boys to stay in line and not run about as they had been doing. When the boys refused to comply, the teacher warned them that he would be forced to throw them out unless they calmed down. One of the boys, perhaps wishing to impress his friends with a display of "heart," challenged the teacher. "Oh yeah, man," the boy said, "whatta you gonna do? Go ahead and touch me. C'mon, man! Try and hit me. Go ahead! *Try your luck!*" The teacher walked away helplessly while the boy's friends patted him on the back.

Expressive language is used to display "heart" in a stereotyped or ritualistic fashion. Thus a third-grade boy who was being physically restrained from attacking one of his classmates by his white male teacher screamed at his teacher: "You shouldn't have touched me, Nigger!"

Many Harlem boys strove to be recognized as "bad," a term that meant "good" in the sense of being worthy of attention, not to be "messed with," able to protect oneself and to get what one wanted. Boys often tried to convince others that they were "bad," but if this was just bluff they were soon found out and were likely to be victimized. Joseph, a fifth-grade boy who tried to act "bad," wanted to associate with a group of classmates who had a reputation for being very streetwise. Somehow, Joseph was never accepted by these boys except as a target for verbal and physical abuse. On one occasion, a teacher was working with Joseph and a small group of boys from his class, trying to stimulate the boys to communicate their concerns in writing. Each boy wrote about a "true" incident in his life that he thought would be of interest to the others and then read his composition to the group. Joseph told a tale of daring and resourcefulness. According to his story he had gone into a store, grabbed an expensive camera, and dashed out; the storekeeper had chased him, but he had been clever enough to get away. The other boys began to ridicule Joseph: "Oh, man, you think you bad." "Yeah, man—you couldn't steal nothin'. A man could catch you and beat your ass." Joseph insisted he had stolen the camera, but he couldn't produce it when challenged. After this incident, Joseph's prestige within his group dropped even lower. He continued to seek acceptance by his peers, but he was accepted only if he played the role of "flunky," a person who could be used and abused. If Joseph could have proved that he had stolen the camera, he might have been elevated to a more enviable status within the group.

Harlem boys frequently used articles of clothing to support their image as tough or daring personalities. Many boys had their particular hats, for example, which they wore to bolster their feelings of adequacy, aided by this culturally defined symbol in playing an expressive role. A young white teacher in a Harlem school was determined to show his fifth-grade pupils that he really accepted them, that he was not going to negate their "black culture." When the boys in his class told him that they did not want to remove their hats in the classroom, he agreed to their wearing hats if they wished. From the teacher's point of view, prohibiting the wearing of hats was an arbitrary white middle-class restriction. To his dismay, he found that the boys continued to group together in corners and have loud conversations ("jiving") punctuated with frequent displays of "woofing," which often escalated beyond the limits of verbal abuse. The boys would not pay attention to the teacher's carefully planned lessons, and he soon became completely demoralized. The teacher had made a fatal error in agreeing so quickly to the boys' demands concerning their hats. What he interpreted as respect for their wishes they had interpreted as weakness. While the boys were wearing their hats, their street identities were being concretely reinforced. The boys felt "hip," "slick," and "bad." They expressed these identities in their usual fashion, with disastrous results for the atmosphere of the classroom.

EARLY SEXUAL AWARENESS

The asexuality that is typical of relations between middle-class preadolescent boys and girls is not found in low-income black communities.[52] We observed a strong sexual awareness on the part of many children in Harlem, even during the elementary school grades. As early as the second grade, girls had to cope frequently with requests from boys to give them some "pussy." In the first grade, children often responded with giggles when the word *pussy* appeared in stories read to them by their teachers. Many of these six-year-olds could already spell the word accurately. It was lavished upon the stairwell walls and was the subject of numerous notes passed among the children as early as the third grade. Girls came up in Harlem having to contend with conflicting impulses: to seek sexual contact with boys as a means of gaining acceptance, pleasure, and an escape from an environment where pain was all too common, and to avoid sexual contact so as to protect themselves from being used and abused by "irresponsible" males.

The early sexual awareness of many children in Harlem was highlighted in one first-grade classroom. A black six-year-old boy had called his middle-aged white female teacher a "cracker." The teacher sought to make the incident a learning experience for the children. She explained to them that she was a person, while a cracker was something one would eat. She then asked the little boy: "Now, Darryl, would you eat me?" The teacher learned her lesson when Darryl replied, "Eat you! Baby, I wouldn't even fuck you!"

For the most part, children's groups in Harlem, in spite of their mistrust of adults, did not seem to develop a constellation of values or behavior that differentiated their behavior substantially from that of many Harlem adults. Many of the problems faced by Harlem children within their peer groups were directly related to their tendencies to imitate, in an exaggerated fashion, the most vivid and exciting behaviors they saw displayed by some adults in their own community. This was particularly true of boys. Early sexual stimulation and awareness served to divert attention from classroom tasks and not uncommonly created anxiety, particular in young girls.

Although some of the girls we knew in Harlem were severely restricted from engaging in street peer-group activities, Harlem parents commonly treated early adolescent girls as if they were women; that is, whatever emotional support they were given as children was withdrawn, and they were expected to function in the home as adults without any allowance for adolescent role experimentation or emotional turmoil. Typically, adolescent girls were warned a great deal about sexual relations and the danger of becoming pregnant. Yet many mothers appeared to accept their teenage daughters' pregnancies without much distress or even great surprise.

> In the ghetto, the meaning of the illegitimate child is not ultimate disgrace. There is not the demand for abortion or for surrender of the child that one finds in more privileged communities. . . . In lower-class families the girl loses only some of her already limited options by having an illegitimate child; she is not going to make a "better marriage" or improve her economic and social status either way. On the contrary, the child is a symbol of the fact that she is a woman and she may gain from having something of her own.[53]

Many ghetto daughters and mothers regard a pregnancy outside marriage as a mistake that is regrettable, but the baby is usually accepted as a member of the girl's family without stigma.[54] Black teenage girls generally regard having a baby as a symbol of womanhood. This symbol of womanhood may be associated with the assumption that parental restrictions are no longer appropriate; on the other hand, having a baby brings on responsibilities that make life more complex and negate the value of the "maturity" assumed to derive from having a baby. The inability of many black fathers to provide financial support for their children accentuates the responsibility of many young black mothers for the care and support of their babies.

PEER INFLUENCE IN SCHOOL

Harlem children brought their ambivalent peer-group dependency into school with them. During the elementary school years this dependency and the conflictful nature of peer relationships steadily increased.

The importance of peer influence on lower-class pupils in general has been demonstrated by Wilson,[55] who studied social climates among sixth-graders in fourteen California schools. The schools were divided into three clearly distinct social strata, following the lines of residential segregation in the community. In one group of schools ("The Hills"), a majority of students' fathers were professionals or executives. In the "Flats," most of the students came from working-class homes. These schools included most of the black population in the area. Between these extremes of social composition and geographical setting was a group of schools with a more heterogeneous enrollment (the "Foothills").

Certain differences in the pattern of student relationships became apparent. In the middle-class schools, parents and teachers supervised the students more closely and had high academic expectations for them. One result of the strong influence of adults on children in these schools was the tendency for many children to select friends on the basis of similarity in academic aspirations and generally to reject those with low aspirations or achievement. In the working-class schools, on the other hand, values were more often communicated laterally among peers, and attitudes toward schooling were largely irrelevant to the students' assessments of one another. Students with low scholastic aspirations were likely to be the group leaders. They gained social support from their peers, and they, in turn, set the pace for them, without adopting the standards of success prevalent in the wider adult community.

Our own observations led us to believe that children in Harlem classrooms had an even greater mutual impact than Wilson found to be the case in other lower-class groups. Because pressing physical and emotional needs, intense personal concerns, difficulties in social relationships, and peer-group orientations to competence interfered with school achievement for many Harlem children in the early grades, they came to feel more and more frustrated in any attempt to be successful in school. They defended against this added blow to their self-esteem by increasingly rejecting the school and their teachers. In this way, the children exacerbated their felt hostility toward and defiance of adult authority.

As the children became increasingly dependent upon one another with each succeeding year, the peer group came increasingly to support many behaviors that ran counter to the objectives and expectations of the school and created an atmosphere that was not conducive to traditional school achievement. By the upper elementary grades, the behaviors supported by peer groups in many Harlem classrooms included continuous talking and socializing as opposed to any individualized, sustained work effort; responding to difficulty or frustration by leaving the room, tearing up papers, or throwing away books; arriving at school with no concern for the hour; and demonstrating skill in verbally putting down children, parents, and teachers.

We have indicated the importance of status within the peer group for many children in Harlem. Since school is where the peer group is for six hours a day, five days a week, school is also a place in which to behave in accord with aspirations to improve one's position relative to one's peers.

The conflictful nature of street peer-group relations was not filtered out by the walls of the school. Fighting was so much of a norm to the children that one sixth-grade boy was very annoyed when he was prevented from boxing with his friend in a classroom to determine, then and there, who could beat whom. He shouted at his teacher, "Damn, man! You can't even fight in peace around here!"

Fighting excited and stimulated the children, but it also frightened many of them. In many elementary school classrooms a large proportion of the children's energies went into watching one another rather than coping with their schoolwork. Many children remained hyperalert to changes in the environment that might be threatening to them. Staring at one another often provoked verbal abuse, which led to conflict. A feeling of tension and barely suppressed excitement often loomed ominously over many classrooms.

In their responsibility to care for younger brothers or sisters, older children often found themselves in situations where they felt duty-bound to beat up smaller children who may have abused their charges. The cry "I'll get my brother on you" was heard frequently in lower grades, and children in upper grades were often sent to the office for hitting younger children. It was not unusual for family feuds to reverberate within the schools, with older children in various grades waiting their turn to fight for the family honor. On several occasions, we saw a child run out of the school after a fight, go home, and return to the classroom with a kitchen knife or an older brother to attempt to hurt or frighten his combatant.

Somehow, the children throughout the school always knew about these fights. They were stimulated by them and were eager to keep them going. The teachers were usually the last to know what was going on and were usually at cross-purposes with the children in trying to put a stop to it.

The prevalent fighting within the schools must be considered part of a widespread pattern of outwardly directed black aggression against other blacks, which created severe problems for the children of Harlem. Many children tried valiantly to act grown-up without much adult emotional support. They displayed an air of bravado and presented themselves as daring, tough, and cunning personalities, but beneath these public masks they seemed to be highly anxious and afraid much of the time. Among the most desperate needs of low-income urban black children is to have adults take a more active role in structuring and relating to their lives so that they can be helped to turn their energies into channels that will lead to ego-building satisfactions rather than spiraling patterns of frustration and self-defeating behavior. Although many children are toughened to the exigencies of a cruel world by successfully coping with demands for early independence, they may never be able to compensate fully, even through peer relations, for the burden of a lonely, unsupported childhood.

NOTES

1. For similar observations, see Lee Rainwater, "Crucible of Identity: The Negro Lower-Class Family," *Daedalus,* Winter, 1966, pp. 172–216.
2. See David P. Ausubel and Pearl Ausubel, "Ego Development Among Segregated Negro Children," in A. Harry Passow, ed., *Education in Depressed Areas* (New York: Teachers College Press, 1965), pp. 109–41.
3. J. L. Bresnahan and W. L. Blum, "Chaotic Reinforcement: A Socio-economic Leveler," *Developmental Psychology,* 4 (1971): 89–92.
4. Claude Brown, *Manchild in the Promised Land* (New York: Macmillan, 1965), p. 415.
5. See Urie Bronfenbrenner, "The Split-Level American Family," *Saturday Review of Literature,* October 7, 1967, pp. 60–66. See also *idem, Two Worlds of Childhood: U.S. and U.S.S.R.* (New York: Russell Sage Foundation, 1970); John C. Condry, Jr., and M. L. Siman, "An Experimental Study of Adult Versus Peer Orientation," unpublished manuscript, Cornell University, Ithaca, N.Y., 1968.
6. See John Janeway Conger, "A World They Never Knew: The Family and Social Change," *Daedalus,* 100 (1971): 1105–38, and Alice Miel, *The Shortchanged Children of Suburbia* (New York: American Jewish Committee, Institute of Human Relations Press, 1967).
7. C. V. Brittain, "Adolescent Choices and Parent-Peer Cross-Pressures," *American Sociological Review,* 28 (1963): 385–91.
8. Henry S. Maas, "Some Social Class Differences in the Family Systems

and Group Relations of Pre- and Early Adolescents," *Child Development*, 22 (1951): 145–52.

9. George Psathas, "Ethnicity, Social Class, and Adolescent Independence from Parental Control," *American Sociological Review*, 22 (1957): 415–23.

10. Suzanne Keller, "The Social World of the Urban Slum Child: Some Early Findings," *American Journal of Orthopsychiatry*, 33 (1963): 823–31.

11. See Jacob Riis, *How the Other Half Lives* (1890) (New York: Hill & Wang, 1957), pp. 134–35. For an informative history of the behavior of children and adolescents in the "good old days," see Frank R. Donovan, *Wild Kids: How Youth Shocked Its Elders Then and Now* (Harrisburg, Pa.: Stackpole Books, 1967).

12. See Urie Bronfenbrenner, "Soviet Methods of Character Education," *American Psychologist*, 17 (1962): 550–63; *idem, Two Worlds of Childhood* (n. 5 *supra*); and Albert I. Rabin, *Growing Up in the Kibbutz* (New York: Springer, 1965).

13. Anna Freud and Sophie Dann, "An Experiment in Group Upbringing," in Ruth S. Eissler, ed., *The Psychoanalytic Study of the Child*, 6 (New York: International Universities Press, 1951): 127–68.

14. See Willard W. Hartup, "Peer Interaction and Social Organization," in Paul H. Mussen, ed., *Carmichael's Manual of Child Psychology*, 3d ed. (New York: John Wiley, 1970), 2: 361–456.

15. D. M. Hicks, "Imitation and Retention of Film-mediated Aggressive Peer and Adult Models," *Journal of Personality and Social Psychology*, 2 (1965): 97–100.

16. Willard W. Hartup and Brian Coates, "Imitation of a Peer as a Function of Reinforcement from the Peer Group and Rewardingness of the Model," *Child Development*, 38 (1967): 1003–16.

17. Robert G. Wahler, "Child-Child Interactions in Free-Field Settings: Some Experimental Analysis," *Journal of Experimental Child Psychology*, 5 (1967): 278–93.

18. Jean Piaget, *The Moral Judgment of the Child* (1932) (Glencoe, Ill.: Free Press, 1948).

19. R. W. Berenda, *The Influence of the Group on the Judgments of Children* (New York: King's Crown Press, 1950).

20. See Raymond G. Hunt and V. Synnerdale, "Social Influences Among Kindergarten Children," *Sociology and Social Research*, 43 (1959): 171–74, and E. K. Starkweather, "Conformity and Nonconformity as Indicators of Creativity in Preschool Children," Cooperative Research Project No. 1967, U.S. Office of Education, 1964.

21. P. R. Costanzo and M. E. Shaw, "Conformity as a Function of Age Level," *Child Development*, 37 (1966): 967–75.

22. T. R. McConnell, "Suggestibility in Children as a Function of Chronological Age," *Journal of Abnormal and Social Psychology*, 67 (1963): 286–89.

23. Ira Iscoe, M. Williams, and J. Harvey, "Age, Intelligence, and Sex Variables in the Conformity Behavior of Negro and White Children," *Child Development*, 35 (1964): 451–60.

24. R. L. Mock and Read D. Tuddenham, "Race and Conformity Among Children," *Developmental Psychology*, 4 (1971): 349–65.

25. Charles E. Bowerman and John W. Kinch, "Changes in Family and Peer Orientation of Children Between the Fourth and Tenth Grades," *Social Forces*, 37 (1959): 206–11.

26. E. C. Devereaux, "Socialization in Cross-cultural Perspective: A Comparative Study of England, Germany, and the United States," unpublished manuscript, Cornell University, Ithaca, N.Y., 1965.

27. Urie Bronfenbrenner *et al.*, "Adults and Peers as Sources of Conformity and Autonomy," unpublished manuscript, Cornell University, Ithaca, N.Y., 1965, and Urie Bronfenbrenner, "Response to Pressure from Peers Versus Adults Among Soviet and American School Children," *International Journal of Psychology*, 2 (1967): 199–207.

28. E. Mavis Hetherington, "Effects of Paternal Absence on Sex-typed Behaviors in Negro and White Preadolescent Males," *Journal of Personality and Social Psychology*, 4 (1966): 87–91.

29. Allan G. Barclay and D. R. Cusumano, "Father Absence, Cross-Sex Identity, and Field Dependent Behavior in Male Adolescents," *Child Development*, 38 (1967): 243–50.

30. Maas, "Some Social Class Differences" (n. 8 *supra*).

31. Bronfenbrenner, *Two Worlds of Childhood* (n. 5 *supra*), pp. 101–2.

32. Lyle E. Larson, "The Relative Influence of Parent-Adolescent Affect in Predicting the Salience Hierarchy Among Youth," paper presented at session of the National Congress on Family Relations, Chicago, October, 1970.

33. Millard C. Madsen, "Cooperative and Competitive Motivation of Children in Three Mexican Subcultures," *Psychological Reports*, 20 (1967): 1307–20, and Millard C. Madsen and Ariella Shapira, "Cooperative and Competitive Behavior of Urban Afro-American, Anglo-American, Mexican-American and Mexican Village Children," *Developmental Psychology*, 3 (1970): 16–20.

34. Ariella Shapira and Millard C. Madsen, "Cooperative and Competitive Behavior of Kibbutz and Urban Children in Israel," *Child Development*, 40 (1969): 609–17.

35. Mirra Komarovsky, *Blue-Collar Marriage* (New York: Random House, 1964).

36. See Elliot Liebow, *Tally's Corner: A Study of Negro Streetcorner Men* (Boston: Little, Brown, 1967), and Ulf Hannerz, *Soulside: Inquiries into Ghetto Culture and Community* (New York: Columbia University Press, 1969).

37. Charles Keil, *Urban Blues* (Chicago: University of Chicago Press, 1966), pp. 8–9.

38. Carlfred B. Broderick, "Social Heterosexual Development Among Urban Negroes and Whites," *Journal of Marriage and the Family*, 27 (1965): 200–203.

39. Joseph White, "Toward a Black Psychology," in Reginald L. Jones, ed., *Black Psychology* (New York: Harper & Row, 1972), p. 48.

40. William H. Grier and Price M. Cobbs, *The Jesus Bag* (New York: Bantam Books, 1972), p. 5.

41. See Alvin F. Poussaint, *Why Blacks Kill Blacks* (New York: Emerson Hall, 1973).

42. William Labov *et al.*, *A Study of the Nonstandard English of Negro and Puerto Rican Speakers in New York City*, Final Report, Cooperative Research Project No. 3288, U.S. Office of Education (New York: Columbia University, 1968, mimeographed), 2: 36.

43. The problem of aggressive competition within the one-sex lower-class peer group is discussed in Walter B. Miller, "Lower Class Culture as a Generating Milieu of Gang Delinquency," *Journal of Social Issues*, 14 (1958): 5–19. On peer-group competition within the black ghetto, see Boone Hammond, "The Contest System: A Survival Technique," master's honors paper, Washington University, Saint Louis, Mo., 1965.

44. Thomas Kochman, "Rapping in the Ghetto," in Lee Rainwater, ed., *The Black Experience: Soul* (Chicago: Aldine, 1970), pp. 70–71.

45. *Ibid.*, p. 72.

46. Roger D. Abrahams, *Deep Down in the Jungle: Negro Narrative Folklore from the Streets of Philadelphia*, rev. ed. (Chicago: Aldine, 1970), pp. 48–49. See also William Labov, *Language in the Inner City: Studies in the Black English Vernacular* (Philadelphia: University of Pennsylvania Press, 1972), pp. 297–353.

47. Malcolm X, *The Autobiography of Malcolm X*, ed. by Alex Haley (New York: Grove Press, 1965), p. 110.

48. Abrahams, *Deep Down in Jungle*, p. 113.

49. Labov *et al.*, *Study of Nonstandard English* (n. 42 *supra*), pp. 69–70.

50. Brown, *Manchild in Promised Land* (n. 4 *supra*), p. 253.

51. Piri Thomas, *Down These Mean Streets* (New York: Knopf, 1967), p. 58.

52. See Joyce A. Ladner, *Tomorrow's Tomorrow: The Black Woman* (New York: Doubleday, 1971). See also Broderick, "Social Heterosexual Development" (n. 38 *supra*).

53. Kenneth B. Clark, *Dark Ghetto: Dilemmas of Social Power* (New York: Harper & Row, 1965), p. 72.

54. See Ladner, *Tomorrow's Tomorrow*, pp. 217–33.

55. Alan B. Wilson, "Social Stratification and Academic Achievement," in A. Harry Passow, ed., *Education in Depressed Areas* (n. 2 *supra*).

6 / COMPETENCE AND PERFORMANCE: THE POLITICS OF INTELLIGENCE

Developmental psychology in England and the United States has been based largely on the assumption that development is a continuous, step-by-step process leading toward an "ideal" or "fully developed" state. This "ideal" state was assumed to be approximated by the white (WASP) middle-class male adult, whose behavior became the standard against which that of all other groups was measured and ranked. Because of their political and economic success, middle-class whites were viewed as having demonstrated superior competence and intelligence in the evolutionary struggle for survival.[1]

Until about 1930, most behavioral scientists shared the general societal belief that blacks were innately inferior to whites and provided "scientific proof" for this belief by pointing out the frequently lower scores of blacks on so-called intelligence tests.[2] We now know that the content of such tests largely mirrored white middle-class life experiences. But beyond this cultural bias in test content, a deeper vicious cycle tended to operate: As members of the white middle class, most psychologists regarded white middle-class behavior as normative and desirable; competence in those tasks in which middle-class whites excelled was labeled "intelligence"; tasks in which other groups excelled were considered of little importance. Intelligence was what middle-class whites said it was and what tests constructed by middle-class white psychologists measured. Once intelligence had been defined in this highly limited fashion, the scores of the tests devised to measure it were used to bolster the argument that the low economic and political status of blacks in America was a result of their genetically determined inability to compete successfully with whites and to adapt to the complexities of the white man's civilization.

The assumption that blacks are less intelligent than whites has remained essentially unchanged in the mainstream of psychological literature since the 1930's. The "evidence" adduced is essentially the same—lower black IQs. But the predominant explanation for the IQ gap has shifted to hypothesized "deficits" in the environment in which black children develop rather than hypothesized deficits in their genes.

Early in the 1960's, many psychologists became increasingly concerned about problems of American education. Much interest and research focused on the newly discovered "culturally deprived" or "disadvantaged" (usually low-income black) child. When focusing on poor reading achievement among middle-class white children, psychologists generally sought the causal factors in methods of instruction (e.g., the phonetic approach vs. the "look-say" method) or inappropriate matches between curriculum content and children's level of development; when the poor reading achievement of low-income black children was their concern, the causes were usually sought in hypothesized deficiencies in the children's cognitive capacities.

"CULTURAL DEPRIVATION"

By the early 1960's it had become academically fashionable to focus attention on particular background variables in the lives of urban black children, such as rundown housing, overcrowding, lack of books and toys in the home, and relatively restricted conversation with adults, and to attempt to establish rather precise connections between such variables and the children's hypothesized underdeveloped cognitive organization. Poor black children were viewed as deficient in basic intellectual capacities as a result of deficiencies in age-appropriate stimulus inputs from the environment:

Visually, the urban slum and its overcrowded apartments offer the child a minimal range of stimuli. There are usually few if any pictures on the wall, and the objects in the household, be they toys, furniture or utensils, tend to be sparse, repetitious and lacking in form and color variations. The sparsity of objects and lack of diversity of home artifacts which are available and meaningful to the child, in addition to the unavailability of individualized training, gives the child few opportunities to manipulate and organize the visual properties of his environment and thus perceptually to organize and discriminate the nuances of that environment. These would include figure-ground relationships and the spatial organization of the visual field. The sparsity of manipulable objects probably also hampers the development of these functions in the tactile area. For example, while these children have broomsticks and usually a ball, possibly a doll or a discarded kitchen pot to play with, they don't have the different shapes and colors and sizes to manipulate which the middle-class child has in the form of blocks which are bought just for him, or even in the variety of sizes and shapes of cooking utensils which might be available to him as playthings.[3]

Such speculation was stimulated by the pioneering hypotheses of D. O. Hebb concerning developmental relationships between stimulus inputs and postulated processes and structures in the nervous system.[4] Psychologists who applied concepts derived from Hebb's work to an analysis of black children tended to see the children in a dehumanized, mechanistic fashion, like cognitive machines with faulty wiring. It is instructive to note Hebb's too modest reflections on his own work, made at the close of the 1960's:

> What I have done is to complicate the connection between stimulus and response. For Watson it was a straight-through connection: If you have a stimulus, you get a response. My theory complicates the pathway so that things can happen in that pathway to keep the message from getting all the way to the end. And one inbound pathway might interact with another, again without necessarily leading to response. But essentially this theory is mechanistic, connectionistic, deterministic and associationistic. And it is not true.[5]

Another source of inspiration for theorists of the "disadvantaged child" was the newly rediscovered work of the Swiss psychologist Jean Piaget. Piaget has constructed a highly influential theory relating the child's interactions with stimulating aspects of his environment to his progressive development of reasoning abilities.[6] However, the realms of feeling and affect and the cognitive processes arising out of interpersonal relations are largely unaccounted for in Piaget's system.

Theorists tended to apply Piaget's concepts to the study of low-income black children and to regard the children's intellectual processes as if they existed in a disembodied form. The children were seen as suffering from insufficiently structured intellects or from "cognitive deficits" arising from insufficient age-appropriate stimulation. These ailments presumably prevented the development of age-expected reasoning abilities among low-income black children, who required special compensatory preschool enrichment experiences to compensate for their "culturally deprived" backgrounds. The children's motives and feelings were ignored or regarded as undesirable distractions that interfered with rational thought processes. Theorists saw programs of early stimulus enrichment as far more important in promoting later school achievement for these children than any attempts to provide emotionally supportive human relationships.

Hunt, among others, has argued:

> Cultural deprivation may be seen as a failure to provide an opportunity for infants and young children to have the experiences required for adequate development of those semi-autonomous central processes demanded for acquiring skill in the use of linguistic and mathematical symbols and for the analysis of causal relationships.[7]

Some cultural deprivation theorists saw the effects of "cultural deprivation" as analogous to the experimentally produced effects of severe sensory deprivation upon young laboratory animals. Kittens and chimpanzees reared for months in darkness became severely impaired in sensory-motor functions and problem-solving ability. Those theorists also saw close parallels between "cultural deprivation" and the sensory deprivation suffered by infants in perceptually barren, understaffed orphanages. These infants suffer severe developmental retardation, particularly in linguistic-symbolic functions. Such theorists presented no evidence to demonstrate that the environments in which low-income black children are reared are, in fact, anywhere near as barren of stimulation as the laboratory or orphanage settings they cited as supporting evidence for their theories on "cultural deprivation" and the "deficits" in intellectual functions that it is supposed to produce. They offered no reliable way to determine the "minimum daily requirements" of sensory stimulation for adequate intellectual development or the age-appropriateness of stimuli, so that we could measure objectively just how deprived "culturally deprived" children are. Cultural deprivation theory to the contrary, we believe that many low-income urban black children are bombarded by sights and sounds during the early years; they are more likely to be overstimulated than understimulated.

By the mid-1960's, "cultural deprivation" theorists such as Hunt and Deutsch offered a more sophisticated approach to "cultural deprivation," which focused on presumed deficiencies in the *quality* of stimuli available to low-income black children rather than on the inadequate amounts of stimulation they received. Other theorists soon singled out verbal communication from adults as an important area of stimulus deficiency. Kagan, for example, argued that a deficiency in communication inheres not in the fact that lower-class mothers talk less to their children than middle-class mothers but in the fact that lower-class children are more deprived of "distinctive vocalization"—i.e., speech directed at the child and unaccompanied by other sensory inputs that might distract him.[8] For "cultural deprivation" theorists, a relative lack of distinctive verbal stimulation hinders the child's development of conceptual categories related to his perceptual experience and his comprehension of relationships between objects and events. These theorists have scrutinized verbal interchanges to locate stimulus deficiencies which presumably would prevent adequate cognitive development among low-income black children. Hunt and Deutsch in particular have expressed little concern for the emotional-interpersonal aspects of human relatedness that might be revealed in verbal interactions between parents and children.

In an apparent misunderstanding of Piaget's developmental blueprint, American "cultural deprivation" theorists became obsessed with the timing and speed of intellectual development; they seemed to believe that for intellectual development to be considered "normal," children had to follow a specific timetable, based upon the progression observed in middle-class white children, so that at each age they "should" perform certain tasks up to an expected standard. Early in the 1960's they entertained the "critical period" hypothesis; if children were unable to perform certain intellectual tasks by certain ages, they would never be able to perform them, because, presumably, deficits in neurological organization caused by early "cultural deprivation" could not be made up. When children in fact appeared to be more flexible than this hypothesis predicted, theorists substituted the "cumulative deficit" argument; if "culturally deprived" children failed to develop intellectually at a "normal" speed because of early "deficits" in neurological or cognitive structures, these early, unremedied "deficits" would make it increasingly difficult—perhaps impossible—for the children to meet age-appropriate standards of intellectual behavior as they grew older. Thus, early "deficits" would become cumulative, preventing age-appropriate intellectual achievements, thus creating new deficits, and so on. To avoid the cycle of cumulative deficits, "cultural deprivation" theorists began advocating earlier and earlier intervention—in the form of compensatory stimulus enrichment—in the lives of low-income urban black children. By 1971, Hunt was arguing that low-income black children were so riddled with "cognitive deficits" by age four that even the Head Start program was too late to prevent the cumulation of intellectual incompetence:

> [Head Start] may be all too often too little and too late to overcome sufficiently the incompetence inculcated during the first four years to enable from a third to half of these children of the persistently poor to succeed in the public schools and later to enjoy full participation in the mainstream of our technological culture. We need a way to intervene in the lives of families of poverty.[9]

In other words, poor black children had a right to live decently, but first they must be "cured" of their "cognitive deficits" and "incompetencies" through government-sponsored intervention in their upbringing, starting almost at birth.

Yet Francis Palmer, among others, found in his observations of young Harlem children that a warm one-to-one relationship with an educating adult and a relatively free adult-child interaction that rewarded the child's initiative were about as important as a well-designed curriculum and formalized instructional procedures in fostering cognitive development and achievement.[10] His subjects, 240 Harlem boys aged two and three, were assigned to one of two training groups, emphasizing, respectively, concept training and discovery. Children in the concept-training group were given systematic instruction in understanding concepts, moving progressively from very simple to complex concepts. Children in the discovery group were provided with the same play materials and instructors as the children in the concept-training group, but the instructors never labeled the concepts for a child or initiated conversations with him. Rather, the adult played with the child, letting him take the lead in the interaction. After eight months, the boys in both experimental groups outperformed a group of control subjects on fourteen of sixteen tests, nine of the differences being statistically significant. The experimental groups even outperformed middle-class children on fourteen measures, four of the differences being statistically significant. When the two experimental groups were compared, the children exposed to the meticulously developed concept-training curriculum performed significantly better than the children in the discovery group on only four measures. On all other measures the discovery children did as well as the others or better. The study thus demonstrated that two-year-old Harlem boys were capable of learning a great deal in only two hours of instruction per week, and that what they were taught seemed less important than the conditions under which they were taught. Similarly, Zigler and Butterfield found that simple increases in motivation to perform well on a test, based upon an increase in interpersonal trust and autonomy, account for many reported instances of test-score improvement among children attending preschool "enrichment" programs.[11]

"Cultural deprivation" theorists want to speed up the production of intelligence among low-income black children to prevent "cumulative deficits" in intellectual functioning, which will, they believe, prevent the children from ever reaching a level of intellectual development sufficient for achievement in school or in later life. However, cross-cultural evidence suggests that middle-class children in Holland[12] during their first two years and in Japan[13] during their first three years tend to score below American norms on measures of sensory-motor and cognitive functioning, even though they catch up to American middle-class children later on. In the United States, Bosco found a large difference between lower-class and middle-class five- and eight-years-olds in the ability to perform complex visual-detection tasks, but no difference between lower-class and middle-class eleven-year-olds.[14] Lower-class children took longer than middle-class children to achieve a given level of proficiency, but they eventually did achieve it, on a task that was not class-biased in informational content.

Similarly, on the basis of his observations of children in an isolated Guatemalan village, Jerome Kagan in 1972 reversed his previous concurrence with much of "cultural deprivation" theory.[15] Kagan and his colleagues administered tests of recall and recognition memory, perceptual analysis, and perceptual inference to children aged five through twelve in Guatemala and the United States. On most tests, the five- and eight-year-old Guatemalan children performed less well than American children, but by eleven years of age, the Guatemalan and American children performed equally well. Kagan also observed that infants in the Guatemalan village spent most of their first year in small, dark huts, were rarely spoken to or played with, and had few objects to manipulate. Compared to American infants, one-year-old Guatemalan infants seemed extremely passive, quiet, fearful, and, by American standards, quite retarded in cognitive and linguistic development. Kagan remarked, "If I had seen infants like the Guatemalans in America prior to my [Guatemalan] experience, I would have gotten very upset, called the police, had the children removed, and begun to make gloomy statements about the fact that it was all over for these children."[16] However, the eleven-year-olds in the same village were gay, alert, active, and, as we have noted, able to perform as well as American children on the tests administered. Apparently, the relative retardation of the Guatemalan infants did not lead to irreversible "cumulative deficits" in intellectual functioning; the Guatemalan children had a slower rate of development than the American children, but by age eleven appeared comparable to middle-class American children in basic intellectual competencies.

Challenging the "critical period" and "cumulative deficit" arguments of the "cultural deprivation" theorists, Kagan now asserts that certain complex cognitive processes will emerge in children in all cultural settings at some time between five and ten years of age, and that the specific timing depends on biological-maturational factors:

> Experience can slow down or speed up that emergence by several months or three to four years, but nature will win in the end. The capacity for perpetual analysis, imitation, inference, language, deduction, symbolism and memory will eventually appear in sturdy form, for each is an inherent competence in the human program.[17]

Although some aspects of the "cultural deprivation" theory relating to intellectual development in general are sound and innovative, the sociocentric and ethnocentric bias underlying the concept, the view of low-income black children as riddled with "cognitive deficits," and the prescription of massive, government-sponsored intervention in black childrearing are, in our view, at best politically naïve, at worst imperialistic. "Cultural deprivation" theorists, by focusing on "cognitive deficits" and "incompetencies," offer lip service to the total society's oppression of the poor and the black. They can righteously point out how resistant poor blacks are to having their "deficits" and "incompetencies" brought under scientific research and treatment procedures. Thus these theorists convert social injustice into intellectual deficiency (blaming the victim) while failing to recognize the confusion between their own vested interests and the needs and strivings of low-income black people. While black communities in the early 1970's were increasingly demanding control over local institutions, "cultural deprivation" theorists were telling black people that they were too intellectually deficient to be trusted with the education of their children. A black world view is either unappreciated or denied legitimacy as a frame of reference for childrearing by these theorists. If only black people will trust the psychological establishment, "cultural deprivation" theorists and the federal government will educate them and their children properly. If blacks object to this patronizing view, their very objection is seen as proof of their "incompetencies."

RACE, GENETICS, ENVIRONMENT, AND IQ

The literature on race and class differences in IQ test performance[18] generally reports that when black and white children at various class levels are compared the black children at each class level tend to score lower than white children.* Although the scores of all children tend to increase with ascending social-class level, black-white differences also increase, because the gains for the white children appear to be considerably greater. Of those psychologists who appear to be convinced that IQ scores are valid measures of basic intellectual competence, two groups have advanced competing explanations for racial differences in IQ performance. One group favors a "cultural deprivation" approach, the other a genetic difference approach.

The "cultural deprivation" theorists tend to be egalitarian and to speak as political liberals. Although they believe that black children do not manifest as much basic intelligence as white children, they trace this state of affairs to deficiencies in the environment related to discrimination and low income, which eventually lead to deficiencies in the children's intellectual capacities. For example, in a highly sophisticated study, Ryckman compared the information-processing abilities of middle- and lower-class black kindergarteners on eight instruments covering a relatively wide array of cognitive behavior.[19] The lower-class children performed less well on measures of language facility than their middle-class peers. Differences in general language performance separated the two groups more clearly than any other measure. "The findings of this study," according to Ryckman, "strongly indicate that lower-class boys of this age do not have

* Regarding the IQ gap between whites and blacks at the middle-class level, it is important to note that, because blacks face problems of discrimination, their economic position is likely to be more precarious than that of whites; consequently, it is impossible to equate white and black samples according to socio-economic class. Black children designated "middle class" are likely to come from families less affluent or economically stable than white children to whom they are being compared. Thus, the IQ gap between middle-class whites and blacks may be in part at least a function of class differences between the two groups.

the necessary language ability to process a wide range of experience." "Cultural deprivation" theorists are optimistic, however, because they believe they can design programs for early intervention in children's lives that will prevent such deficits.

In the late 1960's, a group of psychologists who also believe in the validity of the IQ as a measure of intelligence began to reassert that the primary cause of racial and/or social-class differences in performance on IQ tests is genetic differences. Thus Arthur Jensen argues that racial differences in average IQ are due largely to differences in the gene distributions of these populations.[20]

Compared to "cultural deprivation" theorists, genetic-determination theorists are rather pessimistic regarding the likelihood that early intervention or efforts to equalize educational opportunity will close the IQ gap between social classes or races.

In emphasizing the genetic factor in intelligence, Jensen cites studies comparing white identical twins reared together and reared apart. Based upon these studies he concludes that 80 per cent of the variance found among individuals on IQ tests can be attributed to genetic factors. Although genetic factors probably play a significant role in determining differences between the IQ test performances of individuals from the same population, Jensen's 80 per cent estimate of the genetic component underlying these differences appears to be far too high; behavioral geneticists have demonstrated that the broad-sense heritability for performance on IQ tests may be less than 52 per cent.[21] The importance of environmental factors in determining differences between the IQs of identical twins reared apart was demonstrated by Bloom when, examining one of the most frequently cited twin studies, he looked closely at the differences in the environments in which the twins were reared:

> We have divided the separated twins into two groups. For one group of 11 pairs, each pair of separated twins had very similar educational environments. The rank correlation for their I.Q. scores was $+ .91$, whereas for the eight pairs that had the least similar educational environments, the rank correlation for their I.Q. scores was only $+ .24$.[22]

Jensen goes on to review studies of black-white differences in IQ performance, pointing out that the average IQ of white groups is about 15 points higher than the average IQ of comparable black groups. Then, using his inflated 80 per cent heritability estimate for IQ derived from studies of differences between white individuals, Jensen argues that genetic factors are probably responsible for at least half of the variance in average IQ between groups of white and black Americans. Behavioral geneticists have demonstrated, however, that even if there is a relatively high within-group heritability for some trait (e.g., IQ among whites), this does not necessarily imply that an observed difference between group means (e.g., average IQ of blacks and whites) is also highly heritable.[23] In the absence of data demonstrating comparable heritability of IQ among black Americans as among white Americans, Jensen's use of a within-group heritability estimate to explain between-group differences is a highly questionable procedure.

Scarr-Salapatek studied 3,042 pairs of twins, 36 per cent of them white and 64 per cent black, in an attempt to pinpoint the relationships of heredity, social class, race, and performance on standardized aptitude and scholastic-achievement tests.[24] Her findings call into question the assumption that the genetic and environmental factors that bring about increments and decrements of intelligence act independently of one another in simple additive fashion. After estimating the number of identical and nonidentical twins in the sample and classifying their families according to social-economic status (SES), she compared the test scores. Differences in test scores between the higher- and lower-SES black children were much smaller (5.3 points) than the differences between the higher- and lower-SES whites (16.1 points). Even more important, for both blacks and whites test scores varied more among higher-SES children than among lower-SES children. These findings support the view that heredity and environment influences must be seen as interdependent and interactive, since genetic differences were most likely to be found among the children who grew up in the most favored environments (the middle-class whites) and to remain suppressed or undisclosed among the children who grew up in less advantageous environments (most of the black children). It would appear that children who carry a genetic endowment that could contribute to a high IQ performance in a generally supportive environment may perform no better on standardized tests than genetically less endowed people when they are raised in oppressive-suppressive environments:

> From studies of middle-class white populations, investigators have reached the conclusion that genetic variability accounts for about 75 per cent of the total variance in IQ scores of whites. A closer look at children reared under different conditions shows that the percentage of genetic variance and the mean scores are very much a function of the rearing conditions of the population. A first look at the black population suggests that genetic variability is important in advantaged groups, but much less important in the disadvantaged. Since most blacks are socially disadvantaged, the proportion of genetic variance in the aptitude scores of black children is considerably less than that of white children.[25]

If genetic variability does not account for differences in IQ scores among the black population to the same degree as it does among the white population, the socialization black children experience becomes central to an understanding of their test performance. A study by Willerman, Naylor, and Myrianthopolous is suggestive in this regard. The subjects were a group of children born of black-white matings in urban areas in different parts of the country.[26] Some interesting relationships were found between the mother's race, her marital status, and the IQ of her child at age four. The children who had black mothers and white fathers tended to have lower IQs than children whose mothers were white and whose fathers were black. However, this difference was caused mainly by the particularly low IQs of the sons of unmarried black mothers.[27] A genetic explanation for these differences appears strained since each child, whether a boy or a girl, carried genes from both races, but only the sons of unmarried black mothers seemed to suffer quite low IQs. There were essentially no educational differences among the parents, all groups averaging about eleven years of schooling.

As we have pointed out in earlier chapters, black mothers generally curtail the autonomy of boys more sharply than of girls, and black mothers without husbands often were especially repressive toward sons, in a desperate effort to control their aggressiveness and suppress their demands for attention. Since the IQ test performance of boys generally appears to be more strongly affected by the socialization practices of their mothers[28] (boys are also more vulnerable to unfavorable prenatal and perinatal conditions), the low IQs of the sons of the most disadvantaged black mothers are likely to have been caused primarily by such restrictive socialization practices.

SOCIAL CLASS, RACE, AND IQ TEST PERFORMANCE

If the IQ were a valid and reliable measure of basic intellectual competence, then arguments concerning the precise determinants of this index would be very meaningful. However, we contend, performance on IQ tests is often not a true index of cognitive competence. The positions of both the "cultural deprivation" and the genetic-determination theorists are built largely upon an illusion.

Golden and Birns have endeavored to determine the relationship between social class and IQ test performance for American black infants and young children. In one investigation they compared 192 black children in New York, aged twelve, eighteen, and twenty-four months, from three socio-economic-status groups (welfare families, lower and higher educational-achievement families) on the Catell Infant Intelligence Scale and a Piaget Object Scale. Contrary to their expectations, they did not find any significant social-class differences in performance on these tests during the first two years of life.[29] Since they noted that the black welfare children in the study were more difficult to test and required more effort from the examiner to elicit optimal performance, Golden and Birns conducted a follow-up study in which infants between eighteen and twenty-four months of age from black welfare, black middle-class, and white middle-class families were tested on the same instruments under two different conditions, a standard and an optimal situation.[30] In the standard testing situation, the tester was businesslike and allowed only so much time for response. In the optimal condition, the adult took extra time to establish rapport and allowed as many trials as were necessary to elicit a response. Mothers were asked to elicit a response when the tester failed, and rewards were used to motivate children. The examiners in both situations were white.

Under standard conditions, there were insignificant differences between the mean Catell IQs of the three groups of infants: 94, 98, and 100, respectively. Under optimal conditions the mean IQs for each group rose to 106, 108, and 109, respectively. There were no significant differences between the black and white infants tested in the standard manner. Although all groups profited from optimal testing procedures, the black welfare infants profited the most, performing almost as well as middle-class white and black infants. These findings suggest that many children may be more competent intellectually than their performance on standardized tests under standard test conditions indicates.

King and Seegmiller observed the performance of a group of black male infants living in Harlem (unselected for socio-economic status) on a number of developmental tests.[31] The same boys were tested at fourteen, eighteen, and again at twenty-two months. On the Bayley Mental Scale, the mean level of performance for the black infants was higher than that of the standardization sample at fourteen months, fell to a similar level at eighteen months, and remained stable at twenty-two months. The mean Bayley Psychomotor score of the Harlem infants was significantly higher than that of the standardization sample at all three age levels.

Continuing in the Anglo-American tradition of explaining away every trait in which blacks excel whites as of no importance or as a negative characteristic, Eysenck cites the motoric precocity of black infants as "proof" of their genetic inferiority. He points out that by three years of age American whites have higher mean IQs than blacks. He then cites a (very slight) negative correlation between sensory-motor intelligence in the first year of life and later IQ found in an early study. From exaggerated statements of these various data, he concludes:

> These findings are important because of a very general view in biology according to which the more prolonged the infancy the greater in general are the cognitive or intellectual abilities of the species. This law appears to work even within a given species.[32]

While the first sentence is true, Eysenck presents no data to prove the existence of a within-species relationship between biologically longer infancy and higher adult capacities. Yet he would have us believe that the motoric precocity of blacks is a sign of their biologically shorter infancy, which "proves" that they are a less highly evolved form of the human species than whites.

An additional follow-up study of the black children in the Golden and Birns sample revealed that, while there were no significant social-class differences in Catell IQs at eighteen and twenty-four months of age, there was a highly significant 23-point mean IQ difference on the Stanford Binet at three years of age between black children from welfare and middle-class families.[33] The fact that this difference was almost identical to the 22-point mean IQ difference between the highest and lowest socioeconomic groups of white children aged thirty months to five years in Terman and Merrill's 1937 standardization sample for the Stanford Binet suggests that black and white children have a similar pattern of social-class differentiation in IQ performance during the third year of life.

In speculating about why social-class differences in intellectual performance should first manifest themselves clearly during the third year of life, Golden *et al.* focus on the role of language in cognitive development. During the first two years, most knowledge is acquired in sensory-motor fashion through direct interaction with people and objects. The Catell IQ measures primarily perceptual-motor abilities. The lack of significant racial and social-class differences on Catell IQs during the first two years suggests that the homes of black welfare children supplied sufficient stimulation for the development of sensory-motor intelligence. Beyond the second year, knowledge is increasingly acquired through verbal interaction with other people, and the Stanford Binet tests verbal-symbolic knowledge far more than the Catell scale. Therefore, the significantly lower Stanford Binet IQs of black welfare three-year-olds compared with black middle-class three-year-olds suggest that the middle-class children have enjoyed richer verbal interaction with adults, accelerating their development of verbal-conceptual abilities.

We are in basic agreement that restricted verbal interaction between children and adults slows the linguistic development of poor black children, in the sense that middle-class children are likely to approximate their parents' level of verbal complexity at an earlier age than low-income children are likely to display the level of verbal complexity manifested by *their* parents. On the other hand, a great deal of linguistic development occurs in the context of peer interaction, although this is a slower route than matching the speech patterns of adults. Further, a relatively slow rate of linguistic development does not necessarily indicate a deficit in intelligence, cumulative or otherwise. We have already reported the findings of Kagan and Bosco that lower-class children catch up to middle-class children in performance on tests of basis intellectual processes by about age eleven. We shall discuss linguistic-cognitive development in the next chapter.

Complexity of children's speech is not always a reliable guide to the complexity of their thought processes. Middle-class children may display a verbal precocity that is far beyond the levels of reasoning it may suggest. Conversely, the reasoning abilities of young low-income black children may be more advanced than is revealed by some of their restricted verbal responses in test situations. Piaget has observed that

> . . . a symbolic function exists which is broader than language . . . language is not enough to explain thought, because the structures that characterize thought have their roots in action and in sensorimotor mechanisms that are deeper than linguistics. It is also evident that the more the structures of thought are refined, the more language is necessary for the achievement of this elaboration. Language is thus a necessary but not a sufficient condition of logical operations.[34]

One aspect of basic reasoning is what Piaget calls the ability to "conserve" mentally—i.e., to reason that, even though the appearance of something has changed (as when we pour four ounces of liquid from a tall, slender jar into a short, wide one) certain aspects of the situation have not changed (e.g., even if the level of water is lower than in the previous jar, there are still four ounces of liquid in the new jar). Conservation ability is a basic mental capacity somewhat independent of language. A number of studies report that, up to about age seven, middle-class children manifest conservation ability at earlier ages than lower-class children.[35] But lower-class children tend to catch up during the elementary school years. Mermelstein and Schulman[36] studied six- and nine-year-old low-income black children; about half of the group were from the South and were not attending school; the remainder were from the North and were attending school. In both regions, the children did not manifest much conservation ability at age six, but at age nine both groups did well on conservation problems. These results demonstrate further that a relatively slow rate of development is not necesarily a "cumulative deficit." In the case of the Southern black children, we further see that basic reasoning capacities mature even without the benefit of formal schooling.

COMPETENCE, PERFORMANCE, AND IQ

Regarding the racial and social-class differentiation in IQ test performance reported by some investigators in recent years, some psychologists influenced by studies in linguistics have begun to distinguish carefully between competence and performance; they have begun to question the notion that a given capacity to perform in a certain manner will lead to similar levels of performance in widely varying situations.[37] Such factors as desire to please adults, relationship with the tester, and familiarity with the testing situation are important in determining how hard a child tries to perform well when tested. During the early 1950's Haggard demonstrated that the IQs of lower-class children could easily be raised in only a few days.[38] He gave children three one-hour sessions of training on how to take IQ tests, including explanations of the types of problem found in the tests. Haggard also trained test examiners to encourage the children's efforts so as to enhance rapport between tester and child and offered the children special rewards for doing well on the tests. Under these conditions, the performance of lower-class children on standardized tests improved and their IQs increased sharply.

Palmer has demonstrated that differences between middle- and lower-class black children in scores on standard intelligence and cognitive tests can be reduced by manipulation of certain factors.[39] Black preschool boys from Harlem were divided into socio-economic-class groups. Considerable effort was made to ensure that each child was comfortable and responsive in the testing situation. In contrast to the usual approach, in which a child is brought to a strange place and immediately tested by a strange adult, no child was tested until he had played alone with the examiner for at least twenty minutes. Children were also given time to adapt to the center in which they would be tested, visiting three to five times before the testing began. If the child at any time appeared to be having difficulty attending to the test, testing was discontinued until the next visit. Children progressed through the tests at their own rate, with four to fifteen hours allowed to complete the test battery. Under these conditions, the usual wide performance differences between the socio-economic groups on most cognitive tests did not emerge with consistency at each age level. The one area in which children from higher socio-economic groups continued to show superior performance, even under these "ideal" testing conditions, was on tests of language comprehension and expression.

Zigler, Abelson, and Seitz demonstrated that the typically low scores obtained by young black children on the Peabody Picture Vocabulary test are not necessarily true indications of their cognitive competence by testing the children on two occasions.[40] The first test was administered in standard fashion; the second was administered either by the same tester or a strange adult, following either a play session with the adult or no play session. All the children showed significant gains in IQ on the second testing. They were more likely to gain significantly, however, if they had played with the tester prior to the second testing. The IQ gains in the second testing were therefore due primarily to a decrease in situational test anxiety and an increase in motivation rather than to familiarity with the test or the tester. The resulting improved performance was a more valid index of competence than performance in the standard test situation. It also suggests that increases in IQ following an intervention preschool program do not necessarily reflect remediation of cognitive deficits.

Zimiles, Wallace, and Judson provide an interesting example of how decreasing test anxiety and increasing motivation to do well can in themselves improve test performance and hence IQ scores.[41] In evaluating the effects of different preschool programs, they compared children's responses to individual items on cognitive tests before and after they completed the programs. One of the largest changes in the performance of a group of bright middle-class four-year-olds attending nursery school was their ability to give their first name upon request. It is unreasonable to conclude that these children had to attend nursery school to learn their names; rather, they simply became more relaxed in the test situation and more motivated to respond well. What changed was performance rather than competence.

Social class and ethnicity appear to interact to produce differences in style of reaction to aspects of a test situation. Faced with difficulties in a standard test situation, some children try harder, some refuse to continue any attempt to cope with the task, while still others become passive and quiet. In a study by Hertzig and associates, lower-class Puerto Rican three-year-olds in New York City were compared with middle-class non–Puerto Ricans of the same age on a series of cognitive problems.[42] Two important differences were noted in approach to intellectual problems. The middle-class children were more likely to work at a problem persistently. When the task became too difficult, they were more likely to tell the adult that they couldn't do it or to push the problem away. The lower-class children were more likely to sit passively, saying and doing nothing. These differences were found even when pairs of children from each group were matched for intellectual ability (IQ), so the differences would appear to be indices of behavioral-reaction *style* rather than of levels of competence.

Standardized IQ tests have several shortcomings that penalize low-income and nonwhite children. They usually present questions that have a predetermined "right" or "best" answer. Only the "right" answer gets full credit, and most "wrong" answers receive no credit. The questions and the "right" answers are usually reflective of a single cultural frame of reference. For example, one type of question requires the subject to define words of increasing rarity—but rarity is defined in relation to middle-class white experiences. The following questions from the vocabulary and information sections of the Wechsler Adult Intelligence Scale may be compared with the questions paraphrased from the Dove Counterbalance General Intelligence Test,[43] a test designed by black sociologist Adrian Dove as a "half-serious idea" to demonstrate items that would be familiar to urban blacks:

Wechsler Test	*Dove Test*
1. Who wrote *Hamlet*?	1. What instrument did T-Bone Walker play?
2. Who wrote *Faust*?	2. Who is Bo Diddley?
3. What is *ethnology*?	3. What does "handkerchief head" mean?
4. What does *edifice* means?	4. When is a man called a "blood"?
5. What does *perimeter* mean?	5. Where did "Hully Gully" come from?

A person's score on either test reflects the probability that he has been exposed to the information requested; a low score on either test does not necessarily reflect the lack of basic mental capacity implied by the labeling of low scorers as people of low intelligence.

Another set of questions poses some rather common problems for children and asks them to state what they would do in that situation. For example, one test asks seven-year-olds: "What should you do if you were sent to buy a loaf of bread and the grocer said he didn't have any more?" The only answer for which a child receives full credit is "I would go to another store." Such an answer clearly assumes that more than one store is available and that the neighborhood is safe enough for the child to go anywhere other than where his parent told him to go. Many low-income black urban children answer the question by saying they would "go home"—a perfectly logical answer—for which they receive no credit.[44]

A third class of IQ questions requires children to play word games called analogies. Here again, cultural bias is evident: Children will be asked how a piano and violin are similar, but not how Hully Gully and Funky Chicken are. Another type of problem presents children with line drawings of objects that have an element missing; the children are supposed to discover the missing feature. The pictures used favor middle-class children, for they depict such objects as a thermometer without mercury rather than a door without a double lock.[45]

Class and ethnic differences between children and testers also affect the manner in which they communicate with one another. A white middle-class tester may be misunderstood by a low-income child because of dialect-pronunciation differences. Thus, black children asked to define the word "fur" may reply, "That's what happens when you light a match." Their answer indicates that they have interpreted the word "fur" as "fire" and have given a reasonable, logical reply. Nevertheless, they would receive no credit for it.

In conclusion, psychologists and educators often have confused the poor performance of low-income children, particularly black children, in standard testing situations with a lack of intellectual competence. If they kept these judgments to themselves, the issue of their validity might not be important. However, many psychologists and educators have been quite vocal concerning the presumed lack of intellectual competence of the "disadvantaged child." Such judgments can seriously affect children's lives if they are used as the basis for grouping or tracking children in schools or offered as explanations for the lack of achievement of some groups and for the unequal rewards they receive. The issue of differential sorting of children within the schools, based upon supposedly objective-standardized test scores, and its implications for children's lives will be discussed in detail in Chapters 9 and 10. Chapter 7 will focus specifically upon the linguistic-cognitive competences of low-income black children and the ethnic patterning of mental abilities.

NOTES

1. See Klaus F. Riegel, "Influence of Economic and Political Ideologies on the Development of Developmental Psychology," *Psychological Bulletin,* 78 (1972): 129–41.

2. See R. S. Jones, "Proving Blacks Inferior: The Sociology of Knowledge," in Joyce A. Ladner, ed., *The Death of White Sociology* (New York: Random House, 1973), pp. 114–35.

3. Martin P. Deutsch, "The Disadvantaged Child and the Learning Process," in A. Harry Passow, ed., *Education in Depressed Areas* (New York: Teachers College Press, 1965), p. 170.

4. Donald O. Hebb, *The Organization of Behavior* (New York: Wiley, 1949).

5. "Hebb on Hocus-Pocus: a Conversation with Elisabeth Hall," *Psychology Today,* 3 (1969): 7.

6. See Jean Piaget and Bärbel Inhelder, *The Psychology of the Child* (New York: Basic Books, 1969).

7. Joseph McV. Hunt, "The Psychological Basis for Using Preschool Enrichment as an Antidote for Cultural Deprivation," *Merrill-Palmer Quarterly,* 10 (1964): 236.

8. Jerome Kagan, "On Cultural Deprivation," in David C. Glass, ed., *Environmental Influences: Biology and Behavior* (New York: Rockefeller University Press, 1968), pp. 211–50.

9. Joseph McV. Hunt, "Parent and Child Centers: Their Basis in the Behavioral and Educational Sciences," *American Journal of Orthopsychiatry,* 41 (1971): 28–29.

10. Francis H. Palmer, "Learning at Two," *Children,* 16, (1969): 55–57.

11. Edward Zigler and Earl C. Butterfield, "Motivational Aspects of Changes in I.Q. Test Performance of Culturally Deprived Nursery School Children," *Child Development,* 39 (1968): 1–14.

12. Freda Rebelsky, "First Discussant's Comments: Cross-cultural Studies of Mother-Infant Interaction," *Human Development,* 15 (1972): 128–30.

13. William Caudill and H. Weinstein, "Maternal Care and Infant Behavior in Japan and America," *Psychiatry,* 32 (1969): 12–43.

14. J. Bosco, "The Visual Information Processing Speed of Lower- and Middle-Class Children," *Child Development,* 43 (1972): 1418–22.

15. Jerome Kagan, "Cross-cultural Perspectives on Early Development," address to Annual Meeting of the American Association for the Advancement of Science, Washington, D.C., December 26, 1972.

16. "A Conversation with Jerome Kagan," *Saturday Review of Education,* April, 1973, p. 41.

17. Kagan, "Cross-cultural Perspectives," p. 5. See also *idem,* "What Is Intelligence?" *Social Policy,* July-August, 1973, pp. 88–94.

18. For surveys of such studies, see Ralph Mason Dreger and Kent S. Miller, "Comparative Psychological Studies of Negroes and Whites in the United States," *Psychological Bulletin,* 57 (1960): 361–401; *idem,* "Comparative Psychological Studies of Negroes and Whites in the

United States: 1959–1965," *Psychological Bulletin,* Monograph Supplement No. 70 (1968), No. 3, part 2; and Kent S. Miller and Ralph Mason Dreger, eds., *Comparative Studies of Blacks and Whites in the United States* (New York: Seminar Press, 1973), pp. 185–229.

19. David B. Ryckman, "A Comparison of Information-processing Abilities of Middle- and Lower-Class Negro Kindergarten Boys," *Exceptional Children,* 8 (1967): 545–52.

20. Arthur R. Jensen, "How Much Can We Boost I.Q. and Scholastic Achievement?" *Harvard Educational Review,* 39 (1969): 1–123. Richard J. Herrnstein, "I.Q.," *Atlantic Monthly,* September, 1971, pp. 43–64, and Hans J. Eysenck, *The I.Q. Argument* (New York: Library Press, 1971), basically agree with Jensen's argument, with Herrnstein offering a genetic explanation primarily for social-class differences and Eysenck for racial-group differences.

21. See G. E. McClearn and J. C. DeFries, *Introduction to Behavior Genetics* (San Francisco: W. H. Freeman, 1973), chapter 9.

22. Benjamin S. Bloom, *Stability and Change in Human Characteristics* (New York: Wiley, 1964), p. 70n.

23. See McClearn and DeFries, *Introduction to Behavioral Genetics,* pp. 298–300.

24. Sylvia Scarr-Salapatek, "Race, Social Class, and I.Q.," *Science,* 174 (1971): 1285–95.

25. *Ibid.,* p. 1294.

26. Lee R. Willerman, A. F. Naylor, and N. C. Myrianthopoulos, "Intellectual Development of Children from Interracial Matings," *Science,* 170 (1970): 1329–31.

27. Jensen argues that black males marrying white women are likely to be among the higher-IQ blacks, while white males marrying black women are likely to be low-IQ whites. Thus, he contends, the higher IQs of the children of white mothers in the above study could be due to the genetic effect of the superior black father. See Arthur R. Jensen, *Educability and Group Differences* (New York: Harper & Row, 1973), pp. 228–29.

28. See Nancy Bayley and Earl S. Schaeffer, "Correlations of Maternal and Child Behavior with the Development of Mental Abilities: Data from the Berkeley Growth Study," *Child Development,* vol. 29 (1964), full issue of no. 97.

29. Mark Golden and B. Birns, "Social Class and Cognitive Development in Infancy," *Merrill-Palmer Quarterly,* 14 (1968): 139–49.

30. Mark Golden and B. Birns, "Social Class, Intelligence, and Cognitive Style in Infancy," *Child Development,* 42 (1971): 2114–16.

31. W. L. King and B. Seegmiller, "Performance of 14-to-22 Month Old Black, Firstborn Male Infants on Two Tests of Cognitive Development," *Developmental Psychology* 83 (1973): 317–26. This finding is in agreement with earlier observations of Knobloch and Pasamanick that black infants show motoric precocity throughout the first two years of life. See Hilda Knobloch and Benjamin Pasamanick, "Further Observations on the Behavioral Development of Negro Children," *Journal of Genetic Psychology,* 83 (1953): 135–57.

32. Eysenck, *The I.Q. Argument* (n. 20 *supra*), p. 79.
33. M. Golden, B. Birns, W. Bridger, and A. Moss, "Social-Class Differentiation in Cognitive Development Among Black Preschool Children," *Child Development*, 42 (1971): 37–45.
34. Jean Piaget, "Language and Thought from the Genetic Point of View," in Jean Piaget, *Six Psychological Studies,* ed. by David Elkind (New York: Random House, 1968), pp. 91, 98.
35. See, for example, Harry Beilen, Jerome Kagan, and R. Rabinowitz, "Effects of Verbal and Perceptual Training on Water Level Representation," *Child Development*, 37 (1966): 317–29, and B. B. Rothenberg and Richard G. Courtney, "Conservation of Number in Very Young Children," *Developmental Psychology*, 1 (1969): 493–502.
36. E. Mermelstein and L. S. Schulman, "Lack of Formal Schooling and the Acquisition of Conservation," *Child Development*, 38 (1967): 39–52.
37. See, for example, Michael Cole *et al., The Cultural Context of Learning and Thinking* (New York: Basic Books, 1971), and Jerome Kagan and Nathan Kogan, "Individual Variation in Cognitive Processes," in Paul H. Mussen, ed., *Carmichael's Manual of Child Psychology,* 3d ed. (New York: Wiley, 1970), pp. 1273–1365.
38. Ernest A. Haggard, "Social Status and Intelligence," *Genetic Psychology Monographs,* 49 (1954): 141–86.
39. Francis H. Palmer, "Socioeconomic Status and Intellective Performance Among Negro Preschool Boys," *Developmental Psychology,* 3 (1970): 1–9.
40. Edward Zigler, W. D. Abelson, and V. Seitz, "Motivational Factors in the Performance of Economically Disadvantaged Children on the Peabody Picture Vocabulary Test," *Child Development*, 44 (1973): 294–303.
41. Herbert Zimiles, Doris D. Wallace, and M. Judson, "A Comparative Study of the Impact of Two Contrasting Educational Approaches to Head Start," mimeographed (New York: Bank Street College of Education, Research Division, 1970).
42. M. E. Hertzig *et al.,* "Class and Ethnic Differences in the Responsiveness of Preschool Children to Cognitive Demands," *Monographs of the Society for Research in Child Development,* Serial 117, vol. 33, No. 1 (1968).
43. See "Taking the Chitling Test," in Dushkin Publishing Group, ed., *Readings in Human Development '73–'74* (Guilford, Conn.: Dushkin, 1973), p. 298.
44. See Jerome Kagan, "The Magical Aura of the I.Q.," *Saturday Review of Literature,* December 9, 1971, pp. 92–93.
45. *Ibid.* See also Jane R. Mercer and W. C. Brown, "Racial Differences in I.Q.: Fact or Artifact?" in Carl Senna, ed., *The Fallacy of I.Q.* (New York: Third Press, 1973), pp. 56-113.

7 / COGNITIVE-LINGUISTIC DEVELOPMENT

BLACK ENGLISH VERNACULAR: DEFICIT OR DIFFERENCE?

By 1966, low-income urban black children were being described by many psychologists and educators as essentially nonverbal or so deficient in linguistic skills as to be severely inhibited in the development of intellectual abilities and academic achievement. Describing a group of four-year-olds who, they claimed, represented a "fairly unbiased selection from the lower stratum" of an urban black community, Bereiter and Englemann said:

> Language for them is unwieldy and not very useful. For some of them, speaking is clearly no fun, and they manage as far as possible to get along without it. Others enjoy social speech and use it a good deal in play and social intercourse, but seldom for purposes of learning or reasoning; their language, as they use it, is not adequate for these purposes.[1]

In addition, Bereiter and Englemann tell us, "preschool disadvantaged children are likely to show distressing tendencies to hit, bite, kick, scream, run wildly about, cling, climb into laps, steal, lie, hide, ignore directions, and defy authority." These behaviors are to be considered simply "inappropriate behaviors for the classroom"; the children's social or emotional needs are of little relevance to understanding them. "Cultural deprivation" is essentially to be understood as "language deprivation." The teacher is instructed to "see the task for what it is: *teaching naïve children how to act in a new situation.*"[2] The four-year-old child has no right to want to be held in an adult's lap, nor should he be allowed to cling to the teacher. To remedy the children's linguistic deficiencies, the teacher must restrain them from expressing strong emotions or personal concerns and drill them to behave as the controlling adults would have them behave.

In the late 1960's and early 1970's the linguistic-cognitive-deficit explanation of low school achievement among poor black children came under increasing attack. Anthropologically oriented behavioral scientists began to argue that, instead of being deficient or defective in their linguistic-conceptual systems, black children possess linguistic and cognitive systems that are structurally coherent but different from those of white children. Baratz and Baratz, for example, claim:

> The current linguistic data . . . do not support the assumption of a linguistic deficit. . . . Many lower-class Negro children speak a well-ordered, highly structured, but different dialect from that of Standard English. These children have developed a language.[3]

From the "cultural-deprivation" viewpoint, black children's linguistic-cognitive abilities are *deficient,* unable to meet the demands of the standard school curriculum without preschool remediation; from the cultural-difference viewpoint, they are *different* and require a different curriculum. The two positions have polarized. Their adherents often fail to take into account the fact that poor black children are *bicultural* and *bidialectical:* They are simultaneously inducted into the urban black community and the more inclusive mainstream, white-dominated society.[4] As we noted in Chapter 2, in socializing their children lower-class black mothers have had to take into account the demands of a widening circle of social systems: the black family, the black community, and the wider society. By the time they reached the upper elementary school grades, most of the children we knew in Central Harlem seemed to comprehend most verbal messages directed to them, whether they were framed in everyday standard English or in black dialect and idiom, although occasionally, because of pronunciation differences, *we* had difficulty understanding a word or two spoken by a child, and sometimes a child would interpret our words in a way we had not intended.

In their own verbal productions the children often used black vernacular vocabulary and syntax, but standard English was not a foreign language to them: The dialect they spoke was a variant of the English language. Just as we reject any image of these children as deficient cognitive machines, so we reject any image of the children as exotic primitives. The children were black and poor, but they were Americans—oppressed Americans, Americans with an African heritage, but Americans living in the contemporary United States.

The linguistic-cognitive-deficit theorists rely heavily on the findings of a long line of studies indicating that middle-class children, from infancy onward, generally appear to be more advanced than working-class or lower-class children in most aspects of language behavior: vocabulary acquisition, sound discrimination, articulation, and sentence structure.[5] There are some exceptions to this trend: Inner-city children, black and white, have been found to respond to verbal stimuli with free word associations at a higher rate than white suburban children (from much higher-income families) at the first-grade level; although they fall behind at the third-grade level, they become equal at the fifth-grade level.[6]

The cultural-deprivation theorists view the poorer linguistic performance of lower-class children as indicative of linguistic-cognitive deficiencies, which they trace to qualitative differences in parent-child interaction associated with social-class level. As we noted in Chapter 6, middle-class mothers reportedly present their infants, particularly girls, with more face-to-face verbalizations unaccompanied by competing sources of stimulation than working-class mothers. Middle-class girls are reported to be the most advanced group in the rate of linguistic-cognitive development.

With specific regard to lower-class black children, deficit theorists point to research carried out in schools or school-like settings which demonstrates that black children have greater difficulty than middle-class children (black or white) in using words to classify actions or objects.[7] For example, when shown a series of four pictures, each depicting a person engaging in some activity, lower-class black children had considerable difficulty pointing to the one that showed a person "tying," "pouring," "digging," and "picking." The children were not deficient in experience with the referent actions but, rather, had difficulty applying labels to them. This difficulty in making specific connections between words and referents is related causally by deficit theorists to a relative lack of active verbal interaction between the children and adults in their homes. Deficit theorists see low-income children as less able to use words in thinking, which leads to poor performance on tasks in which words must be used to form categories or express conceptual relationships. Thus, when asked, "Why do these pictures go together?" lower-class black first-graders are more likely to answer: "Because they look the same" or "Because they have legs" than "Because they are all animals." Deficit theorists regard "They are all animals" as a more explicit statement of a concept and, hence, a developmentally more advanced reply; the alternative responses are viewed not as legitimate stylistic ways of ordering perceptions but, rather, as primitive modes of functioning.

The difference theorists argue that many of the researches in support of the conclusion that lower-class black children have linguistic-cognitive deficiencies are based on ethnocentric or racist perceptions. The deficit model is based on the assumption that only standard English as spoken by middle-class whites is acceptable and that any variant, such as the dialects of low-income populations, is a "bad" or "deficient" version. The difference theorists argue that the dialects of low-income whites and blacks as well as their differences from standard English represent parallel development, not deficits.

Cultural-difference theorists claim that no evidence has been found that low-income children have more difficulty acquiring the language of their own community than middle-class children do acquiring theirs.[8] Further, these theorists assert that careful study of the structural differences between the black English vernacular and standard English reveals no grammatical relationship that can be expressed in standard English but not in the black idiom. For example, there is an important distinction between "he workin' " and "he be workin' "—structural forms found in the black English vernacular.[9] "He workin' " means he is working right now; "he be workin' " means he works habitually. In black idiom, the word *be* is employed as an auxiliary to express the habitual tense, to express action that is of long duration. This is a tense found in West African languages but not in standard English.[10]

Children acquire language not so much through imitation as through problem-solving processes. When two-year-olds are presented with statements to imitate, what the children give back is not a verbatim repetition of what the adult said but the results of their own cognitive processing; the children reduce what was said to their current grammar.[11] Thus, "the pencil is green" is repeated as "pencil green," and "the little boy is eating some pink ice cream" is repeated as "little boy eating pink ice cream."

A similar cognitive-processing system has been revealed in studies of low-income speakers in Harlem. When asked to repeat sentences presented in standard English, Harlem boys aged eleven to fourteen demonstrated that some standard English structures were first *understood,* then *translated* to fit the speaker's own syntactic rules, whereas others were simply *repeated* as presented because they were already in a syntactical form used by the speaker. Thus, "I asked Alvin if he knows how to play basketball" became "I aks Alvin do he know how to play basketball," and "nobody ever" became "nobody never." "Money, who is eleven, can't spit as far as Boo can" was repeated as given, as was "Larry is a stupid fool."[12]

It is important to distinguish between the *production* and the *comprehension* grammars of speakers of black English vernacular. Labov and Cohen have reported variability in the grammatical rules followed by black adults in Harlem depending upon the context in which the speech is produced and the speaker's linguistic experience (e.g., his social-class level and his Northern or Southern background). In general they reported differences in the phonological rules used in careful speech and in casual speech. Middle-class black adults came much closer to the production of standard English in careful speech than did working-class black adults. Thus, in linguistic production, middle-class black adults would appear to be more bicultural than working- or lower-class black adults.

Some lower-middle-class black adults who are economically upwardly mobile have been found to display what Labov has called a "hyper-correct" linguistic pattern.[13] This phenomenon is characterized by an extensive shift from black dialect to standard English forms when changing from casual to careful speech; a sharper tendency than any other group to stigmatize the speech of others; less accurate self-reports of their own speech patterns than others—shifting their perception of their own speech toward the standard norm; the most negative overt feelings about their own speech; and the strongest reactions against their own vernacular. The "hypercorrect" pattern of the lower middle class is found more regularly and in more extreme form among black women than among men. The existence of this pattern suggests that a considerable number of upwardly mobile blacks have accepted the standard white view of black cultural characteristics. They appear to regard their own vernacular as "mistakes" in speech rather than as a second dialect or a different speech system. Such blacks are thus caught in a practical and psychological bind. If, in either-or fashion, they reject standard English, they may restrict their job opportunities in a white-dominated society. If they reject the black idiom, they may experience difficulties in relating to family and friends and, to the extent that they perceive their speech as different from a standard that they believe to be "correct" or "respectable," they may suffer damage to their self-esteem.[14]

The conflict involved in the "hypercorrect pattern" may not develop fully until late adolescence, when the youth begins to comprehend the dimensions of economic discrimination against blacks. As we have noted, low-income black children generally seem able to understand both standard English and their own dialect. However, it is not clear how early lower-class black children will make use of different rules when speaking casually and carefully, as black adults have been observed to do. One study has found some distinctions between the verbal productions of lower-class and middle-class ninth-grade black girls in Chicago depending upon whether they were aiming at "school talk" (standard English) or "everyday talk."[15] A young black field worker met with groups of three girls at a time for discussion. In some groups, the worker asked questions framed in standard English and told the girls to answer in their best "school talk" because their recorded speech would be analyzed by educators. In other groups she framed questions in a style that made use of black English forms and told the girls to use "everyday" talk in replying since their answers would be heard only by the field worker. When the lower-class black girls replied to the field worker using "school talk," their speech became a little more like standard English; however, when they replied in "everyday talk," utilizing the black English vernacular, they gave more elaborate responses. While the middle-class black girls also shifted to more standard English when speaking "school talk," they gave relatively elaborate linguistic responses whether talking "school talk" or "everyday talk." Like the middle-class girls, the lower-class girls were able to change their verbal performance somewhat to meet the performance standards of the mainstream society, but they appeared to feel inhibited in performance situations where mainstream standards would be used to judge their competence. The middle-class girls, on the other hand, gave equally complex performances whether the standard for competence was mainstream or ghetto-specific, suggesting that these girls came closer to being fully bicultural than their lower-class peers.

Although poor quality in verbal performance may seem characteristic of many low-income black children in schools that are white-middle-class-dominated, in other contexts, as we have shown, the children tend to be talkative and highly articulate. The respect accorded to the good talker, the man of words, in the black community and the extent to which verbal performance is utilized as a way to achieve status, particularly in street peer groups, suggests the survival in black America of African oral traditions.[16] Black youth may display a distinct variety of verbal skills in the streets: "Rapping," "shucking," "jiving," "running it down," "copping a plea," "signifying," and "sounding" are all aspects of the black idiom. Each type of talking

> . . . has its own distinguishing features of form, style, and function; each is influenced by, and influences, the speaker, setting, and audience; and each sheds light on the black perspective and the black condition . . . on those orienting values and attitudes that will cause a speaker to speak or perform in his own way within the social context of the black community.[17]

Most ghetto children learn to comprehend and communicate appropriately in these styles of talking.

Smitherman argues that the black idiom cannot be viewed apart from black culture and the black experience in America.[18] She distinguishes two perspectives in looking at black English: linguistic and stylistic. From the linguistic perspective, which emphasizes pronunciation and syntax, Smitherman argues that black English is simply one of many contemporary American dialects; it is likely that the linguistic patterns of black English differ from those of standard English only in surface structure. However, although black people use the vocabulary of the English language, some words are selected out of that lexicon and given a special black semantic slant. Smitherman suggests that the following principles apply:

1. Because of the need of blacks for a code that is unintelligible to whites, the words that are given a special black slant are discarded when they are adopted by whites; e.g., blacks no longer speak of a "hip" brother but of a "together" brother.

2. The concept of denotation *vs.* connotation is not applicable to the black idiom. The black idiom is characterized, instead, by shades of meaning along a connotative spectrum. For example, depending upon the context, "bad" may mean extraordinary, beautiful, good, versatile, or a variety of other terms of positive value. Certain words in the black lexicon may be used to indicate either approbation or denigration, depending upon context; for example, "He's my main nigger" means he is my best friend, whereas "The nigger ain't shit" may indicate a variety of negative characteristics, depending upon the context.

3. Approbation and denigration refer to the semantic level; on the grammatical level, the same word may serve two other functions: intensification and completion. Thus, in "Niggers was getting out of there left and right, them niggers was running, and so the niggers said . . . ," etc., the word "nigger" may be devoid of real meaning, serving simply to give the sentence a subject and animate the conversation rather than to indicate approbation or denigration. "Cats" or "guys" or "people" would serve as well.

Turning to the stylistic elements of black English, Smitherman enumerates the following elements that differentiate black speakers of English from white speakers:

1. *Call and response.* A speaker's solo voice alternates or is intermingled with responses from the audience. This is basic to the black oral tradition. For example, the congregation responding to the preacher—"Preach, Reverend," "That's right"—or the street audience responding to displays of repartee with laughter, palm-slapping, and such phrases as "Get back, nigger," "Git down, baby."

2. *Rhythmic pattern.* This includes cadence, tone, and musical quality. Black speakers often employ a pattern that is lyrical and sonorous and generally emphasizes sound apart from sense through the repetition of certain sounds or words. For example, the preacher's rhythm, "I-I-I-I-I-Oh-I-I-Oh, yeah, Lord-I-I-heard the voice of Jesus saying . . . ," or the rhythmic, fast tempo in delivering toasts such as the signifying monkey (see Chapter 5).

3. *Spontaneity.* Generally, a speaker's performance is improvisational, including much interaction with the audience, which dictates or directs the flow and outcome of the speech event. The speaker is casual; he employs a lively conversational tone with a quality of immediacy. For example, a preacher declares, "Y'all don' want to hear dat, so I'm gon' leave it lone," and his congregation calls out, "Now, tell it, Reverend, tell it!" and he does.

4. *Concreteness.* A speaker's imagery and ideas center upon contemporary, everyday experiences, and he conveys a sense of identification with the event being described. For example, the toast teller becomes Stag-O-Lee, or the preacher declares, "I first met God in 1925."

5. *Signifying*. To signify, the speaker talks about the entire audience or one of its members, either to trigger a verbal contest or to hammer a point home, without offending the audience. "Pimp, punk, prostitute, Ph.D.—all the P's—you still in slavery," declared the Reverend Jesse Jackson. Malcolm X delivered this putdown of the nonviolent movement: "In a revolution, you swinging, not singing." The rhythmic alliteration and rhyming in these examples are characteristic of black speakers.

Susan Houston, studying the speech patterns of black and white children in rural Florida, found few important syntactic differences between them.[19] There were real differences, but they were basically in style or pronunciation. In one experiment Houston worked with eighty-six pairs of first-graders from four socio-economic groups: well-to-do whites, well-to-do blacks, poor whites, and poor blacks. She sent one child in each pair out of earshot, then told the other child a story and asked him to re-tell it exactly to his partner. After the retelling, the partner was asked to repeat the story. All the white children and the middle-class black children tended to reproduce details correctly, according to the norms set by the adult in charge. The poor black children took the given instructions as a baseline upon which to demonstrate spontaneous verbal flair. That is, they reproduced general elements from the story but preferred to supply their own details. Thus, 26 per cent of the stories told by the poor black children contained original material, as against 12 per cent or less for the other groups. Cultural-deprivation theorists would find the poor black children linguistically deficient relative to the other groups; difference theorists would stress their creativity and closer contact with their roots in the black oral tradition.

Another finding of Houston's study is worth noting. The poor black children were the most peer-oriented; they generally interacted far more with other children than did the other groups, and this was true whether they were paired with a white child or another black child. They clearly attended to each other more than to the adult, telling their stories to their partners rather than to the adult for her approval.

To summarize, it appears to us that cultural-difference theory offers a more accurate appraisal of the linguistic-cognitive competence of low-income black children than does cultural-deprivation theory. Furthermore, contrary to those cultural-difference theorists who insist that black English must be viewed as a separate language based upon West African linguistic patterns, careful linguistic analysis reveals that it is not based primarily upon West African syntax or grammar, although West African elements are present in the black idiom. From extensive linguistic studies, Labov has concluded that, although black English shows internal cohesion,

. . . it is best seen as a distinct subsystem within the larger grammar of English. Certain parts of the tense and aspect system are clearly separate subsystems in the sense that they are not shared or recognized by other dialects, and we can isolate other such limited areas. But the gears and axles of English grammatical machinery are available to speakers of all dialects, whether or not they use all of them in everyday speech.[20]

Although poor black children may misinterpret some words pronounced by white middle-class speakers because of differences in phonology or usage or unfamiliarity with the vocabulary, there is no reason to believe that the children cannot usually comprehend the basic meaning of sentences utilizing standard English grammar and syntax. Here the distinction between competence and performance is essential. Poor black children often do not utilize certain standard English grammatical forms in their verbal productions, but this does not necessarily mean that by late childhood they are not competent to do so. Performance—what one does with one's competence—is affected by a variety of situational determinants. For example, if one is frightened or tired or in a hurry, his linguistic performance is likely to be affected, although his competence, his mastery of the basic grammar of his language, remains unchanged.[21] A college student may feel a bit anxious when speaking to a professor in a speech course and either restrict his utterances or make mistakes in performance that he is not likely to make under other circumstances. Similarly, low-income black children are likely to freeze up or make performance errors when evaluated by middle-class adults, particularly white adults. However, their poor performance may mask considerable competence. The most significant differences between black English and white English would appear to be in the use made of selected vocabulary and in performance and communication styles.

Cultural-deprivation theorists have a valid point when they observe that middle-class children, black or white, are likely to enjoy richer verbal interaction with adults than their lower-class peers. As we noted in Chapter 2, low-income black parents have had valid reasons, related to survival in a racist society, to quiet young children and wean them early from dependent interaction. However, these theorists grossly underestimate the linguistic-cognitive competence of low-income black children, for reasons we shall outline below. In addition, they confuse a somewhat slower rate of linguistic-cognitive maturation in lower-class black (or white) children with their own reified theoretical construct—a "cumulative deficit" in basic linguistic-cognitive capacity. They assume that low-income black children will never catch up to middle-class white children, and they employ culturally biased tests, on which low-income blacks perform poorly, to "prove" that blacks continue to be linguistically and cognitively incompetent.

Let us look more closely at the criteria employed by these theorists in judging the linguistic-cognitive competence of low-income black children. Bereiter and Engelmann, for example, report that the children respond to adult questioning, if at all, with gestures, single words, or disconnected words and phrases.[22] Such reports are based upon empirical observation. For example, here is a typical complete interview with a black boy carried out in a New York City school by a friendly white interviewer. The adult places an object on the table in front of the child and says, "Tell me everything you can about this."

<blockquote>

12 seconds of silence

ADULT: What would you say it looks like?

8 seconds of silence

CHILD: A spaceship.

ADULT: Hmmmm.

13 seconds of silence

CHILD: Like a je-et.

12 seconds of silence

CHILD: Like a plane.

20 seconds of silence

ADULT: What color is it?

CHILD: Orange. (*2 seconds*) An' whi-ite. (*2 seconds*) An' green.

6 seconds of silence

ADULT: An' what could you use it for?

8 seconds of silence

CHILD: A je-et.

6 seconds of silence

ADULT: If you had two of them, what would do with them?

6 seconds of silence

CHILD: Give one to some-body.

ADULT: Hmmm. Who do you think would like to have it?

10 seconds of silence

CHILD: Cla-rence.

ADULT: Mm. Where do you think you could get another one of these?

CHILD: At the store.

ADULT: Oh-ka-ay![23]

</blockquote>

Here we have a child in a situation where anything he says may be judged "wrong" and lead to shame or punishment. He plays it safe by saying as little as possible, a survival strategy for dealing with strange adults, particularly whites. The child's defensive behavior is not necessarily a function of ineptness on the part of the adult interviewer, for, as Labov has found, a friendly, competent black male adult interviewer from the community obtained similar results when interviewing eight-year-old Harlem boys in the same manner. However, significant changes in both the volume and the style of speech of the same children occurred when the interviewer brought potato chips, making the interview more like a party; brought along one of the child's friends; reduced the height imbalance by sitting on the floor; and introduced taboo words and topics indicating that the child could say anything without fear of retaliation. These changes were striking, as is clear in this interview with eight-year-old Leon in the presence of eight-year-old Greg:

ADULT: Is there anybody who says, "Your momma drink pee?"
LEON: (*rapidly and breathlessly*) Yee-ah!
GREG: (*simultaneously*) Yup.
LEON: And your father eat doo-doo for breakfas'!
ADULT: Ohhh! (*laughs*)
LEON: And they say your father—your father eat doo-doo for dinner!
GREG: When they sound on me, I say "C.B.M."
ADULT: What that mean?
LEON: Congo booger-snatch! (*laugh*)
GREG: (*simultaneously*) Congo booger-snatcher! (*laughs*)
GREG: And sometimes I'll curse with "B.B."
ADULT: What that?
GREG: Oh, that's a "M.B.B." black boy. (*Leon crunching on potato chips*)
GREG: 'Merican black boy.
ADULT: Oh.
GREG: Anyway, 'Mericans is same like white people, right?
LEON: And they talk about Allah.
ADULT: Oh, yeah?
GREG: Yeah.
ADULT: What they say about Allah?
LEON: Allah—Allah is God.
GREG: (*simultaneously*) Allah—
ADULT: And what else?
LEON: I don't know the res'!
GREG: Allah i-Allah is God, Allah is the only God, Allah—
LEON: Allah is the son of God.
GREG: But can he make magic?
LEON: Nope.
GREG: I know who can make magic.
ADULT: Who can?
LEON: The God, the real one.
ADULT: Who can make magic?
GREG: The son of po'. (ADULT: Hm?) I'm saying the po'k chop God! He only a po'k chop God! (*Leon chuckles*)[24]

Leon, a boy who barely responded to a traditional interviewer, is now competing actively for the floor. Both boys seem to have no difficulty in using the English language to express themselves. Revealing a strong peer orientation, they talk to each other as much as to the interviewer.

Cultural-deprivation theorists argue that low-income black children's careless articulation and poor auditory discrimination are signs of incompetence. Here an ethnocentric bias often affects judgment: The difficulties poor black children have in pronouncing many words in the manner of middle-class whites often is no more and no less than the problem white middle-class American children would have if asked to speak like Englishmen. All children learn to pronounce words in the manner of those in their immediate community, but cultural-deprivation theorists impose a single standard as an index of precision in articulation. Similarly, the phonology usually presented in auditory-discrimination tests are the sounds of middle-class white English. Thus, many low-income black children may perform poorly not because they have poor auditory discrimination in any absolute sense, but because some of the sounds on the test are not their sounds.[25]

Cultural-deprivation theorists argue also that low-income black children employ shorter sentences and less complex grammar than more privileged children, indicating linguistic-cognitive incompetence. However, sentence length and grammatical complexity typically are assessed by tests like the one described above, in which a strange adult asks questions such as, "Tell me all you can about the object that is on the table." As we have seen, a child who doesn't trust the adult will purposely reply as briefly as possible. Besides, the test itself may seem silly to lower-class children. Why would an adult ask such a question? Can't he see for himself? What does he really want? What trick is he trying to play? Middle-class children are less likely to see the test in this way because they have more experience in being drawn out verbally by their parents. Thus, such tests may tell us more about the manner in which children relate to adults in an evaluative context than about their basic linguistic-cognitive competence.

Further, psychologists and educators seem to have a bias in favor of long sentences and complex grammar. But sentence length and complexity sometimes hide muddled thought, and short, simple sentences may reveal clarity and precision of thought. As a reading of social-science and education journals soon reveals, involved, cumbersome sentences often do not portray reality accurately or make much sense.

Cultural-deprivation theorists and the teachers they have influenced tend to equate class and ethnic differences in grammatical forms with differences in the capacity for logical analysis, to assume that teaching children to mimic the speech patterns of their middle-class teachers is the same as teaching them to think logically, and to favor and reward children who speak the way they do. This preferred treatment may help some children to achieve in school more rapidly than others and this achievement in turn is often seen as evidence that the higher-achieving children were better equipped intellectually from the start.

CLASS AND LINGUISTIC SOCIALIZATION

As we suggested above, middle-class children are likely to approximate their parents' verbalizations somewhat earlier than lower-class children, perhaps because of differences in the linguistic socialization of the two groups. In one study, it was found that low-income black mothers generally relied on more restricted verbal communications in combination with status-oriented discipline in relating to their children than did middle-class black mothers.[26] When the mothers were asked to teach various tasks to their children, the low-income mothers and their children both displayed a greater tendency to act without taking time for reflection or planning. For example, after briefly demonstrating to a child what he was supposed to do, a low-income mother commonly sat silently by, watching the child try to solve a problem until he made an error, whereupon she would punish him immediately. These mothers frequently failed to structure the learning situation so that the children could learn to recognize and correct their errors. They did not stop the children before they made a mistake and ask them to think about the probable outcome of their behavior. Thus, the lower-class child often learned only that his mother wanted him to do something, although she did not specify clearly what it was; no matter what he did, he would probably be punished.

Helen Bee and her associates have also studied social-class differences in the interactions between mothers and young children.[27] Mothers were observed trying to help children carry out specific tasks and while they were in a waiting room well supplied with toys. Mothers were also interviewed concerning their ideas on taking care of children. In general, lower-class mothers appeared to be much more restrictive than middle-class mothers and more inclined to use negative reinforcements. In the helping situation, middle-class mothers tended to allow children to work at their own pace, offering many general suggestions on how to look for a solution to a problem while pointing out what the children were doing that was right. Lower-class mothers, by contrast, tended to behave in ways that did not encourage their children to attend to the basic features of the problem. They tended to tell the children to do specific things, they did not emphasize basic problem-solving strategies, and their "suggestions" were really imperative statements that did not encourage a reply from the child.

The greater verbal interaction between middle-class mothers and their children seems to be "designed" to help the children acquire learning strategies that they can generalize to future problem-solving situations. The middle-class mothers help their children to attend discriminately to various features of the situation and of their own behavior. This selective attending helps children cognitively to take situations and their behaviors apart and to put the pieces together differently in new contexts, thus increasing the range of situations within which the children can respond adaptively. Middle-class mothers tend to ask many more questions of their children when trying to help them. Thus, they help the children to perceive connections between objects and events. The children are also helped to express connections in words and to formulate general rules independent of the particular context within which they are operating. Lower-class mothers, on the other hand, by instructing children in a manner that does not encourage verbal give-and-take, help their children somewhat to carry out specific tasks, but they do not encourage, and often discourage, a reflective and conceptual orientation to problems.

Studies such as these may be criticized on several grounds. First, the mothers and children were observed in university laboratories, a setting that may be more threatening to lower-class mothers than to their middle-class peers. Thus, the restricted quality of the low-income mothers' performance may have been in part a defense against the possibility of appearing inadequate in the eyes of middle-class observers. Second, the tasks presented by the researchers may have been more familiar to middle-class children, providing a performance advantage. Nevertheless, much of the social-class difference in performance among mothers appears to reflect significant differences in styles of socialization. The behavior of low-income mothers in the laboratory situation is basically consistent with the general socialization orientation of low-income mothers, as discussed in Chapter 2.

Low-income black children have generally not been encouraged to perform linguistically for adult approval or to strive for mastery of skills not immediately necessary for survival. The result is that many such children perform quite poorly in mainstream cultural situations, such as the psychological laboratory or school, in spite of the fact that within their peer group many of them display considerable linguistic-cognitive competence.

The typical middle-class socialization techniques, on the other hand, tend to push children to expand, as rapidly as possible, their capacities for linguistic-cognitive differentiation, categorization, and conceptualization in a widening variety of situations. The parents frequently elaborate on their children's statements, helping them to expand their categorization of experience. They encourage the children to build mental models of experience based on the use of words. By using language to help focus the children's attention on various features of their own behavior and the situations they encounter, middle-class parents provide the children with abundant experience in using the same symbols in a variety of situations. Middle-class children are encouraged to abstract the common meanings of these symbols as used in various situations and to use words as referents for concepts and categories that have generalized meaning, rather than as referents for a narrow range of specific, personalized experiences. Middle-class children are pushed to move beyond the use of language in highly concrete, particularized, situation-specific orientations to the use of language for formal, rule-oriented, conceptually ordered discourse about general aspects of experience. All these skills are socialized by middle-class parents in the expectation that they will be instrumental in the children's future educational and occupational success, helping them to maintain or improve their advantaged position in the social order. These parental behaviors appear to result in accelerated linguistic-cognitive development among middle-class children relative to their lower-class peers, although the magnitude of the differences between them often seems greater than it actually is because of the tendencies of low-income children to perform poorly when tested by adults and because of class and ethnic biases in interpreting low-income children's behavior.

In Chapter 5, we discussed the importance of verbal performance in urban black children's peer groups. We also saw that the shift from adult orientation to peer orientation developed at an early age among urban blacks, stimulated by "push" factors that drive children out of the house and by "pull" factors in the lure of the street. Similarly, among black children in a Southern town, the focus of linguistic socialization has been observed to shift from adults to peers at an early age. Virginia Young, who studied childrearing practices among black residents of a medium-sized town in Georgia, found that about age three there is "an almost complete cessation of the close relationship with the mother and father and a shift in orientation to the children's gang." One of the important features of this change is that

> . . . often speech becomes an indistinct children's patois in contrast to the clear enunciation used by the Knee-baby (younger child) with his parents. Children speak less to adults, and get along adequately with "Yes'm," and "No'm."[28]

We have already noted that low-income black children in the North or the South seemed inclined to direct their verbal performance toward a peer rather than an adult when both peer and adult were available. This relatively early reliance on peers for verbal socialization is likely to delay the child's development of linguistic behavior like his own parents' and to reinforce competence in the language of the streets. While such language is complex, coherent, and creative in vocabulary and style, it is not the language of the schools. Thus, by encouraging linguistic patterns associated with low-income black life-styles and often negating standard English, street peer groups contribute to the child's difficulties in coping with school and his negative attitudes toward school achievement.[29]

CLASS AND ETHNIC PATTERNING OF ABILITIES

We have noted findings that lower-class children tend much more than middle-class children to deal with concrete, emotionally significant features of situations rather than analytically abstracting common features from situations and using words to form more general categories. One interpretation of this finding is that the categorization behavior of middle-class children indicates linguistic-cognitive functioning at a relatively high level of development. Another interpretation of the same data is that young lower-class children tend not to use their abilities to form analytic, formal categories because of their class-based orientation to experience and to the use of language.[30] Both interpretations may be correct. Middle-class children may develop the capacity to utilize language to form analytic, formal categories earlier than lower-class children because the social milieu in which they live encourages and rewards this ability more than is common in lower-class homes. Lower-class children *can* use language to express complex relationships and abstract ideas, but they tend to do so largely in peer-group relationships and experiences which have personal, affective significance rather than in relation to events, objects, categories, and concepts without subjective emotional content.

The socialization of lower-class children, particularly boys, leads to the development of individual identities that are refracted through group relationships more than through individual work and achievement and encourages an orientation toward linguistic competence in relation to expressive interpersonal experiences. For example, Ryan reports that among lower-class white ethnic adults in Boston's West End talk about relatively individualistic, impersonal experiences such as jobs and work was very uncommon in the bars, in delicatessens, and on the corner.[31] Rather, talk tended to center on issues of common concern such as the characteristics of other people and memories of places where the gang got together and events that happened there. Children socialized in this milieu learn to be highly talkative in peer-group situations in which concrete common concerns and emotionally charged experiences are shared and discussed. In such contexts, they strive to be verbally complex and creative because verbal competence leads to affirmation by peers and becomes an integral element of personal identity. Such children will bring an orientation to concretize and personalize experience to school settings, and this orientation will be revealed in their responses to concept-sorting tests.

Drake and Cayton offer a view of urban lower-class black society as they observed it during the 1940's that is reminiscent of Ryan's description of the urban world of lower-class white ethnics:

The world of the lower class is a public world; contacts are casual and direct with a minimum of formality. . . . Conversation and rumor flow continuously—about policy, "politics," sports and sex. Arguments (often on the "race problem"), while chronically short on fact, are animated and interesting. Emotional satisfactions in such situations are immediate. Physical gratifications are direct. There are status bearers within this realm, but they are not the civic leaders and intellectuals. They are, rather, the "policy kings"; sportsmen, black and white, the clever preachers and politicians; legendary "tough guys"; and the good fighters and roisterers.[32]

Some black scholars have argued that this orientation toward direct-feeling encounters with life, although characteristic of lower-class life-styles in general, is basic to the nature of black people and deeply affects their use of language:

Knowledge in Western societies is largely derived from such propositions as "I think, therefore I am." The non-Western heritage of Afro-Americans suggests that knowledge stems from the proposition that "I feel, therefore I think, therefore I am."[33]

The uniqueness of black culture can be explained in that it is a culture whose emphasis is on the nonverbal, i.e., the nonconceptual. . . . In black culture it is the experience that counts, not what is said.[34]

This does not mean that black people don't think or conceptualize their experience symbolically; rather, it means that many blacks (and some counter-culture whites) believe that intellectual analysis disconnected from feelings leads to incomplete knowledge of the world. Dispassionate conceptual analysis requires a fragmentation of experience and a concern with the symbols that represent the pieces of experience, preventing a subjective, empathetic encounter with the total experience. These black scholars are not rejecting intellectual knowledge but, rather, are pointing to another way of knowing, which is a necessary supplement to objective analysis and is basic to black culture. Thus, emanating from a feeling-oriented culture, black verbal expression thrives on what might appear to the analytic mind to be logical contradictions or emotional paradoxes.[35]

Julius Waiguchu maintains that, although black Americans are acculturated to a large extent to white mainstream culture, they nevertheless manifest certain "Africanisms" in their behavior.[36] He argues that the African form of communion with nature survives among black Americans, giving a unique quality to the black experience in America. In a somewhat similar vein, Joseph White illustrates the lack of compartmentalization of life in a feeling-oriented culture with the example of a black youth who goes from participation in a black nationalist rally to a store-front revival to a bar without any sense of contradiction, in spite of the seemingly different life-style each behavior represents, because for him all these activities are the same experience at the feeling level; they are all activities the youth looks forward to every Sunday because he just "dug on it."[37]

The black scholars cited above appear to be making essentially the same point concerning what they believe to be a unique quality of black culture in America. One may debate how much of this feeling orientation is a function of race (ethnicity) and how much of class, since it may be diluted, hidden, or absent among some middle-class blacks and since a similar orientation appears among other lower-class groups; nevertheless, this is an important element in the milieu in which low-income black children are socialized; it affects their orientation toward linguistic-cognitive competence. A psychologist who interprets the concrete, subjective, emotionally toned responses of black children to concept-sorting tasks as signs of linguistic-cognitive immaturity may be in error, responding ethnocentrically to a particular cultural style in experiencing reality. A study of verbal learning ability comparing the performance of 128 black female and white female college students on a paired association learning test, in which the subjects had to quickly relate various three-letter combinations to one another, demonstrates clear differences between black and white learning styles. The performance of the black students was more affected by their feelings of liking or disliking each "word," based on how it sounded to them when they spoke it, while the white students' performance depended less on the affective value of the combinations and more on the extent to which a three-letter combination looked like and sounded like a real word (association value).[38]

Charles Keil has also tried to identify ethnic influences on ways of experiencing the world brought about through socialization in urban black communities. According to Keil, "The shared sensibilities and common understandings of the Negro ghetto, its modes of perception and expression, its channels of communication are predominantly auditory and tactile rather than visual and literate."[39] Keil argues that certain modes of perception and communication are more characteristic of urban black communities than white communities; thus the prominence of aural perception, oral expression, and body movement—the emphasis on the shared sound and feel of experience—sharply demarcate the cultural experience of urban blacks and whites. We have already commented on the importance of verbal performance skills in black communities and some distinctive stylistic elements of the black oral tradition.

Some support for the assertion that black culture socializes particular sensitivity to kinesic cues is provided in a study conducted by Newmeyer.[40] He had preadolescent boys, black and white, act out a number of emotions in an effort to communicate them to observers nonverbally. Black boys were consistently better than white boys at enacting emotions so that others perceived them correctly and also at interpreting the emotions of various other actors. Additional evidence is provided by a study of 160 college students conducted by Gitter, Black, and Mostofsky.[41] Black and white students, each tested by a member of their own race, were shown, in random order, thirty-five specially prepared still photographs of professional actors (of both races) taken while the actors were attempting to portray each of seven emotions: anger, happiness, surprise, fear, disgust, pain, and sadness. The subjects were provided with a list of the seven designated emotions and requested to assign each photograph to one of the seven emotional categories. Black students made significantly more correct judgments of emotion.

Certain nonverbal modes of communication that are important to the life-style of urban blacks may be misinterpreted by whites. Suttles provides an example of such cultural misunderstanding based upon his observations of various ethnic groups living in an inner-city area of Chicago:

> Negro boys . . . have a "cool" way of walking ("pimp's walk") in which the upper trunk and pelvis rock fore and aft while the head remains stable with the eyes looking straight ahead. The "pimp's walk" is quite slow, and the Negroes take it as a way of "strutting" or "showing off." The whites usually interpret it as a pointed lack of concern for those adjacent to the walker. Negro girls provide a parallel in a slow "sashay" that white males sometimes take as an unqualified invitation to their attentions.[42]

The studies of Gerald Lesser and his associates suggest that there is a strong ethnic influence on the organization of mental abilities among children.[43] These researchers tested first-grade boys and girls in New York City on verbal ability, reasoning, number ability, and spatial conceptualization. Equal numbers of children were drawn from four ethnic groups: Chinese, Jewish, black, and Puerto Rican. Each ethnic sample was, in turn, divided equally into middle- and lower-class groups. The performance data were analyzed to determine the effects of ethnicity, social class, and sex on the organization of mental abilities. A number of findings emerged:

1. Differences in *ethnic* group membership produce significant differences in the patterns of these mental abilities. Blacks performed best on tests of verbal ability and reasoning, followed by space conceptualization and number ability. By contrast, the order of performance for the other groups was as follows:
Chinese: space, number, reasoning, verbal
Jewish: verbal, number, reasoning, space
Puerto Rican: space, number, reasoning, verbal
2. Within each ethnic group, the same patterning of abilities was found regardless of whether the children were middle- or lower-class.

3. Within each ethnic group, consistent with its patterning of mental abilities, middle-class children scored higher on each test.

4. Boys scored significantly higher than girls on space conceptualization and on the picture vocabulary subtest in all ethnic groups except one; Jewish girls were superior to Jewish boys on both verbal and space scales.

Lesser and his colleagues had each child tested by an examiner from his own ethnic group, using the child's primary language. Each tester was allowed to extend the length of the testing time to try to establish rapport and allow for fatigue. Each child was tested in a room of his public school during regular school hours. In spite of such precautions, it is difficult to determine whether the results indicate that middle-class children are genuinely more able and competent or whether lower-class children simply performed less well on the tests because they were less motivated to do so. In either event, the results do appear to indicate a genuine ethnic patterning of the mental abilities tapped by the tests, since the relative strengths and weaknesses within each ethnic group were the same across class lines even though level of performance always was higher among the middle-class children. The middle-class children, regardless of ethnic group, were more similar in their scores on each mental-ability scale than were the lower-class children compared from one ethnic group to another. It may be that distinct ethnic patterns of socialization tend to be blurred or lost as families move into the middle class and adopt mainstream standards of behavior.

A replication study with black and Chinese children in Boston revealed that each group there produced the same pattern of mental abilities as their counterparts in New York in both middle- and lower-class samples. Thus, the replication data support the hypothesis of a distinctive ethnic patterning of mental abilities. Higher class position may improve performance in test situations in general, but ethnicity appears to foster the development of different patterns of mental abilities.

One additional finding is worth noting. Social-class differences produced a greater difference in the mental-ability test scores of black children than was the case for any other group; that is, middle-class black children differed from lower-class black children more than middle-class Chinese, Jewish, or Puerto Rican children differed from lower-class children in their ethnic groups. One interpretation of these findings might be that the gap between middle- and lower-class black groups was larger— i.e., the poor black children came from lower-income families than the lower-class children in any other group. Or it might be that the low-income black children were socialized more harshly than the other lower-class children and that this had a greater negative effect on their motivation to perform well.

Lesser's finding that black children performed better on tests of verbal ability and reasoning than on tests of space conceptualization is basically consistent with Keil's finding concerning the prominence of aural perception and expression in the feeling-oriented urban black culture. Black ethnicity may be related to the relatively weak development of certain visual-spatial organization skills not directly related to feeling-interaction between people.

Francis H. Palmer has tested black children on a variety of perceptual and cognitive tasks in Manhattan, on Long Island, and on the Caribbean island of Antigua. He finds that in all these locations three-year-old black children performed significantly less well than white children on visual-perceptual measures.[44] At the same time, the black children did not perform significantly less well on verbal-conceptual items. In fact, three-year-old blacks in Antigua and Long Island (but not Manhattan) actually performed a little better than their white peers on forty-six conceptual items. Thus, it would appear that it is not the ability to manipulate abstract symbols that is poorly developed among the black children but processes related to visual discrimination and/or spatial organization of inanimate objects. Although black children were less proficient than whites on visual-discrimination-organization problems, they could be trained to perform more effectively with relative ease.[45] This suggests that the black children's relative lack of proficiency is a function of socialization. Even if there should be a strong genetic inheritance factor involved in visual-perceptual-information processing, this tells us nothing about how a given individual might have developed under different socialization conditions, since behavior results from gene-environment interaction, not absolute genetic determination, and the number of possible interactions is effectively unlimited.[46] Thus, high heritability for a given perceptual-cognitive ability does *not* mean that the ability cannot be improved by teaching.

Farnham-Diggory studied the ability of black and white children aged four to ten to synthesize pieces of symbolic information.[47] In general, there was little difference between the white and black children on the verbal-synthesis task, but the black children performed somewhat better at putting visual symbols, words, and actions together. On the other hand, there were significant racial differences on the map-like and mathematical tasks, which appeared to require something more like a spatial perception-integration factor. This finding is consistent with the findings of Palmer, Lesser, and a number of other studies.[48] Again, Farnham-Diggory found that training could easily lead to improved performance by black children.

Both sex and social class were significant factors in success on the maplike synthesis test. White middle-class boys scored highest, possibly owing to their greater experience and encouragement in playing with mechanical toys. Black girls performed better than black boys in working-class and middle-class areas. Farnham-Diggory suggests that the girls may have profited from homemaking responsibilities, such as setting the table following directions from mother, so as to increase maplike synthesis ability. Black boys from the lowest income groups performed better than working-class and middle-class black boys; Farnham-Diggory suggests that this may be related to their having learned to be particularly alert to visual signs that told them when to run and where to hide in a dangerous environment. It would appear that success on the maplike task resulted from strengths in somewhat different information-processing systems among each group that excelled.

We suggest that the source of the relative weakness of black children's spatial-perceptual abilities may lie in certain aspects of their socialization into a feeling, people-oriented culture. Consider the following observations on black socialization in a Georgia town:

> One hears five-month-old babies spontaneously imitating single sounds of their parents, and often babies show precociousness which tends to be lost in later childhood when the stimulus falls off. Babies will be distracted by calling their attention to a person, seldom an object. . . . In contrast to this great stimulation of the baby's responsiveness to people, its explorations of the inanimate environment are limited. Few objects are given to babies or allowed them when they do get hold of them. . . . Babies reaching to feel objects or surfaces are often redirected to feeling the holder's face, or the game of rubbing faces is begun as a substitute. . . . Such a degree of inhibition of exploration is possible only because there are always eyes on the baby and idle hands take away the forbidden objects and then distract the frustrated baby. The personal is thus often substituted for the impersonal.[49]

In this milieu babies are kept from crawling on the floor by people holding them and passing them along from one to another. Babies not held by a person or placed on a bed are likely to be put in a walker, usually chaperoned by older children. Such a socialization experience continuously directs attention toward people and away from inanimate objects. With movement and exploration restricted, the child's attentiveness to inanimate objects and spatial perception-conceptualization may develop much more slowly than his attentiveness and perceptual sensitivity to people. It may be that perceptual-conceptual skills related to people develop faster than skills related to inanimate objects in all infants;[50] however, the type of early socialization described above may selectively reinforce perceptual-cognitive development related to interpersonal relations, thus favoring the people-oriented cognition that is highly valued in black communities. The basic elements of very early socialization described by Young among urban blacks in Georgia *may* be shared by low-income blacks in other urban areas and, perhaps to a lesser extent, by upwardly mobile middle-class blacks as well.

In summary, it would appear that black children tend to be stronger in verbal-conceptual intellective abilities than in visual-space-perception-organization mental abilities. The former are emphasized by a culture with a strong oral tradition, which shapes children to achieve peak linguistic performance in emotionally toned peer-group situations. Children from this milieu will perform least well linguistically-cognitively in impersonal contexts where they will be evaluated by adults. In responding to the world, black children are often highly subjective, operating at a basic feeling level that is reflected in their emotionally toned verbal conceptualizations. Thus, among black children, concreteness and subjectivity in verbal conceptualization may reflect an unfragmented feeling approach to experience more than immaturity of thought processes. This approach is likely to be manifested in heightened sensitivity to other people's moods and personal characteristics. Middle-class black children tend to be more acculturated to mainstream cultural patterns than their lower-class peers, so they perform at higher levels on verbal-conceptual tasks. A relative weakness in visual-discrimination abilities appears to cut across socio-economic-class lines among black children. This is a relative weakness, however, and it is easily affected by training.

We suggest that one factor responsible for the relatively poor performances of black children on impersonal, perceptual-discrimination-organization tasks may be related to lack of attention rather than to weakness in perceptual or information-processing abilities. The socialization experiences of black children, particularly of the lower class, may have discouraged attentiveness to spatial-organization aspects of inanimate objects. Thus, in testing situations, the children may pay less attention to certain materials or have more difficulty sustaining attention to the physical features of inanimate objects than children from some other groups. On the other hand, it may be that black children pay more attention to people around them, and this tendency may distract them from impersonal tasks and disorganize their efforts to sustain attention to the inanimate, impersonal features of the environment. We suspect that the reading difficulties some low-income black children have are related to a lack of sustained attention to reading materials.

In many elementary school classrooms we observed that black children were often more attentive to the physical mannerisms of the teacher than to anything she was saying, even when lessons were carefully prepared and of real interest to the children. The children also spent much time watching each other in the classroom. Training procedures that lead to improved perceptual-discrimination-organization performance among children may have their effect as much through directing and strengthening attentiveness to certain features of the environment as through any other route.

NOTES

1. Carl Bereiter and Siegfried Engelmann, *Teaching Disadvantaged Children in the Preschool* (Englewood Cliffs, N.J.: Prentice-Hall, 1966), pp. 39–40.
2. *Ibid.,* p. 41.
3. Stephens S. Baratz and Joan C. Baratz, "Early Childhood Intervention: The Social Science Base of Institutional Racism," *Harvard Educational Review,* 40 (1970): 35.
4. See Vernon J. Dixon and Badi G. Foster, *Beyond Black or White: An Alternate America* (Boston: Little, Brown, 1971); Albert Murray, *The Omni-Americans: New Perspectives on Black Experience and American Culture* (New York: Outerbridge & Dienstfrey, 1970); Charles A. Valentine, "Deficit, Differences, and Bicultural Models of Afro-American Behavior," *Harvard Educational Review,* 41 (1971): 137–57; and Andrew Billingsley, *Black Families in White America* (Englewood Cliffs, N.J.: Prentice-Hall, 1968).
5. See, for example, Mildred C. Templin, *Certain Language Skills in Children* (Minneapolis: University of Minnesota Press, 1957), and Walter Loban, *The Language of Elementary School Children* (Champaign, Ill.: National Conference of Teachers of English, 1963).
6. See Doris R. Entwisle, "Developmental Sociolinguistics: Inner-City Children," *American Journal of Sociology,* 74 (1968): 37–49, and *idem,* "Semantic Systems of Children," in Frederick Williams, ed., *Language and Poverty* (Chicago: Markham, 1970), pp. 123–39.
7. E.g., see Vera P. John and L. Goldstein, "The Social Context of Language Acquisition," *Merrill-Palmer Quarterly,* 10 (1964): 265–76, and Irving E. Sigal, L. Anderson, and H. Shapiro, "Categorization Behavior of Lower- and Middle-Class Negro Preschool Children: Differences in Dealing with Representations of Familiar Objects," *Journal of Negro Education,* 35 (1966): 218–29.
8. See Paula Menyuk, "Language Theories and Educational Practice," in Williams, ed., *Language and Poverty,* pp. 190–211.
9. W. A. Stuart, "Understanding Black Language," in John F. Szwed, ed., *Black America* (New York: Basic Books, 1970), pp. 121–31.
10. See D. Z. Seymour, "Black English," *Intellectual Digest,* 2 (1972): 78–80, and J. L. Dillard, *Black English* (New York: Random House, 1972), pp. 39–72. The habitual tense is not the same as the present tense, and the difference can be important. For example, "my brother sick" indicates that the sickness is in progress but probably of short duration; "my brother be sick" indicates a long-term condition—a distinction that may be missed by a teacher who is limited to standard English (and who might therefore be labeled "culturally deprived").
11. Dan I. Slobin and C. A. Welsh, "Elicited Imitation as a Research Tool in Developmental Psycholinguistics," unpublished paper, Department of Psychology, University of California, Berkeley, 1967.

12. William Labov and P. Cohen, "Systematic Relations of Standard and Nonstandard Rules in the Grammars of Negro Speakers," *Project Literacy Reports,* No. 8, Cornell University, Ithaca, N.Y., 1967, pp. 66–84.

13. William Labov, "Psychological Conflict in Negro American Language Behavior," *American Journal of Orthopsychiatry,* 41 (1971): 636–37. Essentially the same conflict in speech patterns of upwardly mobile blacks is described in Frantz Fanon, *Black Skin, White Masks* (1952) (New York: Grove Press, 1967), pp. 17–40.

14. See John J. Hartman, "Psychological Conflicts in Negro American Language Behavior: A Case Study," *American Journal of Orthopsychiatry,* 41 (1971): 627–35.

15. B. Wood and J. Curry, " 'Everyday Talk' and 'School Talk' of the City Black Child," *The Speech Teacher,* 18 (1969): 282–96. See also Menyuk, "Language Theories" (n. 8 *supra*).

16. See Roger D. Abrahams, "Rapping and Capping: Black Talk as Art," in Szwed, ed., *Black America* (n. 9 *supra*), pp. 132–42, and *idem, Deep Down in the Jungle: Negro Narrative Folklore from the Streets of Philadelphia,* rev. ed. (Chicago: Aldine, 1970).

17. Thomas Kochman, "Rapping in the Ghetto," in Lee Rainwater, ed., *The Black Experience: Soul* (Chicago: Aldine, 1970), p. 51. See also Charles Keil, *Urban Blues* (Chicago: University of Chicago Press, 1966), and Iceberg Slim, *Pimp: The Story of My Life* (Los Angeles: Holloway House, 1967).

18. Geneva Smitherman, "White English in Blackface, or, Who Do I Be?" *The Black Scholar,* 4 (May–June, 1973): 32–39.

19. Susan H. Houston, "Black English," *Psychology Today,* 6 (March, 1973): 45–48.

20. William Labov, *Language in the Inner City: Studies in the Black English Vernacular* (Philadelphia: University of Pennsylvania Press, 1972), p. 64.

21. See Owen P. Thomas, "Competence and Performance in Language," in Roger D. Abrahams and Rudolph D. Troike, eds., *Language and Cultural Diversity in American Education* (Englewood Cliffs, N.J.: Prentice-Hall, 1972), pp. 108–11.

22. Bereiter and Engelmann, *Teaching Disadvantaged Children* (n. 1 *supra*), pp. 34–40.

23. William Labov, "Academic Ignorance and Black Intelligence," *Atlantic Monthly,* June, 1972, p. 60.

24. *Ibid.,* p. 62.

25. See R. Burling, *English in Black and White* (New York: Holt, Rinehart & Winston, 1973), pp. 29–47 and 91–110.

26. Robert D. Hess and Virginia C. Shipman, "Early Experience and the Socialization of Cognitive Modes in Children," *Child Development,* 36 (1965): 869–86. See also *idem,* "Cognitive Elements in Maternal Behavior," in John P. Hill, ed., *Minnesota Symposia on Child Psychology* (Minneapolis: University of Minnesota Press, 1967), 1: 57–81.

27. Helen C. Bee *et al.*, "Social Class Differences in Maternal Teaching Strategies and Speech Patterns," *Developmental Psychology,* 1 (1969): 726–34. See also G. F. Brody, "Socioeconomic Differences in Stated Maternal Child-rearing Practices and in Observed Maternal Behavior," *Journal of Marriage and the Family,* 30 (1968): 656–60.

28. Virginia H. Young, "Family and Childhood in a Southern Georgia Community," *American Anthropologist,* 72 (1970): 282.

29. See William Labov and C. Robbins, "A Note on the Relation of Reading Failure to Peer-Group Status in Urban Ghettos," *Teachers College Record,* 70 (1969): 395–405.

30. See Jerome S. Bruner, *The Relevance of Education* (New York: Norton, 1971), and Michael Cole and Jerome S. Bruner, "Cultural Differences and Inferences About Psychological Processes," *American Psychologist,* 26 (1971): 867–76.

31. E. J. Ryan, "Personal Identity in an Urban Slum," in Leonard J. Duhl, ed., *The Urban Condition* (New York: Basic Books, 1963), pp. 135–50.

32. St. Clair Drake and Horace R. Cayton, *Black Metropolis: A Study of Negro Life in a Northern City* (New York: Harper Torchbooks, 1962), 2: 603–6.

33. Vernon J. Dixon and Badi G. Foster, *Beyond Black or White* (Boston: Little, Brown, 1971), p. 18.

34. Julius Lester, *Look Out, Whitey! Black Power's Gon' Get Your Mama!* (New York: Grove Press, 1969), p. 87. See also Robert H. Decoy, *The Nigger Bible* (Los Angeles: Holloway House, 1967).

35. James Haskins and Hugh F. Butts, *The Psychology of Black Language* (New York: Barnes & Noble, 1973).

36. Julius M. Waiguchu, "Black Heritage: Of Genetics, Environment, and Continuity," in Rhoda L. Goldstein, ed., *Black Life and Culture in the United States* (New York: T. Y. Crowell, 1971), pp. 64–86.

37. Joseph White, "Toward a Black Psychology," in Reginald L. Jones, ed., *Black Psychology* (New York: Harper & Row, 1972), pp. 43–50.

38. Joseph F. Rychlak, C. W. Hewitt, and J. Hewitt, "Affective Evaluations, Word Quality, and the Verbal Learning Styles of Black Versus White Junior College Females," *Journal of Personality and Social Psychology,* 27 (1973): 248–55.

39. Keil, *Urban Blues* (n. 17 *supra*), p. 16.

40. J. A. Newmeyer, "Creativity and Nonverbal Communication in Pre-adolescent White and Black Children," unpublished doctoral dissertation, Harvard University, 1970.

41. A. George Gitter, H. Black, and David I. Mostofsky, "Race and Sex in Perception of Emotion," *Journal of Social Issues,* 28 (1972): 63–78.

42. Gerald D. Suttles, *The Social Order of the Slum: Ethnicity and Territory in the Inner City* (Chicago: University of Chicago Press, 1968), p. 66.

43. Gerald S. Lesser, G. Fifer, and Donald H. Clark, "Mental Abilities of Children from Different Social Class and Cultural Groups," *Monographs of the Society for Research in Child Development,* vol. 30, no. 4 (1964). See also S. S. Stodolsky and Gerald S. Lesser, "Learning

Patterns in the Disadvantaged," *Harvard Educational Review,* 37 (1967): 546–93.

44. Personal communication from Francis H. Palmer, State University of New York at Stony Brook, January, 1973.

45. Francis H. Palmer, "Minimal Intervention at Age Two and Three and Subsequent Intellective Changes," in Ronald K. Parker, ed., *The Preschool in Action: Exploring Early Childhood Programs* (Boston: Allyn & Bacon, 1972), pp. 437–64. Palmer's studies at the Harlem Research Center in New York showed that the area of development most affected by educational intervention at age two and three is the perceptual domain, even though the curriculum used was not specifically designed for that purpose.

46. See Jay Hirsch, "Behavior-Genetic Analysis and Its Biosocial Consequences," in Kent S. Miller and Ralph Mason Dreger, eds., *Comparative Studies of Blacks and Whites in the United States* (New York: Seminar Press, 1973), pp. 34–51.

47. Sylvia Farnham-Diggory, "Cognitive Synthesis in Negro and White Children," *Monographs of the Society for Research in Child Development,* 35 (1970): 2.

48. These are summarized in Thomas Pettigrew, *A Profile of the Negro American* (Princeton, N.J.: Van Nostrand, 1964), pp. 113–14. Pollack suggests that the relative lack of proficiency of black children on visual information-processing tasks may be related to their more darkly pigmented retinas. However, in the Farnham-Diggory study, white boys were far superior to white girls on the maplike synthesis task, and it is unlikely that the white girls had more pigmented retinas. See Robert H. Pollack, "Some Implications of Ontogenetic Changes in Perception," in David Elkind and John H. Flavell, eds., *Studies in Cognitive Development: Essays in Honor of Jean Piaget* (New York: Oxford University Press, 1969), pp. 365–407.

49. Young, "Southern Georgia Community" (n. 28 *supra*), pp. 279–80.

50. See Silvia M. Bell, "The Development of the Concept of Object as Related to Infant-Mother Attachment," *Child Development,* 41 (1970): 291–311.

8 / CHILDREN IN SCHOOL: TOWARD
A TYPOLOGY OF BEHAVIOR PATTERNS

Even in the earliest grades, several rather differentiated personality types can be observed among Central Harlem children. These patterns, described below, represent our attempt to order conceptually the similarities and differences that occurred with some regularity in the behavior of the children. Our categories are relative, not absolute; no child we ever met was a "pure" type, and there were important common denominators in the behavior of all the children. Some children showed traits associated with two or three of the typological categories. Nevertheless, most children we knew in Central Harlem appeared to display certain behavioral traits and qualities to a relatively great degree, so that we could view their behavior as more representative of one of the conceptual categories than of the others.

The types described have their source in our observations in Central Harlem over several years. We conceptualized the children's behaviors, attitudes, and feelings as adaptations to stresses in their lives that we believe are shared to a great extent by other urban black poor and (to a lesser degree) working-class children. We view these adaptations largely as life-styles, ways of organizing experience, not as examples of psychopathology or sociological deviance. Also, these adaptations are presented in relation to the children's lives; they are not measured against a textbook depiction of an average child.

THE AMBIVALENTS

The majority of the children we knew in Central Harlem fitted most closely into the group we have called the ambivalents. The essence of this type is intense and frequent conflict between the desire for dependency, attention, nurturance, and belongingness and the tendency to mistrust others, to expect them to be manipulative and eventually rejecting. Ambivalent children wanted to relate to others with some warmth and friendliness, but they often were pulled in the opposite direction by the desire to appear self-reliant, independent, and without any need for attachments to others. In their relations with adults and with each other, ambivalent children often shifted back and forth between warm, friendly moods and behaviors and sullen, defensive aggressive moods and behaviors, between happy periods in which they appeared lively and full of laughter and unhappy periods in which they seemed depressed and close to tears. Their relationships with their teachers also showed conflicts: They frequently became angry with the teachers and refused to cooperate with them, but soon began to make great demands for teacher attention and approval. If they did not receive sufficient attention, they became frustrated and then angry, repeating the cycle again. Children in this group often expressed emotion freely. Many had relatively few calm periods between their dejected moods and periods of exuberance, excitement, and agitation.

The ambivalent children often tried to follow the teacher's instructions, but they required constant encouragement and recognition. Some sought this recognition through efforts to help the teacher, perhaps by sweeping the floor or straightening up her desk, rather than by devoting themselves to their classwork. When encouraged to do academic work, they claimed that they didn't know what to do even after several explanations by the teacher, and they seemed to require virtually private instruction to move them along, a demand that teachers of classes with twenty-four to thirty-two children usually could not and did not meet.

Many children in this group appeared to be quite sensitive and reactive to perceived inattention or rejection from others, particularly adults. They usually tried to project a self-reliant and confident image, but they were virtually desperate for approval and affection. When discussing home relationships, these children often reported a lack of relatedness to their mothers, with whom they often spent very little time. Many seemed to be seeking surrogate parents to compensate for what they felt was missing in their lives. Girls usually outnumbered boys in this group, but only slightly. In general boys had more dramatic, flamboyant, and frequent mood swings and more erratic responses than the girls.

Ambivalent children often went to great lengths to attract attention, shouting or purposely acting in an aggressive or destructive manner as if hoping that they would be noticed by their teacher or classmates. They often provoked their teachers into issuing stern commands and prohibitions and, sometimes, would oblige the teacher to attempt to restrain them physically.

Teachers reacted with varying degrees of insight to the behavior of the ambivalent children. Some had great patience and understanding and tried to show their acceptance of the children by being nonpunitive. Some were impatient or quite easily provoked and some grew angry and vindictive toward the children. Some of the teachers actually seemed to enjoy the opportunity to be harsh disciplinarians. Most teachers, even those with great insight, patience, and dedication, found that they were not above occasional outbursts of anger as they sought relief from the continuous emotional challenge they faced from many ambivalent children.

It often seemed to us that some of the ambivalent children deliberately elicited punitive reactions from the teacher or regarded them as a true sign of interest; this was particularly true of boys in relation to male teachers. In effect, they seemed to be saying to the teacher, "If you really cared about me, you wouldn't let me act like this!" A display of anger often seemed to reassure ambivalent children that their teachers liked them or at least were interested in them.

Their primary need for personal contact was often expressed by the ambivalent children in attention-seeking through negative behaviors. Many of these children manifested a type of masochism, provoking punishment from teachers by repeating the same behavior for which they had frequently been punished. (Outwardly, of course, the children usually reacted with sullenness or open anger when reprimanded or hit.) As a result of competition for adult attention in their homes, some ambivalent children may have "learned" that behaving in an extremely annoying, upsetting, or dramatic manner was the only sure way to get adults to pay attention to them. When their questions or statements elicited little if any communication from parents, children seemed to learn that adults would listen to them only when they shouted or disturbed them.

Parental inconsistency in responding to children seemed to be a central factor in the outlandish or destructive forms of attention-seeking behavior displayed by many ambivalent children. Many of the parents seemed periodically inclined to display genuine warmth and affection toward the children. Occasionally, some parents actually overindulged the children, sometimes giving them money to buy anything they wanted. This sometimes diverted the children's needs for prolonged attention. Often parents gave enough positive attention to keep the children coming back for more, but the behavior to which parents paid attention most predictably was behavior that became bothersome to them.

On a number of occasions, we found that some children in our classes became receptive to our friendly or affectionate overtures only after an incident in which we had displayed anger over their behavior and intervened to stop them from screaming, throwing objects at other children, fighting, and the like. After each such incident, we made it a point to speak to these children privately, to explain that we accepted *them* but would not accept certain behavior. We tried to make it clear that we had no wish to hurt them, even though we felt strong enough to control them. Finally, we emphatically stated that we would not allow them to behave in ways that prevented them from academic learning and upset others in the class. After these conversations, the children often became much more cooperative. Some showed a desire to sit near our desks. They seemed willing to follow our directions or to take our approval or disapproval seriously for the first time. However, unless continuous attention was provided, these improved behavior patterns were usually short-lived.

Many of the ambivalent children had been nurtured in homes in which an early precipitous decline in adult emotional support was coupled with a great deal of physical and verbal restrictiveness and punitiveness. These children appeared to have formed concepts of affection in which aggression and restrictive controls were meshed with caring and nurturing. The highly authoritarian manner in which they were being reared conditioned such children to order human relations on a power-status basis. Such children found it very difficult to accept straightforward affection from an adult at face value. If the adult was a white teacher, the realistic reasons the children had begun to learn for mistrusting whites made the acceptance of affection even more difficult. But the children were not inclined to readily accept affection from black teachers either without at the same time trying to manipulate them and dominate them in a power contest. For such children, in the typically rigid and simultaneously chaotic ghetto school, a teacher, black or white, had to earn respect by demonstrating that he had the forcefulness and the tenacity to control the children. Once the adult-child power-status roles were clear, the ambivalent children usually overcame their tendency to try to exploit the teacher and were able to accept and display affection openly, although interpretations of rejection and sullen withdrawals by the children remained frequent.

In the earliest elementary school grades, many ambivalent children appeared to be open and direct in seeking attention from adults. But by the middle elementary school grades many of them had essentially given up on adults, in school and at home, and were increasingly seeking attention from peers. However, erratic and impulsive attempts to gain attention from adults persisted for many through the elementary school years, usually with disappointing results, forcing them more and more into a fervent involvement in, if not a commitment to, a street-peer world.

FIVE AMBIVALENT CHILDREN

We first met Clarence when he was in the fifth grade. He had a very expressive face and an infectious smile that reflected warmth and an impish sense of humor. Yet, quite frequently, Clarence walked around with an intensely sullen, pouting expression, sometimes accompanied by barely audible mumbling and grumbling. These two faces—the happy, impulsive, laughing child and the dejected, oppressed, frustrated child—represented the emotional states most characteristic of Clarence. He seemed to alternate between them without spending much time in any more neutral, less intense emotional condition.

Above all, Clarence seemed to crave attention. He would slowly approach each new teacher with ingratiating offers to help clean up his desk or straighten up the room. He took every possible opportunity to try to engage his teachers in conversation about personal matters and concerns rather than about school or schoolwork. When individual work assignments were supposed to be in progress, Clarence frequently approached the teacher to ask for further explanations of the assignment. He often asked the same question a number of times. Each time he came for help, Clarence tried to switch the conversation to personal topics. When the teacher tried to get back to Clarence's original question, Clarence would notice something in the room that needed fixing and would generously volunteer to do the job on the spot. On many occasions, he offered to stay after dismissal time to help the teacher straighten up the room.

Clarence was a warm and likable child, but his intense emotions and his incessant demands for personal attention caused many teachers to regard him as immature and a nuisance. Even teachers who genuinely liked Clarence were not always able to treat his demands for attention, in the midst of thirty to thirty-five other children, with patience and kindness. When Clarence felt rejected by a teacher, as happened frequently when his attempt to conduct a personal conversation or his offer of personal aid was not encouraged, he would walk away pouting and mumbling quietly. For a few hours he would continue to pout and remain in a sullen mood. At these times he was markedly uncooperative, but usually in a stoic, passive way. He would not work on assignments or take part in class activities. Rather, he would sit in his seat and daydream. On occasion, however, Clarence would become openly defiant, usually only when a teacher reprimanded or challenged him concerning his apparent lack of effort or cooperation. After a few hours, Clarence would approach the teacher again with questions that he would try to use to open up personal lines of conversation. He endlessly repeated his cycle of attention-seeking through an ingratiating approach, followed by sullen, pouting withdrawals.

Clarence tried very hard to establish a rather dependent relationship with his teachers. One of Clarence's male teachers used to carry a number of keys on a shower-curtain hook that hung from his belt loop. Clarence managed to get himself some keys and a similar hook, which he hitched to a belt loop in the identical manner. He continuously asked if he could be in charge of opening and closing various closets, which would require that he carry keys around all day. When the teacher gave him this responsibility, Clarence took the job very seriously. His identification with the teacher was so obvious that the other boys teased him. "You think you the teacher," they used to say derisively. These jibes did not discourage Clarence, however. Many times during the day he would go through highly visible rituals of unlocking, straightening up, and locking closets in his classroom.

Clarence gave his teachers very little relief from his continuing demands for attention. He frequently came storming into the teachers' room when the teacher was eating lunch, pushing his way past other teachers who objected to his being there by saying that he had to talk to his teacher immediately; it couldn't wait. Usually the urgent message involved permission to rearrange some aspect of the room or some gossip about other children. Clarence would deliver his question or remarks with great animation while slipping into a seat next to the teacher. He would then try to turn the conversation to personal matters, making himself comfortable for a long stay.

Clarence was never very secure in his relationships with other boys. He would often gain their attention, but this attention was often negative, teasing, and aggressive. Clarence never really became part of any group, although he consciously tried to imitate the walking and talking styles of older boys and young men he knew. He did not seem to have a close friend, nor did any of the other boys appear to consider Clarence a friend. Nevertheless, Clarence often played ball with other boys. He was very sensitive to the status of the boys he associated with, "hanging out" with any high-prestige boys who would accept him and avoiding association with the "lames," the boys who were not a part of street-peer culture activities.

Clarence found a dramatic, flamboyant role for himself as a leader in the peer world one day when he joined the Harlem Cadet Corps. He was given a military-style uniform, which he wore to school each day. The Cadets enjoyed practicing close-order marching drills. Clarence had an exceptional ability to perform the role of drillmaster, organizing the marching of a small group in precise formation with perfect timing. He would march alongside them and exuberantly call cadence for them like a drill sergeant. As a leader, Clarence was extremely authoritarian, screaming at and insulting those who didn't perform correctly. But his rapidly developing skill was so obvious that the boys went along with his leadership style. They bickered among themselves and criticized one another's performances frequently, but Clarence—with great gusto—held them all together.

Most teachers and the school's administration did not regard Clarence's extraordinary leadership ability and showmanship, which were manifested only in the Cadet drills, as worthy of much attention or praise. In fact, many teachers were openly critical of the wearing of military-style uniforms and the performance of military-style drills within the school. Except for his own teacher, Clarence got no positive recognition from adults in the school for his special competence. After he went on to a new teacher, he was discouraged from wearing his uniform and conducting his drill exercises in school. The one area in which Clarence had clearly established competence and self-esteem and had earned high status from his peers was continuously undercut and demeaned by adults in the school. The symbols of relatedness to a highly esteemed group were criticized and rejected. Clarence was reminded endlessly of his poor reading scores and told to get serious and work on his reading, or else he would be held back in the sixth grade. (He was promoted, however, even though he remained more than two years behind in reading.) Thus was a boy with a demonstrated capacity for happiness, great enthusiasm, and emotional relatedness left to flounder in the tug and pull of strong ambivalent mood swings.

One teacher we knew helped many ambivalent children in his class to relate to others with less conflict and to achieve in school. He encouraged all the boys in his class to join the Cadets and to wear their uniforms to school. He made his class into a specially designated division of the Cadets and called the classroom the "barracks" for the "division." (He titled himself the "division commander.") He required two drill periods a day in the gymnasium, about fifteen minutes each. Through the vehicle of the Cadets, with his own doting, mildly authoritarian leadership, this teacher transformed a divisive, sullen, frustrated group of boys into a well-organized group with marked *esprit de corps* and individual self-esteem. He improved reading scores considerably by making reading exercises part of the "duties" of a Cadet and offering Cadet "promotions" for achievement on these "exercises." This teacher was so successful in organizing his class into a self-disciplined group that on days when he was absent his class could be (and was) left alone, with no substitute teacher! The children did the work listed on assignment sheets he left for them and prodded one another not to fool around in the "barracks." Although he enjoyed considerable support from the parents of children in his class, this teacher was considered an undesirable eccentric by most of the staff and administration, was called a fascist, and was socially isolated. After two years at the school, having personally enjoyed his enormous success with his class, he left unceremoniously, and no one seemed to care. It might be added that the school where he taught was one of the few in Central Harlem that had established a reputation for a certain amount of faculty group spirit, an informal and relaxed school atmosphere, and tolerance of differences. Perhaps this teacher would have lasted an even shorter time in most other Central Harlem schools.

Ronald also displayed many characteristics associated with our conception of ambivalent children. Unlike Clarence, he was generally well accepted by other boys. Ronald was a very handsome boy with an engaging smile and a masculine, aggressive, brash quality that helped him to gain status as a leader among the boys. He was also quite popular among the girls in the fifth and sixth grades.

Teachers found Ronald to be either generally friendly or antagonistic, depending upon how Ronald sized up the teacher. With teachers who did not meet his standards Ronald could not help taking advantage of their weakness. He often disrupted the classes of such teachers by clowning and "fooling around." But with teachers who were strong, firm, and warm, Ronald usually tried to be friendly and cooperative. From time to time, he seemed to enjoy having discussions with such teachers, sometimes about school matters and sometimes about personal concerns, often displaying a sharp sense of humor. Even during these discussions, however, Ronald seemed never to be completely open or relaxed; his eyes, his posture, and his movements suggested a wariness and defensiveness that never let down. This lack of trust appeared whether the teachers were black or white, male or female.

While Ronald appeared to desire friendly contact with teachers he respected, unlike Clarence he did not constantly seek their attention openly but was controlled and reserved. About two or three times a week, however, Ronald would manage to create some minor disturbance in his classroom that required teacher attention. When the teacher caught his eye, Ronald would adopt a somewhat sheepish expression and use the opportunity to explain what was on his mind, which usually required a few minutes of personal attention.

Ronald was about two years behind in reading. He often sat at his desk daydreaming when he was supposed to be carrying out an individual work assignment. He was not unmotivated to do some of the work, but he seemed unable to sustain any concentrated effort for more than a few minutes. If the teacher walked over to his seat, Ronald would look up and say, "O.K., I'm doin' my work," and for a few minutes he would make some progress. If the teacher did not come back every few minutes to "push" him, however, the progress ceased. Unlike Clarence, Ronald did not continually claim ignorance concerning his assignments; however, he seemed unable to persevere without constant teacher attention and encouragement.

Although Ronald's moods did not fluctuate so often or so dramatically as Clarence's, he also had frequent bouts of sullen pouting during which he was uncooperative and sometimes openly defiant. These negative moods were most likely to be touched off by the teacher's finding a mistake in his work or reprimanding Ronald for causing some disturbance in the classroom. The moods would not last long, but at their start Ronald would become very hard to reach: He would fling his books on the floor, reject any attempt on the part of the teacher to talk to him, and sometimes walk out of the room and stay outside in the hall for a few minutes. Usually after five or ten minutes the teacher would see Ronald looking in through the doorway, an ingratiating, sheepish grin on his face. When the teacher invited him to come back inside, Ronald approached his seat in a slow-moving gait, apparently relieved that the situation was calm again.

Ronald was looked up to by many boys as a natural leader. He was "streetwise," and he demonstrated his tough, hip, masculine orientation in his tough style of talking and walking, modeled after older boys in the streets. Ronald was known to spend time with a group of boys who were a bit older than he was.

Repartee was not one of Ronald's well-developed skills. He often was at a loss to respond with a one-up insult when challenged. His solution to this dilemma was to change the game to one he could win: He typically responded to any remark that might be shaming with "I'll punch you in your eye, man." He would then push the other boy, put up his guard, and wait for the other boy to strike back so as to make the fight officially "on." Because he had a reputation as a good fighter, boys often backed away at this point. Ronald, thus able to have the last word, now abused his opponent, calling him "faggot," "chicken," or "dumb nigger" —thereby finishing the incident in a blaze of high status for shaming the other boy.

When a teacher assigned children to groups to work together, many boys were eager to be in Ronald's group. Ronald's cooperativeness or lack of cooperativeness could determine whether the group actually worked on an assignment or "fooled around." On a number of occasions, the teacher came over to a group that included Ronald, which had not begun to work on an assignment. Ronald caught the teacher's eye and then called out to the other children: "Hey, man—let's do work!" For a few minutes, the others would follow Ronald's lead and start to do the assignment. If the teacher maintained contact with Ronald, the work could be sustained for much longer; if not, after a few minutes the group would be "fooling around" again.

Ronald associated rather frequently with two other boys in his class, but relations among this trio hardly ever appeared to run smoothly. Each boy was highly aggressive and competitive. Usually one of the three was angry at another, with the third allying himself with one or the other.

In the fifth and sixth grades, Ronald was also continuously linked by the other children with one of the girls in his classes. He did not appear to spend much time with this girl in school, although he showed off quite a bit in front of her when they were together. But the children gossiped frequently about Ronald and Barbara, including much speculation over the sexual involvement of this eleven-year-old couple. Ronald never did much to discourage or encourage these discussions. However, he appeared to enjoy the attention and high status that came from being associated sexually (even if only verbally) with the prettiest girl in the class.

Carla also might be described as an ambivalent child. During her fifth- and sixth-grade years, when we knew her, Carla was a strikingly attractive girl and very much aware of the fact that many boys considered her pretty and wanted to "go with" her. She was popular with the girls as well, even though many girls were jealous of her looks. Carla had a strong need to be at the center of attention, and her attempts to thrust herself forward in many activities antagonized some of the girls in her classes. Many girls liked to be around Carla nevertheless, because ferment or excitement seemed to follow her wherever she went.

Carla was not particularly friendly to most women teachers in the school, black or white, nor did she appear to like them much. She preferred men teachers and a few of the younger, more attractive female teachers. In her relationship with her male homeroom teacher, Carla was quite coquettish and openly sought attention and affection. She frequently came up to the teacher's desk claiming that she didn't understand an assignment, although in fact she was quite bright and able to understand quickly. When she went back to her seat, however, the work stopped after a few minutes. Carla frequently wrote little notes to her teacher about her unfinished work, explaining that she understood what to do when the teacher helped her but that when she was at her own seat she forgot. The notes usually ended with: "Will you please help me?" Carla once left a sealed envelope on her teacher's desk, containing a photograph of herself and a note explaining that she didn't have anyone else to give the picture to.

Carla frequently displayed jealousy when her teacher paid attention to another child. If the teacher was helping a number of children simultaneously, Carla would attract his attention. When the teacher told Carla that he couldn't come over for a few minutes because he was helping another child, Carla would rip her paper out of her book, slam the book shut, and adopt a sullen, pouting expression. At such times she often became openly hostile and verbally abusive to the teacher or to other children.

When Carla went into one of these defiant moods, she was much more difficult to reach than Clarence or Ronald. She could harbor a grudge for an entire day. During these moods, Carla was extremely uncooperative with her teacher yet would refuse to stay in the room if any other teacher came in to teach the class for a period.

Carla had leadership potential. She frequently asked her teacher for the key to the classroom during his lunch period, explaining that she had persuaded some of the girls to go upstairs before the other children came back and "fix up the room." Under Carla's direction, the girls would work hard and clean up or redecorate the room so that it looked very attractive.

Several times during the day, Carla would get together with other girls in the classroom to engage in one of their favorite activities, grooming and fixing one another's hair. While this activity was fun for most of the girls, it was a source of anxiety for some, as it was common to hear blatantly disparaging remarks about the physical features and clothing of some of the girls while it was going on. Such remarks added to the heavy burden of shame endured by the children.

We met Alice for the first time when she was in fourth grade and observed her development for the next four years. She came from a very large family, which eventually had a child in every grade in the school. As the oldest of eight children, Alice was frequently called upon to care for her younger siblings. From time to time her mother would keep her out of school so that she could watch the younger children while the mother had to be away from home.

The most striking feature about Alice was her continual sullenness and even sadness. Alice rarely smiled and hardly ever appeared happy. Most of the time, Alice appeared to be isolated and cut off from others in her classroom. She sat in her seat daydreaming for a large part of each day. Because she was very far behind in reading, a decision was made to give special attention to Alice. A female teaching assistant would take her out of the classroom for about an hour each day and give her individualized instruction. Alice began to look forward to this time. According to her tutor, Alice gradually began to relax after about a week of sullen, silent, stoic noncooperation. She began to talk with her tutor about her home and the other children at school. Basically this talking was a running narrative of frustrations and oppressions, which was the way Alice saw her world. Alice sought to find out all she could about her reading tutor. She would examine the contents of the tutor's purse and question her about each article she found. When the tutor tried to change the subject or get her to read, after their relationship progressed, Alice began to hit the teacher or run out of the room. When caught or restrained, Alice would break down and cry. At these times the tutor would hold Alice close. Alice appeared to enjoy this physical contact, and the teaching assistant usually had to take the initiative of separating from it.

After a few months with the special teacher, Alice began to make noticeable progress in reading. In her regular classroom she made a little bit more effort to do her work, but she still seemed sullen and sad. She did not try hard to get attention from her male teacher but in fact appeared to withdraw from adult attention in her regular classroom.

Alice was not popular with the children in her classes. They teased her a great deal about her family's poverty, about the old clothes she wore, and about her mother's alleged drinking. Alice did not seem able to defend herself verbally or, for the most part, inclined to strike back physically at other children. Alice desperately wanted to be accepted by her peers. When something exciting was going on she would run over to see it and to try to be part of a group. She was frequently rejected, however, and went through repeated cycles of seeking attention and approval from peers, followed by rejection, followed by sullen withdrawal. Alice never cried in her regular classroom.

After Alice had worked with the special teacher for about half a school year, the teacher left the school. It was not possible to offer a replacement for her, as no new personnel were available. Alice became more withdrawn for a time after her special teacher left. She would not try any schoolwork at all. She gradually tried to increase her contact with other girls in her class, but that did not lead to acceptance or belonging. Whatever academic gains had been accomplished through her relationship with the special teacher were completely lost.

Over the next few years, as she matured physically, Alice began to gain a little more acceptance by her peers, and she appeared to channel all her energies in this direction. When she went on to the seventh grade in a junior high school she was barely able to read at all.

When we first met John, in the fifth grade, the characteristic we noticed most was his habit of looking out into space for long periods with a blank expression. John was quite anxious about being approached by adults and seemed very apprehensive when a teacher would walk over and talk to him. Typically, he would sit with an open book and paper and pencil on his desk staring out into space while other children around him were making some effort to work on an assignment. When the teacher came over to inquire about his progress, John would look up with an expression that hovered between a faint smile and an oppressed pout. Very softly, John would say that he didn't know what to do. If the teacher explained the work on the spot and remained there, John would start the assignment, but as soon as the teacher left John went back to staring blankly out into space.

Other children in the class noticed that John accomplished less than they did; some of them teased him and called him stupid. John's poor academic performance, however, was due not to lack of comprehension or reading skill but to high anxiety and a fear of engaging in sustained individual efforts. During the year, John's teacher set up oral reading groups, groups of children who would take turns reading parts of stories aloud to each other while the rest of the group read along silently. On the hunch that John sought recognition from his peers, the teacher placed him in a small all-male group with the toughest, "baddest" boys in the class. Within this context, to everyone's surprise, John demonstrated that he could read quite well, closer to grade level than most other children in the class. He gained some positive recognition when he became the one in the group to whom the others would turn when they were not sure of a word. When he had to work on an individual project, however, John continued to stare out into space, alienated and anxious.

Although John never seemed to seek or to welcome attention from adults, he wanted very much to be noticed and accepted by the high-status boys in his class. Whenever these boys got together to laugh or "sound" or "jive" or play, John would always move quickly to where they were and try to be a part of the action. The boys usually did not take John seriously, however; they seemed to consider him "lame": not "bad," not forceful or dynamic enough to be one of them. John often was the target of insults from these boys: "Hey, John, your head so big it look like a watermelon." "Yeah, John, you better cover up that head when you go in the street, else someone take it home an' eat it for a watermelon." "Aw, don't talk 'bout John, man! He can't help it that his head so big," etc.

John unfortunately made an ideal target. He just stood there with a sheepish grin on his face and took their taunts without answering or fighting back. When the boys felt bored, tension could be reduced and life made more lively by insulting John. It was in this context that some of the high-status boys began to accept John's presence on a somewhat regular basis. He was good to have around for comic relief.

John was commonly teased about his father's absence. Some of the boys used to ask John from time to time who his father was. The boys would argue about whether certain men in the neighborhood could be John's father. When they asked John to confirm or deny their specula-tions, he would laugh nervously and try to change the subject. When some of the boys were in the mood to be especially nasty to John, they would insist that a certain local wino who could regularly be found lying in the streets near the school was John's father.

From time to time, the teasing got to be too much even for John. John would walk away from the other boys, close to tears. He would sit and stare out into space for a while. Usually no more than a day would go by before John was back again seeking attention from the same boys who had teased him—and the cycle soon began again.

THE PRECOCIOUS INDEPENDENTS

A second, much smaller group, which we observed even in the earliest grades in Central Harlem, we have called the precocious independents. The outstanding characteristics of these children were their stubborn, rather rigid self-direction; early functional independence; lack of social cooperativeness; and vigorously carved-out dramatic and forceful identities. The precocious independent children frequently wore strikingly intense, sullen, or angry expressions. Some of them were known to associate with older children who were heavily involved in street-culture activities, but they usually were not friendly or open to adults or even to their peers. Quite often, precocious independent children were socially rather isolated, but their presence was strongly felt in the school; they were rarely part of any group in a classroom or on a grade level. Children in their classes avoided social contact with them; the other children usually did not like the precocious-independent children, but they respected and feared their "badness." Precocious-independent children were frequently involved in conflicts with other children in their classes, wreaking havoc and fear in the schools and streets.

While the independents usually were not liked by their peers, they nevertheless served as interesting or envied models of street prestige for some of them. Their greater knowledge of street life, of the life-styles of older children, adolescents, and adults, enabled them to offer information and gossip to some of their peers concerning goings-on in the bigger world of the ghetto. This enhanced the independents' status. Their wider associations with older people and their superior knowledge, combined with their style, potency, and emotionality, made them the most immediate and convincing "worldly" models available to the children—especially the ambivalents—to be respected, admired, or envied, but usually at a safe distance. The independent was, in short, "older" than his peers.

While the independent as an ideal type experienced a serious mistrust of others, and of life in general, he displayed a high degree of self-confidence. Aggressive defenses, anger, self-direction, and daring apparently enabled him to bury his fears and anxieties.

The precocious independents did not get along well with most teachers. They frequently insisted on doing something other than what a teacher had asked or told them to do. When they ran into difficulty on assigned work, the precocious independents would not seek help but typically would stop working and give violent vent to their frustration by tearing up papers and throwing books on the floor. When a teacher tried to point out errors in their work, these children stubbornly refused to admit that they had made any mistakes at all. Often they would grab their paper away from the teacher, tear it into pieces, and walk away shouting: "I ain't doin' this jive!"*

* Other children often tried to withhold their work from the teacher, but they would do so either secretly, by hiding the work, or by anxiously or tearfully crumpling it up and throwing it in the wastepaper basket. Even if they engaged in a "tug of war" over a piece of work, this was usually an act of desperation to prevent the possibility of appearing incompetent. The independent, on the other hand, handled such encounters with steely defiance.

Unlike the ambivalent children, the precocious independents did not seek teacher attention overtly, nor did they welcome it. Their distrust of all adults and their need to maintain the appearance of tough, cunning self-sufficiency were profound. More than any of the other types of children, the precocious independents tended to be openly suspicious of and hostile to white teachers in racially oriented terms, although they did not get along well with black teachers either. The precocious independents were the children most likely to respond to white teachers by calling them "cracker" or telling them to "keep your white hands off me!" On the other hand, the precocious independents were also more likely than other children to call their black teachers "niggers" or "black motherfuckers" and to warn them to "keep your black hands off me."

Presumably one way of helping children is by building up their weak areas to allay their anxieties and fears. But the independent, despite his mistrustful feelings, aggressiveness, and stubbornness, which could border on the pathological, remains in many respects a strong individual. Usually he not only did not welcome a relationship with a teacher but actively resisted any effort to establish one. If he did begin to accept a teacher-initiated approach, this frequently led to an endless flow of demands, defeating the possibility of an enduring relationship.

The few teachers who persisted sometimes found the child gingerly flirting with a desire for attention, but rarely would he allow consistent friendly overtures. He insisted on taking extensive liberties once he began to accept some attention, and he almost always maintained his tough exterior, reserving the right to breathe defiance even as he accepted a semblance of adult friendship. He implied that he regarded himself as virtually the equal of the teacher.

If a disagreement caused him to flare up, he usually pronounced escalated demands, renewed his threats, or even severed the relationship. Whereas most children are eager to make up after an altercation with an adult, one could never be certain if the independent truly wished a reconciliation.

To a considerable extent, it was the independents' very success in vigorously defending against the traumatic features of living, while initiating his own brand of trouble, that interfered with any desire for trust he had and prevented him from entering into true friendships with adults or children.

Some of the precocious independent children became skilled in reading. Most of them seemed to have considerable raw intellectual potential. But the intellectual capacity of the precocious independents was channeled largely into survival skills and the defensive reactions needed to "make it" in the street world with the bare minimum of adult help or support. In spite of their early, uncanny ability to hustle, scrounge, and "go for themselves" in the streets, most precocious independent children failed to achieve significantly in school. Their general unwillingness to take direction and to enter into cooperative efforts with teachers or other children usually hindered any efforts to channel their intellectual potential into sustained traditional school-achievement activities.

Independents who are bright or high achievers are likely to draw much attention in both ghetto and mainstream settings, largely because of their dramatic (or melodramatic) personalities. These independents are the most likely to achieve conventional forms of success as adolescents and young adults, provided that they receive educational and training opportunities.

Independents of preschool and elementary school age probably could be taught to curb their aggressiveness and to cooperate, at least minimally, and handle interpersonal conflict. Young independents, we believe, could even be socialized to accrue a rudimentary social consciousness. However, unless independents undergo resocialization as preschoolers, we predict that it will be extremely difficult for them to develop even a minimal level of trust and cooperation with others.

Most of the precocious independents were boys. The few girls who fitted into this group tended to be more stoical in their refusal to cooperate rather than dramatic, flamboyantly daring, and defiant, as were most of the precocious independent boys.

Parents and neighborhood school aides reacted with mixed feelings to the style of the precocious independent boys. On the one hand, they took a certain pride in their tough, hip, adult manner. They were miniature "bad niggers," future quickwitted strong men and ladykillers. On the other hand, they seemed destined for a life of trouble. They were the ones who "ain't supposed to die a natural death."

Larry, for example, displayed nearly all the behaviors we associated with our category of precocious independents. We first met Larry in the fifth grade. He had been in most of the other fifth-grade classes in the school, causing the teachers so much trouble that each insisted he be placed elsewhere. We were struck by the intense, penetrating gaze which Larry would turn on other people in combination with a sullen facial expression. We never saw him smile.

The first day in the class, Larry did not wait to be assigned a seat but picked one out himself and went directly to it. When his teacher pointed to a number of other seats, Larry stubbornly refused to move. He loudly offered various comments on each alternative such as: "I ain't gonna sit next to that big head!" The teacher at last agreed that Larry could remain in the seat he had chosen, and for the moment Larry seemed content. Before the day was over, however, Larry was engaged in a fight with another boy who claimed that Larry had taken something from his desk. Larry was winning the fight quite easily. When the teacher approached to intervene, Larry began running about the room and toppling chairs over. He challenged the teacher to try to catch him, at the same time exclaiming that the teacher could not, and better not try to, do anything to him.

The teacher waited for Larry to calm down and kept him isolated in a part of the room for a few minutes. When he asked Larry to talk about what happened, Larry explained that he hadn't done anything; the other boy was against him because Larry had beaten him up in the street. The teacher acknowledged Larry's ability to beat up any boy in the room but also stressed his own responsibility to protect the other boys; he could not allow Larry to beat up others in his classroom. The teacher and Larry came to a shaky understanding: Larry would not be allowed to beat up any child in the room but would take a chance and complain to the teacher the next time someone tried to "mess with him"—just to see whether the teacher could solve the problem.

Larry did not trust adults at all, any adults, black or white. He could not allow himself to rely upon an adult for help or nurturance. If he felt an inner urge to be dependent, he defended against this desire vigorously by avoiding contact with adults or relating to them in an openly hostile manner. Unlike most of the ambivalent children, he did not seek adult attention or help, nor did he have difficulty functioning independently. Like many of the precocious independents, he was able to read nearly on grade level and could carry out independent work assignments successfully. The key factors determining whether Larry would complete an independent work assignment were his mood at the moment and his perception of the teacher's power. If Larry was not particularly preoccupied or sullen, and if he believed the teacher was powerful but not arbitrarily or unnecessarily punitive, he would work silently and diligently at his seat. If Larry did not feel like doing an assignment, or if he did not respect his teacher, he would refuse to do the work and could not be persuaded. When Larry had completed an assignment he would bring it to his teacher and hand it to him directly and abruptly. He would not wait to discuss the work or receive any praise; he would simply return to his seat. For many months, Larry was highly indignant if any error was found in his work. He would refuse to recognize an error—"That's *right, man!*"—and often grabbed a paper with an error and tore it apart. He often tore up and threw away his perfect papers as well; he did not want to have them displayed on the walls, as the ambivalent children always did. Larry's attitude appeared to be—"See, I did it; you didn't think I could (would)"—but he could not allow himself to care too keenly about his work, just as he would not allow himself to care too deeply about people.

Larry had a number of fights in his classroom during his first few weeks in the class. He refused to let the teacher help in resolving conflicts although he had grudgingly said that he would; he was constantly busy defending his small claim on life and could not allow himself to let down his defenses and rely on any adult. Larry's fighting in the classroom gradually stopped, chiefly because the other boys became increasingly fearful of him and tended to back away from fights with him or to invite teacher intervention, but also because Larry began to develop a certain respect for his teacher and seemed eager to avoid continuous confrontations with an adult whom he could not easily manipulate. Larry's relationship with his teacher became peaceful coexistence based on clearly defined power-status boundary lines rather than warm friendship.

Larry's relationships with his peers were quite conflictful. He was not well liked by the boys in his class, most of whom were quite fearful of him and tried to keep their distance, even though some were clearly in awe of his defiant independence. Larry, on the other hand, appeared to regard most of the boys in his class as "lame" and showed no interest in joining any of their cliques. He associated mostly with older boys in the street who were deeply involved in street-culture activities. On two occasions, policemen came to the school to question Larry about burglaries in the neighborhood in which boys he often associated with were suspects.

Larry had learned early in life how to "hold his own," even if it meant a lonely existence. One day, Larry's class was playing in the schoolyard. A number of older boys, a few inches taller and much heavier than Larry, came over to him as he was playing alone with a basketball. They wanted to use the basketball and the basket Larry was monopolizing. Larry refused to surrender the ball. As the teacher, who saw what was happening from the other end of the yard, began to approach the scene, one of the older boys knocked the ball out of Larry's hand. Larry swung hard and punched the older boy in the eye, causing him to reach up and hold his eye in pain. The older boy looked reluctant to continue the fight even though his associates were "sounding" on him for letting that "little midget" hit him. The teacher at that point intervened and persuaded the older boys to leave the yard. Larry looked up at his teacher with an expression that approximated a grin. The teacher took the expression to mean: "I wasn't afraid of him. You didn't have to protect me like the others. But it was O.K., you did good." That was the closest Larry ever came to acknowledging dependency on a teacher or saying "thank you."

It is possible that the precocious independent is a kind of "aggressive fatalist." His persistently hostile and suspicious view of his surroundings seems to contain a note of fatalism. But he characteristically does not feel humbled by fate. Some independents clearly felt oppressed, but they struggled angrily, spitefully, tenaciously, and often courageously. This child who wrestles with his world is reminiscent of American folklore heroes, the rugged, brooding, bitter, or confused individuals who fight lonely, stubborn battles against futility and danger. The independent calls to mind the mountaineer or the frontiersman, the hermit or the cowboy. Thus viewed historically, the independent may be seen as a uniquely American character: an urban cowboy, spawned from the assertive, aggressive elements of the Northern black experience. The independent embodies, in exaggerated form, a contemporary response to some major features of the black ghetto predicament, notably the problematic outsider position of subjugated low-income urban black America. His is the most individualistic response to be found in the slum streets. Forged by members of a people whose hope and trust and autonomy have been woefully damaged, it shows stubborn, willful, defiant autonomy, pride, and shamelessness.

THE SUBMISSIVES

A third group, representing a significant minority of the children we observed in the earliest grades in Central Harlem, we characterized as submissives. The key features of children in this group were their tendency to be quiet, inactive, nonassertive, stoic, and socially isolated. Such children usually spoke to an adult only if they were encouraged to do so, and even then their speech would be brief and hard to hear. The submissives rarely asked a question of teachers or openly displayed curiosity in a classroom. They showed little inclination to speak to or play with other children. They spent much of their time silently watching other children but seldom joined in their play. Even in their relative isolation, submissives were not playful with toys or other inanimate objects. They usually handled objects tentatively and made little use of them. A few of them could be pushed to the point where their inhibitions weakened and they would show an angry or even a violently aggressive side. These outbursts were usually less an expression of an aroused sense of offended dignity than the venting of frustration.

Submissive children tried their best to follow the teacher's instructions. They were not openly antagonistic or uncooperative. They displayed very little emotion outwardly. Their faces were often expressionless, their eyes pained, dull, or unfocused. Some submissive children seemed to be in a daze; others even seemed to be in a hurt condition much of the time. (Some may have suffered from nutritional deficiencies or debilitating physical illnesses.) In spite of their efforts to cooperate, submissive children spent most of their time doing nothing unless an adult was standing by to direct their actions.

Some of the other children permitted submissives to have at least marginal contact with them on an individual basis and in their groups. Such relationships depended a great deal on the emotional status and behavioral repertoire of a particular submissive child. Sometimes submissive children became much more animated as they grew older. The excitement of peer-group life would draw them out—typically in "follower" roles. Thus some submissives could avoid, at least partly, dwelling for long periods in their inert, sometimes morbid states. Most of them found some way to enjoy some social involvement, at which time their otherwise stoic or oppressed appearance took on a bedraggled, gentle cheerfulness.

In prekindergarten classes in Central Harlem we saw quiet, submissive children coming to school with their mothers. Typically, the mothers left the children at the classroom door with no kiss, no "goodbye," no "I'll pick you up later," not even a "be good." The children rarely cried and often did not say goodbye to their mothers. They usually stood silently at the door until someone in the classroom asked them to come in.

Once in the classroom, these children ordinarily would not take off their coats until told to do so. They would then, typically, sit down at a table and stare vacuously across the room. The initiative or self-confidence needed to get up and select a toy or a game and play with it was not evident in these children. They would accept a toy if it was handed to them, but they handled it tentatively, gingerly, and without much expression.

The quiet, submissive children frequently did not answer when spoken to. When they were eating, for example, they might not answer a simple question like "Do you like this juice?"

After being in a preschool class for a while, some of the quiet, submissive children began to speak in a whisper. Many teachers found that such children responded most when they were treated like two- or three-year-olds. They often enjoyed being tickled or playing "hide and seek" with an adult who pretended not to be able to find them. These children seemed to be not so much frightened as emotionally deadened. Generally, as they progressed through the elementary school grades, most submissives became more active than they were in preschool, owing largely to peer influence.

Submissives varied in the extent to which they succeeded in inhibiting their anger, hatred, and aggression. They also differed in the content of their inhibitions. Some were hampered in their capacity to manipulate their environment pleasurably and meaningfully; some characteristically suppressed their anger, frustration, and aggression (in varying degrees); others were apparently more fearful of expressing their dormant liveliness; and a few erected inhibitions in all these areas.

Some of the overcontrolled submissives occasionally surprised peers, siblings, or adults by sudden outbursts of agitated anger. These outbreaks usually were not escalated frontal assaults but convulsions, cries of outrage signifying a desperate desire to escape from torment.

Submissives whose meekness and conformity were related to an inhibition of spontaneity did not tend to explode. This subtype is stoical, controlled, conforming, sometimes invisible, with little experience in exerting a pleasurable, successful impact upon the environment, and a fear of trying. Such children are incapable of exploratory and imaginative behavior. They find it harder to act than to modulate anger and frustration.

By being stoic, invisible children, the submissives hoped to reduce interpersonal friction and stay out of trouble. They were too inhibited or too weak to do much more than complain softly or suffer quietly while studiously trying to avoid compounding misfortune and deprivation. Some submissives succumbed entirely in childhood; these were the most wretched and the most pitiful. In the submissive group, boys outnumbered girls significantly; there were at least twice as many boys as girls in this group.

Randolph displayed many behaviors typical of the children we have called submissives. We first met Randolph in the fifth grade. When we spoke to his previous teachers, most of them hardly remembered him at all. He was so quiet and unobtrusive that he could sit in a classroom all year and be barely noticed. Randolph hardly ever spoke above a whisper. He made no demands for attention on his teacher or other children. He was socially isolated and apparently unattached to other people. If told to sit in his seat all day he would do so with no complaints, demands, or self-assertiveness.

Randolph, like most submissives, was a quite pleasant child. He did not look deeply unhappy. He seemed to be almost smiling most of the time, but the half-smile was more like a mask than a child's expressive face. Randolph's eyes generally stared out into space blankly. In his actions (or lack of them), as well as in his facial expressions (or lack of them), Randolph rarely showed a strong emotion. When relating to an adult, Randolph usually lowered his head and looked up occasionally, fleetingly, tentatively, avoiding prolonged eye-to-eye contact. (This avoidance of eye contact appeared to be more a personal than a cultural trait, since it was not shared by other types of children.)

When given an individual assignment, Randolph would make some effort to start working. Typically the teacher's attention would be drawn to one of the ambivalent children in the class who, in various ways, were making bids for personal attention, and the teacher would not get around to checking on Randolph's work. When he did, he would find that Randolph had very little written on his paper. He had started, but as soon as he ran into difficulty, he stopped. He did not ask for help or try to get teacher attention. He simply sat there doing nothing until the teacher came over. When the teacher asked where the problem was, Randolph would explain it in a bare whisper. If the teacher told him how to proceed, Randolph would begin working again, but as soon as he ran into difficulty again he would sit and do nothing until the teacher came back or asked him to do something else.

Unlike the ambivalents and the precocious independents, the submissive children almost always made an effort to cooperate with adults. Randolph would carry out simple requests without any overt resistance. In carrying out tasks independently, however, Randolph could not display autonomy and initiative. His behavior easily became disorganized, and he withdrew frequently into the safety of inactivity.

Submissive children appeared to lack even minimal self-assertiveness, spirit, and liveliness. Things happened to submissive children; they did not make things happen. Submissive children suffered misfortunes in stoic silence. For example, on one occasion Randolph was in the gymnasium with his class, standing on the sidelines quietly watching some boys play basketball. One boy threw the ball hard at another boy who had the good sense to duck. The ball crashed into Randolph's head. Randolph did not utter a sound, not a scream or complaint or protest, even though a large bump had been raised on the side of his head. He simply walked to another part of the room and stood there observing some other children playing. He made no attempt to elicit teacher attention or aid.

Randolph was a social isolate, like most submissive children. He rarely played with other children and was rarely included in their activities. He was typically an observer, infrequently a participant. The other children usually regarded submissive children as different from themselves and paid no attention to them, positive or negative. If a boy in the class picked on Randolph, which didn't happen often, another boy usually would intervene on Randolph's behalf: "Quit messin' with Randolph, he's my man, Jim! You mess with Randolph and you messin' with me!" Those who defended Randolph were not likely to pay attention to him in any other context. Submissive girls were more likely than submissive boys to be included in some social activities, such as jumping-rope games, but generally they were relegated to the mechanical task of turning the rope over and over.

Randolph came from a family of nine children in which he was a middle child. As near as we could tell, he went directly home from school every day and stayed in his apartment. The other children said they rarely saw him in the street except for coming to and going from school.

Placing the submissives into a historical-cultural perspective, we found them to be an anachronistic child type, few in number. Their behavior patterns and sometimes aspiration levels were once appropriate to a dominant Negro type of the older rural South, but these patterns are, on the whole, not applicable to economic and social conditions in Northern cities. The submissives stand in sharp psychological contrast to the stark Northern Rebels, the independents.

THE MAINSTREAMERS

We observed the group we have called the mainstreamers from the early grades in Central Harlem. We chose the term "mainstreamers" to denote the greater physical and behavioral resemblance of these children to children from the mainstream of American society (middle-class white children), in contrast to the ambivalents, precocious independents, and submissives. We do not mean that the mainstreamers had lighter skin or more Caucasian features than their peers. Rather, somehow they looked more like descriptions in child-development textbooks, which rely on norms derived from white middle-class children: Generally the mainstreamer children had relatively bright, clear, shining eyes; their faces had a pleasant, contented expression; they appeared to be less oppressed, better cared for, better fed (sometimes overfed); and they were often dressed in newer, neater, cleaner clothing. The mainstreamers looked like children rather than little adults. They were neither extremely inhibited nor impulsive, as was the case, one way or the other, with children in the other groups. In addition, many of them were quite assertive and also showed defiance and aggressive behavior.

Although we are not certain of the reasons, the mainstreamers definitely looked different to us from other children in the school. We believe they looked different to other adults as well, because most of the children whom we would have categorized as mainstreamers in the various kindergarten and first-grade classes seemed to wind up in the same class from the second grade on. In our first year in a Harlem elementary school, we often watched children walking in the halls and tried to guess which classes they belonged in. If a child had the characteristics we are now associating with the mainstreamers, we generally predicted that he would be in the highest-achieving class for his grade level. If such children were in the kindergarten or first grade, we predicted that they eventually would go to the "best" class in the second grade. Usually we were right.

The mainstreamers generally were friendly to adults, but if not they were at least cooperative and usually obedient. Mainstreamers did not make the continuing or excessive demands for teacher attention associated with the ambivalents. They were much more self-assertive than the submissives, but not nearly so independent or stubbornly self-directed as the precocious independents. The mainstreamers did not display the frequent mood swings associated with the ambivalents. While they were not always happy, neither were they usually sullen or depressed.

Teachers generally liked the mainstreamer children better than the other children, in part because they seemed to learn more of what the teachers were trying to teach them and were relatively easy to control (without being deadened, like the submissive). More than most children in the other groups, mainstreamers were developing mainstream culture skills during the elementary school—i.e., reading near grade level, writing, and mathematics skills, mastery of standard English. They were able to work independently on assignments given to them by their teachers, to pay attention to a school task, and to work more persistently on an assignment, with less need for constant support and direction than either the ambivalents or the submissives. The mainstreamers also became more involved with their schoolwork, took it more seriously, and were more open to guidance or criticism than the precocious independents.

The mainstreamers appeared to exercise much more self-control than the ambivalents, without being as stubborn as the precocious independents or as inhibited as the submissives. They appeared to be in closer touch with adults, and more involved in relationships with adults than children in the other groups. Some of the mainstreamers were children of parents who worked as aides in the schools. Some of the parent-aides made it a point to look in on their children's classrooms from time to time. In general, parents of mainstreamers were more likely to come into the school of their own volition to see how the children were progressing than the parents of children from the other groups. These parents were more likely to be in the PTA or otherwise active in school affairs.

In their relationships with other children, the mainstreamers were not likely to involve themselves in frequent bickering or in physical fights. Mainstreamer children teased one another quite a bit, but they tended to avoid showdowns. Usually they would talk or shout out a conflict rather than come to blows.

It was not only in the schools that the mainstreamer children became segregated from most of the other children in their community. After school, such children usually did not become as much involved with street-based peer groups or their activities as ambivalents or precocious independents. This was quite noticeable as far as the boys were concerned, because boys usually became more dramatically involved in early street peer-group activities. The mainstreamer boys usually were considered "lames" by the precocious independent and most of the ambivalent boys, who did not associate with mainstreamer boys except sometimes to "shake them down" for money. The mainstreamer girls were more likely than the boys to have some relationships with children from the other groups; some mainstreamer girls and some ambivalent girls spent time together, went places together, and considered themselves friends.

We don't wish to picture the mainstreamers as "ideal" children. In some ways, some of the precocious independents and some ambivalents were more admirable. Some of the mainstreamers may have been overcontrolled and dependent upon adults. But as a group the mainstreamers appeared to be more comfortable physically and psychologically than the other groups and better able to meet the demands made of them by the school. The mainstreamers were the group most likely to be successful in moving into working-class and middle-class occupations and lifestyles. In fact, of the small number of upper-elementary-school-aged children from Central Harlem who were sent to schools in predominantly white neighborhoods by their parents under the voluntary Open Enrollment program in New York City, most were clearly of the mainstreamer type.

In the mainstreamer group, girls outnumbered boys by about two to one. The majority of the black female teachers with whom we worked in Harlem grew up as mainstreamer children in Harlem and on its periphery. (This became apparent to us as we came to know these teachers and to hear them tell how markedly different their own childhood experiences were from those of many of the children in their classes.) The black male teachers often had not been so sheltered from ghetto street activities as their female counterparts, but most of them had had a great deal of adult support, direction, and guidance—characteristics more commonly associated with the mainstreamer pattern than any of the others we have described. A graphic example of a mainstreamer orientation in socialization and development was provided by a black female teacher in her late thirties who wrote a paper about her childhood for us as an assignment (aimed at developing greater insight into the needs of children) in a class in developmental psychology:

> I lived in the Inner City when I was a child, but I wasn't a part of it. My parents did not let me go out to play with the neighborhood children, we had friends that lived far away and we would visit on the weekends. We were never told that we weren't allowed to play with them, but we were always busy when the children came around. We were told that we were important, if we only had bread we set the table and followed the same traditions as a middle-income family. We were black and proud as the black race now is saying that black is beautiful, not meaning that the features of every black person are beautiful, but beautiful inside, with pride, independence and security that they were robbed of ever since slavery.

As we said earlier, no single child was a pure type; most children showed some characteristics associated with more than one of our typologies. Thus many mainstreamers appeared to experience a good deal of ambivalence concerning themselves and their community, as well as the larger society. But these ambivalent feelings did not usually lead them to the erratic, shifting behaviors characteristic of the ambivalent group. Many mainstreamers appeared to cope with their ambivalence by striving toward upward mobility, an effort in which they were obliged to reject many identifications and associations with the major part of the population in their community. In addition to ambivalence in the mainstreamers, we observed some submissive tendencies in a good number of ambivalents and the development of mainstreamer skills (reading) in some of the precocious independents.

Paul, a chubby fifth-grade boy who wore dark-rimmed glasses, displayed many characteristics typical of mainstreamer children we knew.

When we met him he was in the highest-achieving class of his grade in an elementary school in Central Harlem. He had been in the highest-achieving class since first grade. Paul's mother was a parent-aide in the school and frequently spoke with his teacher to check on his behavior and academic progress. Paul's older sister had also been in the best classes in the grade two years ahead of Paul's. Teachers and other children generally were aware that Paul's mother kept a close eye on him and that she was active in school affairs.

Paul always came to school very neatly dressed. He often wore a tie with a dress shirt, and it was not uncommon to see his mother stop him when he was running around in the schoolyard to bawl him out about looking "such a mess." Paul carried his books in a briefcase, which made him stand out among other boys his size, who usually carried their books under their arm. All in all, Paul looked like a "student," or what most of the teachers appeared to want their pupils to look like.

Paul usually had a pleasant expression though occasionally we would see him sullen and pouting, most often when he was being shouted at or had just been bawled out by an adult, often his mother. Paul smiled often, and we saw him laughing and apparently having a good time on many occasions. He was an active boy who enjoyed running and playing exuberantly with other boys, mostly from his own class but also from other classes. He displayed a good deal of spirit and often was restless in his classroom. Teachers could calm him down by reminding him that they would speak to his mother if he didn't "behave" (which meant sit still, be quiet, and do what he was told). Paul seemed somewhat ambivalent concerning his mother's attentiveness to him: On the one hand he seemed to resent her attention and her tendency to treat him "like a baby"; on the other hand he seemed to love his mother very much, to derive security from his close relation to her, and he did not appear eager to challenge or antagonize her and jeopardize their relationship. Paul was not exactly a "goody-goody"; he enjoyed going along with peers in rough-and-tumble play and mischief, often at a teacher's expense. But teachers could and did exercise a great deal of control over Paul's behavior by threatening to talk to his mother. This threat caused Paul enough anxiety for him to exercise self-control, to "get serious," to stop "playing around."

Teachers often tried similar threats in attempts to control ambivalent and precocious independent children, but usually without success. Many of these children would respond by saying: "So what?" or "She won't come!" Many mothers and a few fathers would come, but often they were themselves experiencing difficulty in controlling their own children and so could not help the teacher much. In general, the threat of sending for a parent was far more likely to lead to a change in pupil behavior if the pupil was a mainstreamer than if he was an ambivalent or a precocious independent. Submissive children simply did not present problems of control for teachers.

Like many children in his class, Paul was reading about on his grade level. He seemed to enjoy reading. When he had finished assignments in his class, he often would select a book and spend a few minutes reading by himself. He usually completed individual assignments in his classroom, though not without some prompting and threatening by his teacher. Paul did not make great demands for teacher attention, although he generally was friendly toward adults. He seemed less interested in getting a teacher's attention than in enjoying himself by playing with other boys in his classroom. In spite of his desire to have fun with the boys, Paul was able to pay sufficient attention to his assignments to get his classwork done. His mother made sure that he did his homework every night.

In his relationships with boys in his class, Paul was active and outgoing. He was competitive and could "hold his own" with other mainstreamer boys, but the mainstreamer boys' relationships were not so conflictful as relationships of ambivalents and precocious independents. Although Paul played with some boys from other classes in the schoolyard, he avoided many of the "baddest" boys who were patterning their behavior after street-culture models. These boys generally did not pay much attention to Paul; they considered him "lame" and did not wish to do battle with Paul's mother, whose presence in the school most children were quite aware of.

SOCIALIZATION AND BEHAVIOR PATTERNS

We cannot be sure what was responsible for the differentiation of Central Harlem children into the types we have described. The socialization factors that we believe were very important influences include the degree and extent of adult attention and emotional support the children had received before and during their school years. Also of great significance, we believe, were the extent to which children had faced restrictions on autonomous strivings for mastery and effective coping with objects and people in their environment and the nature and extent of punishment the children experienced in their preschool and school years.

In contrast to the mainstreamers, the ambivalent, precocious independent, and submissive types seemed to represent different patterns of coping with somewhat common predicaments: the early loss of adult attention and support (relative, but significant), in combination with early restrictions on autonomy and initiative and an abundance of physical punishment and verbal abuse. These features appeared to be rather common in the lives of the ambivalents, the precocious independents, and the submissives. We cannot determine with certainty why, out of a roughly common matrix of experiences, some children will develop an ambivalent style of life while others will develop a precocious independent or sub-missive style. The answer must lie in the interaction between each child's unique physical and emotional constitution and modes of reacting to stimulation, on the one hand, and the particular variations on the sociali-zation practices listed above that the child instigated and responded to over time. Modern developmental research has demonstrated that, from earliest infancy, each child presents his parents with a particular constel-lation of characteristics ("primary reaction tendencies"), which influence the parents' responses to the child as well as setting some limits on the ex-tent of their ability to mold the child to their desired image.[1]

The submissive children appeared to be generally unable to cope ac-tively with demands for early self-reliance or independence in an environ-ment that was frustrating, usually restrictive, intimidating, and filled with danger. To a much greater extent than other types of children, the sub-missives have attempted to withdraw to small islands of safety by being undemanding, inconspicuous, restrained, resigned, and quiet. To obtain small satisfactions while avoiding frustrations and punishments, these children have largely given up the hope of autonomous action, active satisfactions, or individual initiative. The submissives generally appeared to have lost the courage to be curious, to question, or to attempt mastery over many aspects of their environment. Behind much of their lackluster, submissive behavior and resigned attitude were an avoidance of challenge and a search for serenity.

The precocious independents somehow have dramatically risen to the challenges imposed by minimal adult support, abundant frustrations, and extensive punishments. At an early age, they appear to have developed real competence in taking care of themselves in a limited number of areas, but they became rather closed to their own impulses to be depen-dent upon others, to enter into social cooperation, or to care deeply about anyone or anything. Many precocious independents maintained a rebel-lious, exploitative, or intimidating style in their social relationships, which began rather early in life.

Although we saw some of the same phenomena at work in all the types we have described, it was in the precocious independents that elements of an early identity foreclosure were clearest: attempts to create stability in stressful young lives by fixing self-images and behavioral roles to a small number of tough, older-boy life-style possibilities, avoidance of alterna-tives, and elimination of ambiguities or contradictions.[2] This phenome-non of early identity foreclosure led to the fixation of rather limited, sometimes impoverished self-definitions as many of the children, espe-cially the precocious independents and submissives, tended to depend heavily upon certain sets of behaviors and attitudes as rather rigidly de-fining and delimiting their selves in many ways. For these children, early adaptions to severe stress apparently became deeply entrenched definitions of what one was and what one could be. The independents defiantly spat in the face of life through active defense. The submissives hid. Both these personality styles eclipsed much potential personal development.

The ambivalent children occupied various points on a continuum between the submissives and the precocious independents. They generally attempted to maintain more social relatedness than the submissives and precocious independents. They often continued to try to become personally involved with and dependent upon adults, including teachers, and they often sought adult attention—not uncommonly, through extreme behaviors. Often ambivalent children had experienced considerable inconsistency in their relationships with adults, and their erratic behaviors and moods seemed to be at least in part related to this aspect of their lives. Quite commonly, ambivalent children we knew were cared for by a number of parental figures, simultaneously or in sequence, and they had to adapt to broken attachments and varying adult demands. Some ambivalent children openly expressed concern over whether they could continue to live with one relative or would have to be sent to another relative to be "kept" for a time.

The ambivalents were the group most susceptible to early peer influence, because they so often sought support, affiliation, and intense belongingness wherever they could find it. The precocious independents were less open to peer influence from children their own age, but they often sought to model their behavior after youngsters older than themselves.

In many ways, many ambivalent children appeared to be better cared for physically than most precocious independents and many submissives, but the quality of parental care and involvement accorded to ambivalent children varied over a wide range. Although many of the children were presented with an austere front and received frequent beatings and hostility from adults, many had relationships with adults that concomitantly permitted friendliness and satisfaction and that often were not so oppressive as the relationships with adults or older children commonly experienced by the submissives or precocious independents.

Because so much of their energy was devoted to attention-getting, support-seeking, and power manipulations of others (children and adults), many ambivalent children suffered in their ability to cope with relatively independent, task-oriented problem-solving and learning behaviors in school. Personal alienations and concerns over unmet needs, centering on interpersonal relationships, preoccupied them and led to frequent disorganization of efforts toward conventional school achievement.

The mainstreamer children as a group generally appeared to have at least one adult in their lives who took an active and continuing interest in directing their behaviors toward conventional school achievement. These children often had a sense of themselves as "special" or "different" from

the majority of their peers. This feeling was reinforced by the more frequent preferential treatment they enjoyed from teachers, but it usually
originated in their relationship with a highly supporting and directing
adult in their homes. In general, though, with some exceptions the mainstreamer children appeared to be better cared for physically and emotionally than children from all other low-income groups in Central Harlem. They remained more open to flexible and conforming relationships
with adults, but their relationships with children were likely to be somewhat more limited than those of the ambivalents. This relative limitation
primarily involved restriction of their choice of associates to children of
their own type and emphasized a small number of friends rather than
affiliation with larger groups.

Children with characteristics of the types described above can be found
in any public school in any community. But the proportion of each type
and the intensity and extensiveness of the behavior associated with each
would vary from community to community. In communities in which exclusion from participation in the mainstream of American society is less
frequently the rule than in Harlem, because of racism, political powerlessness, and economic exploitation, we might expect to find more main-
stream-type children and fewer ambivalents, submissives, and precocious
independents. We cannot overlook the relationship between the socialization experiences of Central Harlem children and their need to learn
how to survive as blacks in a white-dominated country and in a community that in many respects is an exploited internal colony.

The submissives and the independents are the most burdened by distrust. They are similar in their strong perceptions of people and life as
malevolent. Therefore both are likely to feel anxious or depressed, especially when they sense that they are beginning to feel dependent on another person. Their response to these perceptions of malevolence and
feelings of discomfort differ radically, however. The submissives tend to
"hide," to withdraw from dependent contacts, but if an adult or child
persists in trying to establish contact many submissives may tentatively
and marginally accept friendly overtures. The independents' dependency
anxiety triggers withdrawal, anger, rejection, or aggression. They tend to
be aggressive toward others to ward off potential feelings of affiliation,
which portend becoming dependent upon others. By fighting with others
they make it almost impossible for themselves to face rejection. By consistently engaging in limited "wars" they protect themselves against the
malevolence of others; they are, in a word, "independent."

One reason the independent responds aggressively to his basic distrust
is that he has an unusual amount of self-confidence. His estimate of his
own personal characteristics—sometimes including his intelligence and social adroitness—is high. He may not love himself much in the traditional
sense, but he believes in himself and feels special. This helps him to bear

not believing in others. He goes on, he does not give up. The submissive, by contrast, feels lost and helpless in his perception of the world as malevolent. He tries to suppress this perception because he is incapable of dealing with it actively. Therefore, while he has, like the independent, significantly given up on trusting the world, he may accept a dependent relationship because his only defense lies in ingratiation or defiant withdrawal. Thus he may sometimes find it easier to accept overtures than to remain lonely and withdrawn.

The submissive has no active capacity for aggression in response to perceived malevolence in part because he is much more burdened with shame than the independent. This contributes to his doubts of his own resources (a differentiated form of feelings of mistrust). The independent, on the other hand, suffers much less self-doubt, largely because he has reacted to shame by aggressively incorporating his sense of personal "badness" into his self, sometimes to the point of a powerful, defiant shamelessness, which tends to give a positive valuation to his "badness." In addition, as he grows older he may actually feel that his "badness" is part of a positive identity, as black ethnic elements that are positively valued by large segments of the black community (but not the white) are assimilated into the shameless defiance so characteristic of the independent.

Ambivalents in general view people and life more optimistically than either the independents or the submissives. They also generally see themselves more positively and are less afflicted with doubt and shame than the submissives. But ambivalents who do not share this optimism inevitably develop anxiety because of their mistrustfulness and their insatiable need for dependency. When their dependency needs are met, ambivalents tend to become more like mainstreamers. When their dependency needs are not met, they tend to veer away from people in a manner reminiscent of independents and to assume some of their mannerisms.

Ambivalents represent by far the largest group of children. Moreover, the ambivalents' dilemma runs throughout the lives of most of the children, probably as the outcome of family, peer, and school socialization and the black predicament in America, today and in the past; the ambivalent type is meaningfully related to the other types. If one closely observes low-income urban black children today, in fact, the cross-fertilization of these types becomes apparent. Among the illustrations we have presented, Ronald, for example, showed some behaviors associated with the independent, but his strong ambivalence generally submerged the precocious independent in him. Carla's ambivalence was colored by aggressive manipulation reminiscent of an independent's behavior. Clarence cried a lot, but when he was not crying he could easily be mistaken for an independent because of his dramatic style and emphasis on masculine

characteristics and mannerisms. He could talk tough and strut like an independent and would violently assault another child from time to time.
John showed many submissive traits.

Randolph was almost a "pure" submissive. But Alice, who often was
depressed and would sulk for long periods, thus resembling a submissive,
was explosive; she would suddenly become violently aggressive in a manner resembling some of the independents and some of the high-strung
ambivalents.

Finally, while stoicism was most characteristic of the submissives, it
clearly showed up in the independents and was about equally shared by
mainstreamers and ambivalents.

Ambivalents are children who have neither given up, as the submissives have, nor clearly gone another way, as have the independents. They
stand torn between their desire for adult and peer attention, acceptance,
and guidance and their suspicion and doubt. Usually lacking both the
achievement skills and orientations of the mainstreamers and the commitment to the streets and to deviancy that typifies the precocious independents, the ambivalents represent vast numbers of children suspended in a
restless limbo. Caught between mainstream and street-influenced alternatives, most ambivalents gravitate toward the latter. Yet their greater
flexibility leaves them more open to mainstream opportunities than the
independents or submissives are. Even during adolescence they may be
expected to take considerable advantage of such programs as open college enrollment. Because they have not internalized self-defeating patterns or values as a group, their fate will be significantly influenced by
the nature of the opportunity structure as well as by the activism-
optimism theme of the black liberation movement.

NOTES

1. See Richard Q. Bell, "A Reinterpretation of the Direction of Effects in
   Studies of Socialization," *Psychological Review,* 75 (1968): 81–95,
   and Alexander Thomas, Stella Chess, and Herbert G. Birch, *Tempera-
   ment and Behavior Disorders in Children* (New York: New York University Press, 1968).
2. For a discussion of early identity foreclosure and research findings concerning this phenomenon among urban lower-class black adolescent
   males, see Stuart T. Hauser, *Black and White Identity Formation:
   Explorations in the Psycho-Social Development of White and Negro
   Male Adolescents* (New York: Wiley, 1971).

9 / THE INTERACTION OF TEACHERS AND STUDENTS

THE SORTING PROCESS

Teachers and administrators responded differently to the four types of children described in Chapter 8, generally showing a marked preference for those in the mainstreamer group. In fact, such children usually were separated from the others and, during the first two or three grades, grouped together to form the high-achievement class or classes in each grade. In the remaining classes, little was expected of the children and little was achieved.

Achievement in elementary school depends on a behavioral-attitudinal factor, involving obeying the teacher's instructions, getting along with others, being satisfied with a reasonable amount of attention, and wishing to please adults, and a work-skill factor, consisting of those skills and abilities needed to master the contents of the curriculum, such as elaborated verbal abilities (comprehending and speaking), well-developed perceptual-discrimination skills, and the ability to relate to or create a symbolic significance for objects.[1] In making judgments concerning a child's intellectual potential and appropriate group placement, however, teachers and school administrators typically give considerably more weight to their impressions of the child's behavioral-attitudinal functioning than to his academic skills and abilities. Children who do not respond to adults or to other children in the approved manner are adjudged "immature," "incompetent," or at least unlikely to achieve academic success and, on the basis of such judgments, are assigned to groups that are generally expected to fail academically. What the school thus "accomplishes" is the segregation and concentration into a few classroom groups of the children who are most unwilling, unable, or ambivalent concerning the open expression of dependence upon adults, those who experience the most difficulty relating to adults and to each other. This procedure tends to ensure a respectable level of academic achievement in the one or two "top" classes, but at the same time it ensures a very low level of achievement in the other classes, made up mostly of non-mainstreamer children.

In the schools where we taught, sex discrimination became apparent early in the sorting process. There were at least twice as many girls as boys in the mainstreamer group that made up the top class. As one went from the "best" class to the "worst" on any grade level, the proportion of boys steadily increased, so that the "worst" classes usually were about two-thirds boys. A few precocious-independent boys usually turned up in the "best" first- and second-grade classes; however, as they became more involved in street life and began to perceive school success as less and less related to their lives, present or future, they became more and more antagonistic and uncooperative, so that many of them were reassigned to one of the "worst" classes for "safekeeping." By the third grade, the "worst" class in each grade had usually become, in effect, a "maximum security" class to "control" the most "deviant" children, the troublemakers, the "incorrigibles," the children for whom teachers and supervisors could see no good future.

Research in recent years has documented the nature and extent of the sorting process in the early school grades, particularly when children are poor and black. One study, for example, focused on the criteria used by teachers in making judgments concerning the intelligence of children in two Head Start programs.[2] Each teacher was asked to rate the children in her class according to her judgment of their intelligence. In addition, IQ tests (Stanford Binet) were given to obtain a more objective measure of the children's intellectual performance. The correlations between teacher's ratings and "objective" measures (assuming, for the moment, that performance on an IQ test is a measure of intelligence) were low in one of the two Head Start centers studied. Those children whom the teacher rated as more intelligent were more likely to carry out an activity initiated by the teacher, to follow directions, and to be cooperative in their interactions with the teacher; they appeared to display less aimless, nonpurposive behavior and were more likely to be verbal (in school), to seek teacher attention (in "constructive," work-oriented ways), and to be aware of what went on around them than their peers who were rated as less intelligent. The child rated as more intelligent also "looks happy most of the time, shows joy openly, and is an active, exuberant participator." The children rated as more intelligent thus resembled those we have described as mainstreamers.

Additional evidence on the sorting process in ghetto schools has been reported by Rist,[3] who observed teacher-child interaction in a kindergarten class in a low-income black neighborhood. On the eighth day of school, the teacher made permanent seating assignments, grouping the children around three tables. At table 1, she placed all the children on whom she had called frequently to lead the class in the Pledge of Allegiance, read the weather calendar, come to the front of the class for "show and tell," take messages to the office, take the roll, pass out materials for class projects, etc. These children were kept physically close to the teacher and had a high degree of verbal interaction with her. They used standard English more frequently and black English less often than the others. Table 1 children also were somewhat different in appearance from the other children; for example, they all wore clothes that were clean, relatively new, and pressed, while the children at tables 2 and 3 wore old and often dirty clothes. The children at table 1 generally displayed more ease in interacting with the teacher; children at tables 2 and 3 would often linger at the periphery of groups surrounding the teacher instead of crowding around her, as table 1 children did. In short, the children the teacher selected to form the table 1 group were mainstreamers, most like middle-class children. All the nonmainstream children were placed at tables 2 and 3.

The teacher's preferential treatment of some children appeared to be based on her perception of the differences among the children in appearance and behavioral styles and her belief that certain behavioral and cultural characteristics were more important than others for school achievement. The children who did not possess these characteristics were assigned to groups accorded low status by the teacher. The children at tables 2 and 3—kindergarteners, it will be recalled—were described by the teacher as "failures." The teacher not only expected more learning and achievement from the table 1 children but helped to ensure that her expectation would be fulfilled by devoting a large proportion of teaching time to them and directing relatively little control-oriented behavior to them, holding them up as models for the remainder of the class and continually reinforcing them positively by telling them they were "special." As the children moved from kindergarten into the first and then the second grade, the table 1 children remained together as the highest-achieving and most favored group. Their high-status position and the preferential, supportive treatment established in kindergarten continued, producing a widening achievement gulf between these children and all the others.

During the late 1960's the idea that pupils' level of school achievement was shaped by teachers' differential expectations for them received substantial support through the publication and widespread acceptance of *Pygmalion in the Classroom,* by Rosenthal and Jacobson.[4] The central concept behind this investigation was the self-fulfilling prophecy, the proposition that one's prediction (expectation) of another person's behavior somehow tends to be realized, either in the eyes of the predictor or, through some form of communication and influence, in the actual behavior of the other person.[5] Rosenthal and Jacobson set up an experiment in a San Francisco elementary school designed to create expectations in teachers that some pupils might show superior intellectual performance during the coming school year, and to observe the impact of these expectations upon the pupils' performance during the year. At the end of one school year, teachers were informed (falsely) that children in the school were being given a new kind of test developed by Harvard psychologists to predict future academic gains; the children were actually given a standard intelligence (IQ) test. The following September, 20 per cent of the children—about five in each class, chosen at random—were designated potential academic "spurters," and their new teachers were told that these were children who could be expected to show unusual intellectual gains in the year ahead. Thus, it was planned that the difference between these children and an undesignated group of children who constituted a control group would be entirely in the minds of the teachers. All the children were given the same test again four months after school had started, at the end of that school year, and again in May of the following year. According to Rosenthal and Jacobson, the results indicated strongly that children from whom teachers expected greater intellectual gains showed such gains.

Because these results were so widely accepted as proof of teacher self-fulfilling prophecy in the classroom, it is important to consider carefully the data on which they are based. Robert L. Thorndike has performed a valuable service by offering a critical review of these data.[6] Thorndike's analysis reveals beyond question that the scale of measurement upon which Rosenthal and Jacobson based their argument in *Pygmalion* is extremely untrustworthy.[7] Yet we believe that their basic conclusion, that self-fulfilling prophecies operate in the classroom, is substantially correct.

Recently Rosenthal has accumulated evidence to support his argument for the Pygmalion effect in the classroom.[8] He has proposed a four-factor theory to explain the influences that produce self-fulfilling prophecies in classrooms: teachers who expect their students to achieve create warmer social-emotional climates around them, give more feedback to them about their performance, teach more material and more difficult material to them, and give them more opportunities to respond and question. (It is a mistake, however, to overgeneralize this argument, for some children who are expected to achieve don't, and some who are not expected to achieve do. In any analysis of teacher-child interaction, one must also consider the effects of the children's expectations upon the teacher's behavior, something we shall look at later in this chapter.)

In spite of serious flaws in their methodology, Rosenthal and Jacobson performed a service in bringing the self-fulfilling-prophecy concept to public attention. This concept applied to education means that from the vast array of human attributes, every culture selects for cultivation those few that meet the requirements of successful functioning within that system. Children who possess these characteristics, which adults expect will contribute to success in high-status occupations, are likely to receive favored treatment in the schools, thus ensuring the frequent confirmation of initial expectations. American schools operate to socialize and sort out those children who are best able to adopt the behavior requirements of employees within a corporate-capitalistic, technocratic political economy. Among these behavioral characteristics are strong impulse controls and the subordination of emotion to rational-conceptual thinking; the willingness to channel attention and energy into somewhat autonomous efforts to achieve high levels of performance, in a dispassionate manner, on tasks often unrelated to one's personal motives and desires; cooperativeness; and willingness to accept direction from those in authority. Schooling thus functions to adapt children to characteristics of work in an advanced capitalist country—such characteristics as job fragmentation, hierarchical lines of authority, bureaucratic organization, and unequal reward. In order for most individuals to succeed, first in school and then on the job, they must accept and come to view as natural these possibly unattractive, relatively undemocratic aspects of work.

Although the schools nominally are charged with the responsibility for promoting cognitive growth, a larger view of the relationship between schools and the political economy suggests that their primary functions are inculcation of the personal-social behaviors and moral outlooks suitable to the work-role requirements of large corporations; the early sorting of children into groups based largely upon the extent to which the children display such personal-social behaviors; and the conferring of credentials (diplomas, degrees) upon those who successfully meet these behavioral criteria. These credentials, required by employers for entry into most better-paying, high-status jobs, are withheld from those who do not behave "properly," thus barring access to such jobs. In a country in which there is wide support or at least lip service for democratic precepts, egalitarian ideologies, and a liberal ethos, the sorting of children into groups that receive unequal attention and rewards in school and in later life must be defended on the ground that it rests on objective assessments of differential ability and merit rather than on personal, class, or race prejudice. Therefore, those behaviors that are believed to be required for success in the political economy are often labeled by those with power as indications of "intelligence" and "competence," and children are observed and tested for signs of such behavior in school. Rather than leave the assessment of "intelligence" and "competence" to teacher judgment alone, mass-produced standardized tests are used to define and measure these attributes "objectively,"—the former as IQ points, the latter as scores equal to "grade norms" on tests of reading achievement, which through word-games assess familiarity with specific words (vocabulary) and the ability to match designated multiple-choice answers with the content of paragraphs (reading comprehension). The fact that middle-class children tend to score higher than lower-class children on such tests is used as justification for the unequal rewards they will receive within the social order; unequal rewards are seen as the inevitable competitive outcome of differential merit in intelligence and competence. Those children who, upon entry into school, provide more signs of the behaviors considered to be intelligent and competent by teachers and administrators—i.e., those who appear middle class—receive favored treatment, are expected to achieve, and usually are separated from those viewed as less likely to succeed. Thus, the schools function significantly to maintain class and caste advantages by reinforcing and maintaining the initial advantage of white middle-class children (and those who most resemble them) in adapting to the demands of the social order, legitimizing this perpetuation of unequal rewards by conferring and withholding the credentials required for employment while professing the meritocratic view that rewards are always based upon objective assessments of intelligence and competence.[9]

David C. McClelland has recently criticized the naïveté of many psychologists who have helped to perpetuate social inequality through their dissemination of intelligence tests:

> . . . suppose you are a ghetto resident in the Roxbury section of Boston. To qualify for being a policeman you have to take a three-hour-long general intelligence test in which you must know the meaning of words like "quell," "pyromaniac," and "lexicon." If you do not know enough of these words or cannot play analogy games with them, you do not qualify. . . . You, not unreasonably, feel angry, upset, and unsuccessful. Because you do not know those words you are considered to have low intelligence, and since you consequently have to take a low-status job and are unhappy, you contribute to the celebrated correlations of low intelligence with low occupational status and poor adjustment. Psychologists should be ashamed of themselves for promoting a view of general intelligence that has encouraged such a testing program.[10]

The relevance of success on such word games to successful performance as a policeman is dubious; yet on the strength of such measurements people are sorted into different status levels in the social order in a manner justified as objectively meritocratic. Other credentials a man has—his habits, values, accent, clothing, and connections by education and family—determine how acceptable he is to management and business associates and, hence, substantially affect his entry into and success in the job.

In the early grades in Harlem, it was common for teachers and supervisors to judge that children who were not mainstreamers had very low intelligence and little potential for academic achievement. In making such judgments, they were often responding to differences in the behavior patterns of the children rather than to differences in intelligence, learning ability, or achievement strivings. This is not to say that there is no relationship between school behavior and intelligence; certainly there is a reciprocal-interactive relationship between the development and use of various components of intelligence, the social-emotional aspects of a child's behavior, and cultural definitions of competence. However, teachers and school administrators often had decided opinions about how children should look and function, and they often tended to equate intelligence, competence, and ability with middle-class white behavior styles. They often failed to see the intelligence and competence manifested in the survival strategies of precocious-independent and many ambivalent children, because these strategies made the children hard to control and manipulate. In addition, ambivalents, precocious-independents, and submissives looked considerably different from the white middle-class model most often associated with future economic and social success (not an unrealistic expectation in a racist society). Therefore such children were often regarded as less deserving of time and attention than the few mainstreamer children in the school, who, it was believed, had a chance to "be somebody" in America. It was common for school personnel to develop a perception of most children in Harlem schools as essentially less capable than white children; they saw them as children whose failure was, after all, basically their own fault and that of their families rather than the fault of the teachers or the school.

Because the ambivalent, precocious-independent, and submissive life-styles largely represented attempts to cope with stressful life conditions within the ghetto and in an oppressive society, they did limit the uses children made of their intelligence and did curtail their willingness and ability to strive to accomplish impersonal, cognitively oriented tasks in school. For example, fifty Harlem first-graders were observed over the course of a year by a school psychologist because the children's teachers reported that they were having learning or behavior problems.[11] All of them showed a great deal of fear and anxiety in their reactions to a testing situation, related to preoccupations with violence and punishment. Much of their behavior in the testing situation appeared to be rigid and non-achievement-oriented, as if they had learned to act in a manner they believed to be safe, particularly in a mainstream, white-controlled situation. The children often seemed to be pretending not to know or care rather than risk punishment by doing the wrong thing. Children in a community like Central Harlem obviously present greater problems to teachers attempting to implement standard achievement goals than do children in more affluent communities. But to use this fact to justify segregation and preferential treatment of the mainstreamer children, as we have noted, exacerbates the conflicts of the other children and fosters teacher-pupil antagonism.

The promise of assignment to a class at the top of the grade, a class of "nice," "normal," "reachable" children, was often used to reward teachers who had suffered through a number of years with groups of "difficult" children ("putting in your time"). A common hope of many committed but demoralized teachers in the Harlem elementary schools was, "Well, if I can just survive this year, maybe next year I'll get the 'one' class."

Placing the submissives, the precocious-independents, and the ambivalents together in large classroom groups only intensified the characteristics associated with their life-style adaptations. In such classrooms a submissive cannot get enough personal attention, support, and encouragement from an adult to bring him out; a precocious-independent child is not encouraged to learn to trust and become less rigid, because his stubbornness and defiance often bring him into conflict with the teacher and the other children; an ambivalent child goes through cyclical periods of frustration and anger as his attempts to relate dependently to adults often are responded to unsympathetically.

A frequent result of this situation is that teachers fail to have sufficient impact upon the children to help them cope with the academic demands of school. Most of the submissives, precocious independents, and ambivalents fail to achieve normatively in school. Their failures only exacerbate their personal shame and doubt and decrease the chances that they will achieve the credentials required for steady, well-paid employment in later life.

Because Harlem schools did not have the facilities, the programs, or the personnel to meet the needs of most children, the schools failed to be sufficiently supportive of the children much as many parents had failed to be very supportive of the children. Early withdrawals of parental attention and support led many children to turn to one another at an early age. The school's failure had somewhat the same result: Many children became much more involved with status-related concerns in their peer group as they moved into the upper elementary grades than with schoolwork or school achievement. School became a place where children went more to meet their peers and to have fun with them than to work, study, or achieve academically.

During the 1960's, the question increasingly raised was, What differentiates the small percentage of ghetto children who achieve academically from the majority who do not? The answer throughout the 1960's and still to a large extent is basically that the children who achieve in ghetto schools display characteristics and behaviors quite similar to those of academic achievers in white communities—e.g., a positive self-concept, substantial impulse controls, directed individual achievement strivings, and a willingness to accept direction from adult authorities.[12] Positive self-concept may be both a contributor to and a result of successful school achievement and positive feedback from adults.

In a study comparing eighty high- and eighty low-achieving children in

Central Harlem carried out in the mid-1960's, it was found that the high achievers had better self-concepts and more impulse controls, which appeared to be closely related to the teacher's positive perception of them and to their cognitive efficiency; their cognitive strengths lay chiefly in conventional verbal-informational areas, which they approached with accuracy and considerable control.[13] There appeared to be considerable anxiety and tension in the entire sample of Harlem children, coupled with intellectually passive and unassertive behavior; however, the high achievers were less handicapped in this respect; they had more effective mechanisms for dealing with anxiety and tension in school situations even though they sometimes appeared to be too controlled and conforming.

An analysis of home and family variables in the backgrounds of the children revealed some important differences between the groups.[14] Compared with the mother of a low achiever, the mother of a high achiever typically expressed greater interest in and sensitivity to her child as a specific individual, and she used less severe punishment for misbehavior. Although most mothers expressed concern for education, the parents of the high-achieving children were themselves better educated and were rated significantly higher in concern for education than the mothers of low achievers. The mothers of high achievers appeared to have greater knowledge of and sophistication regarding the nature and functioning of the school system and broader social issues. At the practical level, they were more likely to implement their desire to have the children progress academically by providing more structured, better cared-for homes and more adequate study facilities; their children had significantly better school-attendance records than the low-achieving children. The mothers of high-achieving children appeared to be better off economically than the mothers of low-achieving children; they held higher-level jobs, and their apartments had fewer persons per room. Thus, it would appear that the high achievers within the lower-class black community came from somewhat better socio-economic circumstances than their low-achieving peers. As Davidson and Greenberg conclude,

> . . . it may be that the high achievers started with some advantages in the cognitive, ego, and affective areas and came from somewhat better homes. Whatever the source of the initial advantages, the school probably magnifies them through the practice of homogeneous ability grouping and the tendency for teachers to show greater approval to the more favored children, thus setting up a self-perpetuating spiral effect. Possibly, also, teachers lack an understanding of the learning abilities of lower-class children and their expectations of them are too low.[15]

Zena Blau, studying white working-class preadolescents in Gary, Indiana,[16] also found that maternal aspirations for children's school achievement and maternal childrearing practices were significantly related to the children's school achievement, but in a different way for boys and girls. The white working-class girls' level of school achievement was highly influenced by their mothers' aspirations for them, even though maternal childrearing practices varied considerably. This was not the case for boys, whose school achievement was more related to their mothers' childrearing practices than to their mothers' aspirations for the boys' school success. Blau relates the differential impact of maternal aspirations on boys and girls to the working-class tendency to socialize children differentially by sex. From their early years, girls are given more warmth and attention and are disciplined less harshly. Perhaps for this reason they tend to behave in a manner likely to please their mothers; thus, the higher the mother's educational aspirations for the girl, the harder the girl is likely to try to achieve in school. For boys, on the other hand, the combination of less warmth and attention and harsher discipline appears to weaken the desire to please their mothers; thus, even when a boy's mother has high scholastic aspirations for her son, he may become so alienated by her childrearing practices that he will not try hard to please her by achieving in school. The paradox is that, even though working-class parents generally have higher educational aspirations for their sons, the daughters achieve in school at a higher level than the boys.

We suggest that most boys, white or black, as they progress through the elementary school, are caught between lessening or ambivalent desires to please their mothers, on the one hand, and an increasing desire to be "one of the boys," on the other. For working- and lower-class boys who experience less maternal warmth and attentiveness and more coercive discipline than their middle-class peers, the mothers' aspirations for the boys' school achievement rarely can compete with the lure of the masculine peer group, which does not support striving for school achievement. Those lower-class boys who are socialized more as girls are socialized—i.e., with relatively more warmth and attentiveness—are most likely to try to please their mothers through school achievement (if their mothers have such aspirations for them) and to resist the attraction of masculine street groups. Such boys are more likely to work out some compromise in which they continue to strive to meet their mothers' aspirations while they nevertheless become and remain "one of the boys."

The presence of a father who is well educated and whose occupation depends upon school-related learning may significantly reinforce maternal efforts to influence a son's school achievement. A relatively uneducated father who is a blue-collar laborer may also influence his son toward achieving in school by providing a positive evaluation of scholastic success. On the other hand, more typically the blue-collar father, working under conditions that require conformity and submission to authority and in a world that reinforces sex-role segregation, is not too likely to expect or demand from his son continuous striving for academic success, particularly if such striving is seen to contribute to a lack of conformity in behavior at home and an orientation to life, including closeness to the mother, that might be viewed as effeminate.[17] Thus, working-class socialization patterns encourage the development of characteristics in children that are more adapted to lower- than to higher-status jobs; and the sorting process in school tends to keep children at this level of the economy.

In Harlem schools, children usually know very well which class is the "one" class, the "best" class, the class expected to achieve; and they know that the "six" class, the "worst" in the grade, is for children who can't read or who are "the baddest." This knowledge of assignment to a group labeled unintelligent by teachers and stupid by other children generated an additional burden of shame and doubt and added a special intensity to their tendency to reject the school's values and demands. The children in the "best" class, encouraged by the school staff to see themselves as special, brighter, and of more worth than the others in the school, developed a somewhat elitist mentality.

MOTIVATION AND SCHOOL ACHIEVEMENT

The drive to perfect a skill, to accomplish a task more efficiently or quickly, to produce a better product, or to do something well in accordance with perceived standards of excellence seems to have its origin in high levels of parental involvement in the early years of childhood. It develops, at least in part, out of performance standards established and enforced by parents, reinforced by parental approval and affection.[18] When a child has been allowed to remain emotionally dependent on his parents, the withdrawal (or threat of withdrawal) of parental love because of his failure to behave in accordance with parental standards is likely to cause the child anxiety. If it is not too severe, this anxiety will energize his efforts to meet parental standards so as to keep or regain their approval.

As we have noted, many Harlem children did not maintain the intense involvement with parents associated with the development of strong achievement motives and were not "pushed" by parents to master cognitively oriented tasks. Even those who were so encouraged were generally not allowed to be sufficiently dependent—nor did they receive enough emotional support or stability—to make the potential withdrawal of love a potent motivator for behavior that would please their parents (or later, teachers). Most of the achieving children we knew had a close relationship with at least one adult who provided some combination of emotional support and achievement "pushing."

Some of those children who had not learned to read well in the elementary school grades gave up trying. Others habitually tried to hide their lack of reading ability. Most, however, were unable to channel their anxiety into achievement-oriented behaviors as they fell farther behind in the functional reading skills required for school achievement each year. An even more important factor disrupting any consistent efforts toward school achievement was the pressing physical needs of the children and their intense emotional concerns related to the lack of nurturance, acceptance, direction, consistency, and protection.

If we look behind the school achievement of more advantaged children, we are likely to find that intrinsic motivation for learning often has little or nothing to do with their behavior in school. Many middle-class elementary school children become resigned to the fact the school is (and has always been) a rather authoritarian place run by adults. They learn that the important thing to do in school is to find out what the teacher wants them to say or write—the "right answers"—and to say or write them upon request. They learn that "being good" in school means not getting out of your seat unless the teacher says it is all right to do so and always knowing the "right answers" (even if you don't care much about the subject or understand what the answers mean).[19]

Because of their characteristically intense dependency relationship with their mothers, most middle-class children have been socialized successfully to achieve in school. Middle-class elementary school children generally seem to be able to relate to teachers much as they relate to their mothers, hence displeasing the teacher by not knowing the "right answer" causes them anxiety. Even if they are somewhat frustrated in school, they are generally comfortable enough and secure enough to channel their anxiety into directed striving to meet the demands of teachers.

Many Harlem children had extreme difficulty pursuing intrinsic motives to learn or playing the school's game. In their efforts to learn they became easily disorganized and tended to relate ambivalently to teachers. In displeasing their parents, they often ran relatively little risk of significant emotional or material loss, especially when the displeasure was related to failing in school (an everyday occurrence in Harlem). And what could most teachers in a traditional school do? The teachers (like the parents) could not give the child enough emotionally or materially to make him willing to strive to please them; nor could they force him to do so. When Harlem children encountered difficulty or boredom in school, they did not have enough comfort or security to overcome frustration by increased task-oriented efforts. And so the children turned away from their teachers, as many had turned away from their parents. By the second grade, most teachers found that the force exacted by the children's peers in the classroom and throughout the school almost counterbalanced the teacher's impact.

PEER INFLUENCE AND ACHIEVEMENT

Because teachers had become largely irrelevant to most Harlem children by the upper elementary grades, and because the early sorting process increasingly forced children who were most susceptible to group influence into the same classes, peer-group activities came to command much of the attention and energy expended by the children in most classrooms. The often conflictful nature of the children's relationship to one another, exacerbated by the frustrations of the classroom, led to a heightening of tensions in the classroom. Many of the children spent a lot of their time in the classroom watching each other somewhat nervously until finally something happened—an exchange of insults, a confrontation, a fight. There was a great deal of teasing, shaming, and open aggression, and the defenses used against them often were seen frequently in classes below the "best" one.

The ambivalent children appeared to be more susceptible to peer-group influences than the other types of children. They responded more openly to their own dependency needs than either the precocious independents, who tended to avoid dependent relationships when available, or the submissives, who became resigned to a lack of opportunity for such relationships. Some of the precocious independents became clique or gang leaders because of their audacity and resourcefulness. Through their defiant attitudes and displays of physical and verbal power, they often set the tone for group activity. Other precocious independents seemed to be "loners," having no real affiliation with any other children. Such children were often quite unpopular, even feared by the other children. The submissives were either socially unattached or were on the fringes of a group of more outgoing children.

Most of the children became so caught up in the group that a single incident could keep them agitated and disorganized for an entire day. One fight, one wild outburst against a teacher or by a teacher, one complaint, any potentially dramatic event could start a chain reaction of nervous impulsive behavior, which the children could not control or stop. This common susceptibility to excitement resembled the condition that Redl and Wineman have called "group psychological intoxication."[20] In such situations, a great deal of new anxiety was generated continuously, which further disorganized the children's achievement-oriented efforts.

Teachers in Harlem frequently complained that they could not get the children to pay attention during a lesson. This is an age-old problem for the schoolmaster, but today theorists of intellectual development are saying that children are intrinsically motivated to learn, that they have natural curiosity and a desire to know more about the world. The implication is that, if children don't pay attention to their lessons in school, the fault must lie with the curriculum or the methods of teaching. It is often suggested that children should be allowed to involve themselves more in exploring, experimenting, manipulating, discovering, and planning their course of study. It certainly can be argued that a great deal of curriculum content in the ghetto schools is patently irrelevant to the everyday experiences of the children and that by avoiding personally significant or controversial issues, it provides a distorted image of the real world. However, similar charges can be leveled against the curriculum being presented to children in more affluent areas, who nonetheless are learning to read. Many city children have never visited a farm; yet they find some interest in a story entitled "A Visit to the Farm," and they learn to read it. Conversely, many children in Harlem who had the new reading materials prepared to deal somewhat more realistically with the world of urban minority-group children were still grossly retarded in reading. These facts suggest that, despite their contributions, new reading materials cannot alone produce much achievement on the part of low-income black children, at least not in traditional classrooms.

Some children may have difficulties in focusing or sustaining attention that have little to do with the curriculum or the teaching methods used. We do not know how often such impairments are a major contributor to a lack of school achievement. However, research on children with learning problems highlights their potential importance. For example, reading retardation and difficulties with symbolic learning in a sample of seventh- and eighth-grade boys of normal intelligence have been associated with their tendency to be less attentive to the stimuli involved in learning tasks than children without these problems, and studies of children with behavioral or learning disorders diagnosed as the result of minimal brain dysfunction indicate that disorders of attention are a common problem among this group.[21] Davidson and Greenberg, in their comparative study of "high"- and "low"-achieving Harlem children, found that difficulties on perceptual-motor tasks were more common among their sample than in other groups of children of the same age, with the low achievers displaying significantly more perceptual-motor impairment than the high achievers.[22] Most of the perceptual-motor impairment was judged to be caused by "emotional interference"; in only 10 per cent of the cases was there suspicion of brain damage. Nevertheless, since minimal brain damage is often associated with premature birth, and since the rate of prematurity is quite high among low-income blacks, it is possible that a substantial minority of cases of low reading achievement among low-income black children (particularly boys, who appear to be more vulnerable to nervous-system disorders than girls) have an organic basis.[23]

Another important factor related to attentiveness is the poor nutritional status of some low-income black children.[24] Children who are poorly nourished or undernourished are generally less attentive to the environment and more likely to be distracted from schoolwork by their own visceral sensations; they may therefore become unable to sustain attention to school tasks.

Various problems associated with urban poverty put low-income black children at high risk for a variety of physical illnesses that can lead to frequent absences from school, with consequent interruptions in sequential learning or impairments in functioning in school. Medical examinations of 542 Harlem youths aged twelve to fifteen revealed that two thirds had at least one medical condition (not counting dental problems) that deviated significantly from what physicians considered normal, and that one in three had at least two of these conditions.[25] One fifth of these children had vision and eye problems; one sixth were found to have respiratory-tract disorders; and one sixth had heart or blood-pressure abnormalities. One fifth reported having frequent colds and another fifth reported frequent headaches.

Living in the inner city, low-income black youth are exposed to certain noxious substances that can have deleterious effects. For example, the New York City Department of Health estimates that, at any moment, as many as 30,000 inner-city children between twelve months and six years of age may have absorbed a significant amount of lead into their bodies by eating peeling paint and plaster containing lead.[26] A study comparing a sample of primarily low-income New York children classed as hyperactive with a non-hyperactive control group found that the hyperactive children had significantly higher levels of body lead.[27] Heroin is another noxious substance that circulates extensively in the ghetto. Harlem Hospital reports that one in every twenty-nine babies delivered there is the child of an addicted mother, and no one knows how many other such births are not diagnosed or reported.[28] By the fifth or sixth grade, many Harlem children know where to obtain heroin, and a small minority are tempted to experiment with it before they reach their teens.

The inconsistency in daily life experienced by some Harlem children may also lead to the tendency to be inattentive. When a child is faced with an environment that presents him with many stimuli he cannot effectively organize, order, or predict, he may begin defensively to restrict his tendency to be attentive to novel situations.

In addition to neurological impairment, nutrition and health problems, and inconsistency in daily life, there are personal-social factors that deflect the attention of many ghetto children from their schoolwork. The anxiety frequently aroused in disorganized Harlem classrooms often leads to an inability to focus attention upon schoolwork. Piaget, from whose work experts on the "disadvantaged child" borrow many concepts, did not give much consideration to the role of emotions in intellectual development. He studied children who were reasonably secure by giving them non-threatening tasks to perform in familiar, safe situations. We think that frightened, anxious children are unlikely to be as open to new experience or to take such delight in problem solving as Piaget's subjects. Such children would be more likely to display defensive behavior—lack of trust, unwillingness to take a chance on being wrong, a traumatic response to errors, lack of perseverance on difficult tasks, and an inability to sustain attention on a problem. The inclination to explore and manipulate the environment and to utilize physical and intellectual skills in problem solving is most likely to be manifested by children whose physical and emotional needs have been reasonably satisfied, children who have been reasonably safe and protected.

Bruner's distinction between coping and defending is useful in attempting to understand problems in attending to school work.[29] Coping behavior involves paying attention to a problem and trying to comprehend and act upon the requirements for a solution. Defending involves the development of strategies for avoiding stressful situations or escaping from problems that jeopardize personal safety. Children who have experienced serious difficulties in interpersonal relationships in the past are likely to channel energies that might otherwise go into carefree exploration and attempts to master the environment into defense, frequently scanning the environment for "things that will hurt." Anything perceived as a potential threat may lead to anxiety and attempts to escape contact and avoid danger. For many Harlem children, accustomed to a great deal of ridicule and physical punishment, this perceptual alertness to potential danger requires so much energy and attention as to make coping with schoolwork very difficult.

Classroom situations or aspects of subject matter at times may have aroused threatening personal-subjective mental associations by stimulating aggressive fantasies and impulses or the fear of aggression from others. Attempts to master a difficult task may have led to protective withdrawal of attention and effort, so that the child's already eroded self-esteem would not be dealt another blow by acknowledging or having others perceive still another inadequacy (which could lead to punishment).

In a classroom of children who often sought to discover others' inadequacies and expose them in stinging repartee, who were easily moved to physical aggression, paying a great deal of attention to other children rather than to books or lessons was unavoidable for many children already predisposed to defensive perceptual operations. The sorting process, which tended to group together the children who were most likely to be concerned about their personal adequacy or safety and to behave in ways that exposed the inadequacies or threatened the safety of others, intensified the problem.

Several of our fifth- and sixth-grade pupils seemed to have some vague insight into the causes of their relative inability to concentrate on lessons. Just before an important test, a number of children who seemed motivated to do well would ask us if they could go into another room or move a chair into a relatively isolated corridor outside the classroom to take a test or work on a lesson away from the other children. Once we spent about half the school year with a fifth-grade class in an old, dilapidated school building and then moved into a brand-new classroom in a completely new school building. The new classroom had bookcases and movable tables and chairs, unlike the old classroom. After experimenting with different arrangements of the furniture, the children decided that they would like to move the bookcases away from the wall and distribute them around the room. It soon became clear to us that the children's idea was very useful in dealing with the problem of attention. The final arrangement brought small same-sex groups together (four to six to a table grouping) with a bookcase strategically placed near each group so that it became, in effect, a barrier screening out distracting and overstimulating perceptions. As a result of this simple maneuver, the children seemed more relaxed, there was less teasing and fighting, and the development of a work orientation (as opposed to the socialization-affiliation orientation noted previously) became possible. A number of the children seemed to make significant gains in achievement following the move to the new room.

In an extensive survey of racial and class differences in school achievement, Coleman and his associates found that schools had little influence on a child's performance on standardized IQ and achievement tests that was independent of his family socio-economic background and the socio-economic background of the school.[30] Most subsequent reanalyses of the data bearing on cognitive performance have supported this conclusion.[31] However, these studies do not establish any clear relationship between school resources and children's emotional-social development. Because schools apparently have had little effect upon children's cognitive-test performance independent of their status in the existing social order, and because such test performance is used as the basis for denying entrance to better-paying jobs, the inequalities imposed upon low-income-family children by the society and mediated through their home, neighborhood, and peer environments appear to become relatively fixed during the elementary school years.

In isolating specific correlates of school achievement, Coleman and his staff found that "attributes of other students account for far more variation in the achievement of minority group children than do any attributes of school facilities and slightly more than do attributes of staff."[32] Further, among the lower-achieving black and Puerto Rican groups, achievement seemed to be more dependent on the characteristics of fellow students than among the higher-achieving white and Oriental American groups. Apparently the strengths and weaknesses that poor children bring to school are largely determined by their ethnicity and social class and are not significantly changed by their experiences at school. The influence of teachers, school facilities, and curriculums is often overshadowed and counteracted by the influence that low-income black children have upon one another, once they are homogeneously grouped through the sorting process.

On the basis of our own observations, we believe that the schools of Harlem have had very little positive influence on the majority of the pupils who passed through their doors, and a negative impact upon many of them. On the other hand, it appeared to us that the children actually changed the school environment to make it a little more congruent with their street world, rather than the school having any significant success in encouraging an alternative life-style among most of the children.

RESOCIALIZATION OF THE TEACHER

In our previous discussion of the self-fulfilling prophecy in the classroom we drew three conclusions: First, we are confident that the self-fulfilling prophecy does in fact operate in the classroom. Second, because of the extensive, rather uncritical attention this concept has received, it has been overgeneralized as an explanation of teacher-child interaction and low achievement. Third, there is a tendency to view teacher-child relationships as unilateral rather than reciprocal, which fails to take into account the child's behavior and personality as contributing to the interaction. Here, we shall consider the impact upon teachers of children's expectations and behavior, as well as the impact of the school as an institution.

Until the early 1960's, almost all the literature directly addressed to the slum child's schooling explained academic failure in terms of characteristics of the individual child and/or his immediate family and subcultural milieu. This literature was increasingly criticized during the mid-1960's, especially by those who were attempting to call national attention to the plight of the children. Such writers tended to lay primary or exclusive blame on the teachers and school administrators for black children's low achievement. In addition, they made some attempt to understand the role of the school as a social and cultural institution in perpetuating injustice and inequality. However, they seemed insufficiently aware that the children and the school did have an effect upon teacher behavior and attitudes.

After a few days in a ghetto school, it was common for teachers to forget that their professed aim was to foster children's learning and achieving. They gradually lost the feeling that they were in a meaningful job, let alone a profession. The teacher's assumption, unvoiced but understood, was that teacher and children were engaged in a contest. This might result, in part, from prior race and class prejudice, perhaps developed from rumors and media reports of the "slum school" as a blackboard jungle, but more often it resulted from assorted difficulties with individuals and groups of school children during the teacher's first days on the job. This resocialization of teachers into a contest mentality also stemmed from the children's sense of schooling as a contest in which one could be bored, shamed, and made to feel inferior. It was common for a child or several children to advise their new teacher that iron-clad authoritarian control was the way to handle the class or a group of children in it. Teachers would frequently receive friendly advice offered by a former student regarding the incoming class: "Teacher, you be nice, they be mean; you be mean, they be nice."

Most teachers began with some sensitivity or desire to succeed, but in a matter of days, weeks, or months they became more or less desensitized, irritable, angry, or numbed by this demoralizing experience. A number of newly appointed teachers after a few days were already thinking of leaving Harlem. It had taken some of them four years of college to "prepare" for this fight. Think what this says about our society and our educational enterprise! Yet it happened each September.

Most of those who stayed changed. No doubt all jobs tend to affect the personalities of those who hold them. In teaching as it is now constituted, one must continually ask children to do various things that one feels will contribute to their learning and socialization, and to classroom order as well. But prolonged experience in asking and demanding things of children—not unlike the sort of thing parents do—for several consecutive hours five days a week changes people. Continued asking and demanding as a way of relating to children is a central core of teacher behavior as it now exists. Underneath this behavior often lies not only the wish to help children learn intellectual and social skills but also the fear that one's ability to control the classroom will be undermined. The teacher tries to "teach" children about respect, so that his basic authority to regulate their behavior will not be challenged.

Whether his ultimate concern is protection of preferred ways of doing things, fear of being humiliated at the hands of the children, or fear of jeopardizing his reputation and his job, the teacher abhors any challenge to his authority, whether earned or imposed, useful or restricting. For whatever reason, in Harlem the concern with control in the classroom permeated teachers' behavior and mentality. A deadening atmosphere of containment pervaded many of the classrooms. Teachers continually demanded that children obey them in attempts to strengthen their authority. They also demanded that the children do various things related to achievement. Drill, practice, and repetition were heavily stressed. But efforts to teach large classes as a single group and a lack of consideration for timing and pacing in the use of traditional techniques frequently resulted in futility. Thus, failure in attempts to teach influenced teachers under pressure to drift into, actively adopt, or reinforce authoritarian attitudes and behaviors that stressed controlling and quieting children as their main objective. These, in turn, resulted in reinforcement of the teachers' fear of the children, which became acute if a teacher was unable to stabilize the class through effective management or blatant authoritarian rule.

In the schools of Central Harlem, then, the authoritarian aspects of traditional schooling were heightened and intensified, with an inevitable effect on the teachers' personalities. It was tragic to watch ardent and idealistic new teachers struggle to maintain their excitement and commitment to making a positive difference in the lives of the children. Most of them soon turned sour, their kindness, interest, concern, and predilection for reason and fairness diluted or stifled as these young teachers were pressured by children, administrators, and other teachers to adopt an authoritarian demeanor and take up autocratic rule.

None of us is free from authoritarian attitudes and behaviors; few of us experienced much real democracy in our schooling, from kindergarten through high school or college. In the slum school, though, even those teachers who were inclined to encourage initiative and self-direction in children found that their efforts had far less impact than they had hoped. The question became, how much frustration could these novice teachers endure before they, like the veteran teachers, would devote their energies to controlling the children through authoritarian measures. Teachers did try to some extent to influence the children's attitudes, to impress upon them the traditional virtues of obedience, studiousness, respect, and constraint.

As we have said, most young children in Harlem seriously mistrusted adults; they anticipated that adults would use arbitrary power to hurt or limit them; they expected little attention, help, or protection from adults. These attitudes and expectations were reinforced by school personnel, most of whom were unequal to and felt burdened by the problems the children presented. The children, in frustration, increasingly turned to each other rather than teachers and thus created a precociously strong and potentially explosive classroom peer culture—one that was quite resentful of adults and that carried heavy grudges. These children, in schools that were not committed and structured to meet their needs, would openly violate school rules and display contempt for school personnel. The children did not feel they had much to lose, because they saw the school year after year engaged in an unsuccessful holding action while they themselves fell farther and farther back.

Many teachers concentrated their efforts on making children submissive because of their own fear and a hardening moral indignation regarding the uncooperative, defiant attitudes of the children. The teachers became hostile toward the children because they resented the perceived necessity to devote so much time and energy to classroom management.

Critics of life in ghetto schools often fail to recognize that the anger and hostility of many teachers stemmed from the children's failure to pay attention to lessons when the teachers tried their best to teach. The general atmosphere of demoralization, disrespect, and futility contributed to the verbal hostility in many classrooms.

Some teachers told sharply rather than asked gently, mainly to try to make themselves understood, to make children obey, to save themselves from minute-to-minute combat. While racism and disrespect for children often played a part in the hostility and ridicule teachers directed at their pupils, the efficacy of sometimes brutal treatment in forcing children's compliance strengthened many teachers' belief that it was the only way to relate to the children. Large classes, lack of materials, and bureaucratic impediments also contributed to the teachers' desire to discourage autonomy and initiative in children and made the children feel that school was not a place to find warmth, protection, and friendship.

The teachers' use of language changed as they became more authoritarian and more directive, away from complex, explanatory sentences toward more restrictive, controlling signals. We believe that this change resulted, first, from some teachers' difficulty in making themselves understood by the children and, second, from the teachers' aggressive and defensive battle for control with the children as the balance of power shifted between them.

A new teacher typically set out to try to give the children what he thought they needed—that is, he spent a lot of time pressuring the children to pay attention, to be obedient, passive, and quiet. Such demands also were calculated to establish order, which most teachers needed to feel comfortable. Since the children had gone that route before in their homes and with former teachers, they were commonly inclined to offer substantial resistance. Even when they wished to comply, to be docile and "good," children whose needs were all too pressing, whose frustrations were highly abrasive, and who had been made defensive and resentful by previous responses of teachers would typically be thrown into painful and confusing ambivalence or would rebel or withdraw. The school's power to inculcate or reinforce ambivalence, rebellion, or withdrawal was enormous. The intensity and pervasiveness of the emphasis on domination of the children and the undercutting of initiative perhaps constitute the most marked difference between the cues commonly transmitted to poor black school children and those that middle-class children are likely to receive from their teachers.

Teachers who had been accustomed to relating to others in a rather egalitarian manner had more difficulty managing their classes than teachers to whom a system of positional ("pecking order") control came more naturally. Most new teachers came to utilize a positional-control system during their first or second year on the job. Those who did not had severe "discipline problems" or could be counted upon to quit. In their classrooms, a large minority of the children became relatively free to try to call the shots, to beat the teacher in gaining the upper hand. "How to teach the urban child" books that deny, ignore, or minimize the "combat zone" atmosphere of the typical classroom simply overlook a plain fact of ghetto classroom life.

Teachers were usually at a loss to establish an atmosphere inviting both to the children and to themselves. After a while the teachers' authoritarian attitudes, their coerciveness and bitterness, made the children more and more sullen, negative, antagonistic, and apathetic. It took great emotional and professional resources for any teacher to avoid total classroom deterioration. Some worked very hard for very long hours (including after school preparations); some spent most of their time attacking and defending against the children; others floundered anxiously or apathetically. A few became truly accomplished and continued to grow in competence, both in curriculum areas and in relating to the children.

In some classes there was no continuous conflict. When a teacher who was expert as a controller was assigned to a class that had potential as a conventionally middle-class group, the teacher was often able to get the children to work harder and achieve more in reading, writing, and math. The teacher's control of such a classroom was likely to be less harsh, at least overtly. Nevertheless, often in these classrooms teachers would tell and the children would usually do what they were told. The atmosphere usually would be characterized by austerity that hampered intrinsic motivation, mastery behavior, and discovery. The children in these classes were learning the three Rs pretty well but their enjoyment of learning and thinking and their initiative, self-direction, cooperativeness, and exploratory techniques in learning situations remained sorely underdeveloped. White society, college training, and the ghetto schools themselves were hardly taking that sort of achievement seriously for black children. The ideas of Dewey, Piaget, A. S. Neill, Bruner, and others were seen essentially as items for consumption by white teachers working with white children, especially middle- and upper-middle-class children. Education majors and teachers were seldom encouraged to pursue methodologies and curriculums that were capable of stimulating the fullest possible development of black children.

Within the deteriorated circumstances of Harlem classrooms, the individual teacher's strength of personality and his durability determined his effectiveness. No other factor was so important. Teacher techniques, acquaintance with curricula, and even motivation took a back seat to their personal strengths as individuals. The teacher's warmth, reliability, concern, tenacity, confidence, and planfulness were the most important factors determining whether anything worthwhile would happen in a classroom in Central Harlem.

Strong teacher motivation and imagination could make an impact in a classroom, but success usually required forcefulness, tenacity, reliability, and continuous planning and on-going assessment. Some deeply committed young teachers firmly believed that if only they could make learning exciting for the children through various forms of motivation, the children's learning would blossom. They were sometimes bitterly disappointed. A single strategic flaw in an otherwise skilled teacher could result in her undoing in the classroom. One young teacher ran a chaotic classroom because she did not say "no" to her children often enough, and when she did she somehow failed to make the children believe in her will to discipline them.

During the summer vacation, this same teacher tutored several of her most difficult children with amazing success. Apparently working with a few children diminished her need to control them, and the impact of a personalized relationship brought out the best learning experiences the children had ever had and helped them grow as individuals as well. This experience and countless reported similar experiences suggest that, in order for most lower-class and blue-collar children to become more motivated and task-oriented in learning, to develop more autonomy and initiative, schools must become more personalized and more homelike, at least until the middle elementary years. Adults who recognize and relate to the children's concerns and interests, both personal and task-oriented, can sustain them in their desire to become intellectually as well as emotionally mature. Harlem is filled with children who spend much time and energy resisting and combating adults in and out of school and who need more opportunity to enjoy childhood and to immerse themselves in it.

Many Harlem children were sorely tempted to vent their hostilities on anyone they felt would not hit back at them—which could include their teachers. Again, such a situation created defensive feelings in the teachers involved and encouraged a round of manipulative forays in the classroom.

One should not get the impression that the Harlem classroom atmosphere was never friendly and relaxed. Even in some chaotic or rigidly run classes, there could be many moments of pleasant informality between teachers and children—oases amidst the hostility and futility. Classrooms could also be found in which the children and their teachers liked each other. Sometimes a teacher liked the children but found that many of them remained mistrustful of her feelings. Sometimes a group of children could have liked a teacher who did not, in turn, like or respect many of them. One could see children who were subtly abused or neglected by their teachers and who nonetheless liked the teachers and wanted their attention and support. Time and again a particular child, especially an ambivalent type, tried to win his teacher's approval but received swift rejection—if not open hostility. Nor was such a child always a demanding, relentless attention-seeker; sometimes he was merely a child fighting for his self-esteem who wanted the teacher to recognize him in a favorable light. The teacher commonly did not have the time, energy, or inclination to meet his wishes.

NOTES

1. See Talcott Parsons, "The School Class as a Social System: Some of Its Functions in American Society," in *idem, Social Structure and Personality* (New York: Free Press, 1964), pp. 129–54.
2. M. B. Holmes, D. S. Holmes, and Arlene S. Friedman, *Interaction Patterns as a Source of Error in Teachers' Evaluation of Head Start Children,* Final Report, Grant No. OEO-4152 (New York: Associated YM-YWHAs of New York, 1968).
3. Ray C. Rist, "The Self-Fulfilling Prophecy in Ghetto Education," in Joseph McVicker Hunt, ed., *Human Intelligence* (New Brunswick, N.J.: Transaction Books, 1972), pp. 123–62.
4. Robert Rosenthal and Lenore Jacobson, *Pygmalion in the Classroom: Teacher Expectation and the Pupil's Intellectual Ability* (New York: Holt, Rinehart & Winston, 1968).
5. See Robert K. Merton, *Social Theory and Social Structure* (New York: Free Press, 1957), pp. 421–27.
6. Robert L. Thorndike, review of *Pygmalion in the Classroom* in *Teachers College Record,* 70 (1969): 805–7.
7. Thorndike does not question the validity of the raw scores on the IQ tests, but only the scale of measurement converting raw scores to mental ages. For Rosenthal's reply to Thorndike, see "Empirical *vs.* Decreed Validation of Clocks and Tests," *American Educational Research Journal,* 1969, pp. 689–91. Thorndike's rebuttal, "But You Have to Know How to Tell Time," appeared in the same issue, p. 692.
8. Robert Rosenthal, "The Pygmalion Effect Lives," *Psychology Today,* September, 1973, pp. 56–63.
9. See Samuel Bowles and Herbert Gintis, "I.Q. in the U.S. Class Structure," *Social Policy,* January–February, 1973, pp. 65–96, and Martin Carnoy, ed., *Schooling in a Corporate Society* (New York: David McKay, 1972).
10. David C. McClelland, "Testing for Competence Rather than for 'Intelligence,'" *American Psychologist,* 28, no. 1 (1973): 4.
11. Janet S. Vosk, "Study of Negro Children with Learning Difficulties at the Outset of Their School Careers," *American Journal of Orthopsychiatry,* 36 (1966): 32–40.
12. See B. Mackler, "Blacks Who Are Academically Successful," *Urban Education,* 7 (1970): 210–37.
13. Helen H. Davidson and James W. Greenberg, *School Achievers from a Deprived Background* (New York: Associated Educational Services, 1967).
14. *Ibid.* See also James W. Greenberg and Helen H. Davidson, "Home Background and School Achievement of Black Urban Ghetto Children," *American Journal of Orthopsychiatry,* 42 (1972): 803–10.
15. Davidson and Greenberg, *School Achievers,* p. 148. See also B. Mackler, "Grouping in the Ghetto," *Education and Urban Society,* 2 (1969): 80–96.

16. Zena S. Blau, "Maternal Aspirations, Socialization, and Achievement of Boys and Girls in the White Working Class," *Journal of Youth and Adolescence,* 1 (1972): 35–57.

17. See Melvin J. Kohn, *Class and Conformity* (Homewood, Ill.: Dorsey Press, 1969).

18. See Vaughn J. Crandall, Ann Preston, and A. Rabson, "Maternal Reactions and the Development of Independence and Achievement Behavior in Young Children," *Child Development,* 31 (1960): 243–51, and Bernard C. Rosen and Roy G. D'Andrade, "The Psychosocial Origins of Achievement Motivation," *Sociometry,* 22 (1959): 185–218.

19. On middle-class children's feelings and concepts regarding school and the motives behind their school achievement, see Philip W. Jackson, *Life in Classrooms* (New York: Holt, Rinehart & Winston, 1968); Mary A. White, "The View from the Pupil's Desk," *Urban Review,* 2 (1968): 5–7; and John Holt, *How Children Fail* (New York: Pitman, 1964).

20. David Wineman and Fritz Redl, *Children Who Hate: The Disorganization and Breakdown of Behavior Controls* (New York: Free Press, 1951).

21. A. Harry Walters and I. Kosowski, "Symbolic Learning and Reading Retardation," *Journal of Consulting Psychology,* 27 (1963): 75–82. See also J. E. Peters *et al.,* "Presumed Minimal Brain Dysfunction in Children," *Archives of General Psychiatry,* 16 (1967): 281–85.

22. Davidson and Greenberg, *School Achievers* (n. 13 *supra*), p. 75.

23. For insights into this question, see Benjamin Pasamanick and Hilda Knobloch, "The Contribution of Some Organic Factors to School Retardation Among Negro Children," *Journal of Negro Education,* 27 (1958): 4–9; *idem,* "Retrospective Studies on the Epidemiology of Reproductive Causality: Old and New," *Merrill-Palmer Quarterly,* 12 (1966): 7–26; A. A. Kawi and Benjamin Pasamanick, *Prenatal and Paranatal Factors in the Development of Childhood Reading Disorders* (New York: Kraus Reprints, 1959); and Cecil M. Drillien, *The Growth and Development of the Prematurely Born Infant* (Baltimore: Williams & Wilkins, 1964).

24. See Herbert G. Birch and Joan D. Gussow, *Disadvantaged Children: Health, Nutrition and School Failure* (New York: Grune & Stratton, 1970).

25. A. F. Brunswick and E. Josephson, "Adolescent Health in Harlem," *American Journal of Public Health,* October, 1972, supplement.

26. New York City Department of Health news release, October 9, 1969.

27. O. David, J. Clark, and K. Voeller, "Lead and Hyperactivity," *The Lancet,* October 28, 1972, pp. 900–903.

28. David Burnham, "The Heroin Babies: Going Cold Turkey at Birth," *New York Times Magazine,* January 9, 1972, p. 18.

29. Jerome S. Bruner, *Toward a Theory of Instruction* (Cambridge: Harvard University Press, 1966). Bruner's term "defending" refers to reactions to a distorted image of reality, a perception of danger that exists

mainly in the perceiver's mind. We have expanded the meaning to include the tendency to be perceptually vigilant and reactive to a *real* threat to safety or well-being. The development of a heightened vigilance against danger in the environment is an aspect of the adaptive socialization of black children to life in a racist society in which blacks face real dangers not generally part of the experiences of whites. Dixon and Foster include "oppression/paranoia" defined as "a high degree of sensitivity to situations perceived as dangerous" among the aspects of a black world view reflecting the black experience in America. See Vernon J. Dixon and Badi G. Foster, *Beyond Black and White* (Boston: Little, Brown, 1971), pp. 16–17.

30. James S. Coleman *et al., Equality of Educational Opportunity* (Washington, D.C.: Department of Health, Education, and Welfare, 1966).

31. See Frederick Mosteller and Daniel Patrick Moynihan, eds., *On Equality of Educational Opportunity* (New York: Random House, 1972), and Christopher Jencks *et al., Inequality: A Reassessment of the Effect of Family and Schooling in America* (New York: Basic Books, 1972), pp. 52–109.

32. Coleman *et al., Equality of Educational Opportunity,* p. 302. For further evidence of the effects of lower-class school children on each other, see U.S. Commission on Civil Rights, *Racial Isolation in the Public Schools* (Washington, D.C.: U.S. Government Printing Office, 1967), pp. 77–91.

10 / CHILDHOOD PERSONALITY AND ADULT LIFE-STYLES

The roots of adult adaptations to oppressive life circumstances may often be found in childhood. Here we shall consider further implications of our childhood typology and of the sorting process within the school for adult life-style and achievements.

PATHWAYS TO ACHIEVEMENT

A longitudinal study by Kraus of children from kindergarten to their adult years provides results that are congruent with our developmental analysis of the effects of political oppression and of social and economic inequality.[1] Two New York City elementary schools were studied, one in Brooklyn and one in Harlem. The former, with a majority of white children, received most of its pupils from a "low-middle-income" housing project. The children's parents were mainly white-collar workers, skilled laborers, and civil service employees. Only one or two children qualified for free lunch. In the Harlem school, parents were mainly unskilled and semiskilled laborers. The children, mostly black, came from depressed areas. One third of them qualified for free lunch during their seven years in elementary school.* The children who formed the basic research population were studied when they entered kindergarten in 1953 and at intervals throughout their school career until they completed the ninth grade.

* Most of the Harlem schools where we observed or taught had even poorer pupil populations than this and were virtually all black. We rarely saw a white child in these schools. The school in the Kraus study, therefore, is not what we regard as a typical "hard-core" ghetto school of the 1960's or early 1970's.

Contrary to the conclusions of Rosenthal and Jacobson (p. 204) , Kraus and his project staff found that teachers' knowledge of IQ scores had "no effect" on their expectations of pupil performance or on actual performance: "At no time during the elementary and junior high years did an IQ score determine promotion or retention, or class placement or rejection in the ordinary class."[2] It was found that these school decisions were made solely on the basis of "class performance." But class performance "usually" meant "reading achievement"—which cannot qualify as a comprehensive, objective evaluation of a child's abilities and competencies. Since successful performance on standardized reading tests, as on IQ tests, is based on a familiarity with standard English vocabulary and on the selection of multiple-choice answers that coincide with the testers' judgments—both of which introduce social-class and ethnic biases —reading tests may be almost as subjective as IQ measurements. Thus, one may question the extent to which either score provides an objective basis for evaluating young children and for making administrative decisions when children are very young that apparently affect their life-styles and success in later years.

In the Brooklyn school, a larger percentage of boys than of girls read below grade level until the fourth grade. From then on the boys read better than the girls. But in the Harlem school a greater percentage of boys than of girls read below the norm throughout the entire range of grades:

> The most significant measure was the score obtained on the third-grade reading-achievement test. There is a high correlation between this score and all subsequent reading, mathematics, and intelligence-test scores and with general performance on the junior and senior high school level. There were no "late bloomers," and for most of our children in both schools, third-grade reading achievement might have been used for purposes of prediction even beyond the high school years.[3]

We suggest that, while reading achievement appears to be a less class-biased measure than IQ on which to determine class placement, it may actually lead to injustices in shaping individual and group destiny. Our experience and the literature suggest just that. As we related in Chapter 9, certain children came into kindergarten able to express their dependency needs in appealing ways, ready to please the teacher and get along with their classmates, and so forth. These behaviors are what teachers and administrators are culturally conditioned to recognize, enjoy, and encourage. Children who displayed them were more likely to be placed in the "best" first-grade class, in which privileged group the teacher would be disposed to push them harder to read than was true of children in other classes. These other children were likely to come from homes that were poorer, in which discipline was somewhat harsher and the person-to-room ratio less favorable, etc. They were less appealing to teachers principally because they were less like middle-class children and, therefore, less promising as achievers.

Thus, while the sorting process may originate in family and household background differences, the school plays an important role in determining who will read above, at, or below normative standards. By the third grade one can see the effects of a process that begins as early as kindergarten to sort children in terms of their behavior and attitudes and then, during the next year or two, sorts them on the basis of their reading-test perform-ance. This test performance, we assert, is affected by the earlier sorting along the dimension of middle-class deportment and attitudes.

Other evidence indicates that the third grade is the critical period for children's educational careers. Bloom, for example, presents data show-ing that grades one through three represent "the most important growing period for academic achievement and that all subsequent learning in the school is affected and in large part determined by what the child has learned by the age of nine or by the end of grade three."[4]

What we are suggesting is that a class-oriented sorting process signifi-cantly determines well before the third grade which children, particularly among boys, will become peer-oriented and which will be more respon-sive to adult direction. Those children who are adult-oriented and in other ways more "middle class" at the time they enter the school are more likely to learn to read at normative or higher levels, will tend to be grouped together, will mutually influence one another toward reading achievement, and are more likely to be expected and encouraged to learn to read by their teachers.

Learning to read, in turn, is a crucial determinant of the sorting proc-ess. Middle-class behavior and reading readiness become inextricably in-tertwined in kindergarten or first grade, mutually reinforcing each other and determining a child's class placement. If the child in kindergarten or first grade shows signs that he is ready to read, he stands a chance of go-ing to the best or second-best class in the grade, where his peer contacts and his teacher are likely to influence him to become more adult-oriented and a better reader. If the child shows little reading readiness in kinder-garten or first grade (as was true, we found, of peer-oriented children), his chances for academic success are virtually nil, for he will almost cer-tainly be streamed into a class below the top two on grade, where he will associate mostly with other children who suffer the double jeopardy of a strong peer orientation and little readiness to read. Thus, by the time the child is eight or nine years old his ability (or lack of ability) to read and his adult (or peer) orientation have usually mutually reinforced each other through a sorting process that the school directs.

The fact that by the third grade a child's reading-test or intelligence-test score apparently predicts his subsequent educational career and his future life-style and success means, in essence, that by eight or nine years old he must make more of a commitment to either a relatively middle-class or street-oriented life-style.[5] Our contention is that the school participates in an insidious process that results in functional illiteracy by helping to forge a school-alienated life-style among children in which reading achievement becomes largely irrelevant. A few children are encouraged in their mainstream development and learning patterns but most of them (the ambivalents and precocious independents) have been socialized by age nine to resist adult direction and support while developing a style of life oriented to being "one of the gang." Another small group of children (the submissives) also tends to be overlooked by teachers and does not expect adult support or encouragement. Hopelessly alienated from adults but not deeply committed to the street-based group, these children languish apathetically.

The HARYOU Report presented data comparing the academic performance of children in Central Harlem with that of other New York City school children, relative to national norms on standardized reading, arithmetic, and IQ tests.[6] From the third grade through the eighth, the achievement levels of New York City children on the average were on a par with those in the nation, but by the eighth grade the New York children had slipped almost a half-grade behind. The Central Harlemites showed an even more disastrous pattern. In the third grade, their achievement levels were one year behind those of all New York City children; by the sixth grade they had fallen nearly two years behind; and by the eighth grade they were nearly two and a half years behind New York City levels and three years behind national norms. On IQ tests, Central Harlem children exhibited a decrease in mean scores from the third to the sixth grade; the scores recovered slightly by the eighth grade but were still lagging behind third-grade performance. New York City pupils, by contrast, showed a slight but steady increase in IQ and by the eighth grade matched national norms. From such statistics one can see that the longer Harlem children stayed in school, the greater the percentage who failed to perform up to national norms on standardized achievement and IQ tests. The period of sharpest decline in test performance was between the third and sixth grades. Most Harlem children from the third grade onward never attained grade-level performance on reading or arithmetic tests.

The major explanations offered for this precipitous decline in performance have been fragmented and one-sided. The tendency has been either to blame racism or indifference on the part of the teacher or to suggest that "cultural deprivation," leading to cumulative deficits in intellectual processes, is the cause. We have discussed the cultural-deprivation argument in Chapters 6 and 7, citing evidence that, even though low-income children tend to develop linguistic and cognitive abilities at a relatively slow rate, most of them do catch up to middle-class children by

about age eleven, even though this may not be revealed by their performance on traditional IQ tests. At the very least, we must question any explanation of the low reading performance of poor black sixth-graders
that assumes the major determinant of such academic failure to be the
children's lack of age-appropriate mental abilities.

On the other hand, the argument that the decline in reading achievement is the result of low expectations and lack of commitment on the
part of teachers is, at best, a partial explanation. As we argued in Chapter 9, some teachers try valiantly to teach children to read, only to have
their efforts counteracted by distracting peer activities in the classroom
and the generally demoralized atmosphere in the schools. When the
teacher could see his efforts continually frustrated by forces within and
outside the school over which he had little control, he often sought to re-
trench to more energy-conserving and psychologically safe strategies and
classroom techniques.

Even if sorting continues beyond the third grade, our impression is
that it is the expanding peer influence, more than any independent effect
of schooling, that increasingly determines a child's life-style and life
chances. From the third grade on, peer influence is perhaps most important in reinforcing personality traits and life-style adaptations initially
shaped in the home.

In recent years some black teenagers have been given a second chance
to achieve academically through college open-admissions programs and
new recruitment policies that permit individuals with low high school
achievement records to enter college and work toward a degree. These
programs are based on the assumption that, although individual achievement and behavioral patterns tend to remain stable, they *can* respond to
modifications in the social structure. Moreover, should black academic
and economic achievements rise fairly rapidly in connection with increased educational opportunities or increased family assistance, we
might suspect that black poverty is not, by and large, a result of ethnic
traits but is a result of white racism and class discrimination. In short,
if a more open and beneficent social system is shown to be associated
with an increased rate of success among blacks, there would be less theoretical justification for implicating lower-class behavioral patterns and
personality structure in the causation of poverty.

Our finding that most of the achieving children in Harlem, particularly the boys, did not seem to affiliate much with street-based peer
groups has been documented by Labov and Robbins, who found striking
correlation between low reading ability, generally low academic achievement, and membership in a street-based peer group for ten- to twelve-
year-old boys in Central Harlem.[7] Conversely, higher reading ability and
academic achievement were strikingly correlated with nonmembership in
such a peer group.

The long-range effects of deepening involvement with street peer groups are suggested by a study that compared samples of young men (black and Mexican American), aged twenty-one to thirty, who had grown up poor in urban ghettos. At the time of the study, some were striving for conventional success through school or employment; others had been unemployed or underemployed for two years.[8] The former (mainstreamer) men had experienced school positively, remembered having had some academic success, enjoyed sports, and had good relationships with school personnel. Those who were not conventional achievers remembered school negatively in regard to academic achievements and conflict with school authorities. In adolescence, the mainstreamer men's self-esteem was already related to ideas of conventional achievement, while the others' depended on having a successful reputation among peers on the streets. The conventionally achieving men had positive attitudes toward representatives of mainstream society and were able to maintain relationships with peers who were not involved in gang activities. The nonachieving men, on the other hand, were alienated from representatives of mainstream society, were more dependent on approval from peers, and admired street people and "delinquent" peers. The achievers had received more parental encouragement, emotional support, and discipline. They appeared to possess high self-esteem associated with productive activities as children. Their primary loyalty was to their families; that of the nonmainstreamers was to the streets. The study indicates that, for those who grew up in the ghetto, striving for and achieving conventional employment success are heavily influenced by assimilation into mainstream life-styles within the ghetto. A lack of conventional employment success, or a lack of striving for it, is influenced by dependence on approval from peers and assimilation into street life-styles and street peer-group activities. We propose that the sorting process in the school helps to push different groups of children in one direction or the other.

Note that we are suggesting that the schools encouraged and reinforced mainstream life-styles and a striving for conventional forms of achievement among a small minority of ghetto children.[9] We are *not* suggesting that such striving brings these children, as they grow up, the same economic returns they might receive if they were white. An examination of the data on race differentials in returns from investment in education suggests that through the 1960's many black school dropouts may have behaved in an economically rational manner: Whereas whites generally make up the income lost by remaining in school longer through gaining more lucrative and stable employment, this is not necessarily true for blacks.[10] Relatively well-educated blacks tend to earn higher incomes than relatively uneducated blacks, but at educational levels short of graduate school, the gap is not always large enough to make up for the cost of the additional years the educated remain outside the labor market. The street world provides boys and adolescents with models for how to survive in the ghetto while conventionally underemployed or unemployed and thus suggests some exciting or escapist (although very stressful) life-styles in a society that practices employment and wage discrimination on the basis of race and tends to measure a man's worth by the amount of money he has.

ADULT LIFE-STYLES AND CHILD TYPES

On the basis of a survey of 1,651 Northern black men and women aged twenty-one to forty-five in 1966, Crain and Weisman found associations between certain personality traits, educational achievement, and adult income.[11] High self-esteem and internal control, for example, were related to adult achievement. A person was rated high in self-esteem if he indicated a perception of himself as unique, "a good and talented person, better than the average person in some ways." A person was rated high in internal control if he responded to questions by indicating self-perception of the ability to control his destiny. The researchers propose a fourfold typology as follows:

Internal Control

Self-esteem:	Low	High
High	Drifters	Accepters
Low	Militants	Achievers

The group with both high self-esteem and high internal control (the "achievers") have the highest levels of education and the highest incomes; the "drifters" rank lowest in both categories.

The *achiever* adult most closely resembles our mainstreamer child type. Most achievers and mainstreamers are self-assertive but also relatively controlled in that, although they are capable of becoming openly angry when others frustrate or oppress them, they tend not to respond with violent aggression, wild mood swings, or emotional outbursts. The achieving black adult (in the mid-1960's) perceived racial oppression and discrimination as "weak" or "surmountable." Like a middle-class white, he believed that he was capable of succeeding on his own.

The *militant* adult type most closely resembles our child precocious independent type, and some ambivalents. All these types are self-assertive and competitive and have difficulty controlling aggression. Even though the adult militants and the child precocious independents tend to trust their ability to cope with many problems, achievement is often elusive because their assertiveness, aggression, audacity, and apparent shamelessness lead to conflict with those in authority, particularly whites. Although they may feel personally competent, they perceive less control over their future life since they feel personally oppressed by blocked opportunity.

The *accepter* adult type resembles our child submissives and a few mainstreamers. A small percentage of submissives might, on occasion, suddenly explode aggressively, but the majority strongly inhibit their anger, as do the adult accepters and some mainstreamers. On the other hand, whereas the adult accepters are depicted as knowing how to achieve (but often failing to do so because they are passive), our submissives showed little such knowledge. It may be that some submissives learn how to achieve in low-level jobs, aided by their powerful inhibitions against aggression, which tend to keep them out of trouble. Whereas the adult accepter showed relatively high internal control, which was also associated with inhibiting aggression, our child submissives mainly showed the latter characteristic. It is possible that some submissives, once they secure a job as an adult, will be sufficiently diligent and will find their efforts sufficiently rewarded (reinforced) to make them believe that success is possible as a result of hard work.

The *drifter* adult resembles some of our ambivalents and the potentially explosive submissives. The drifters and those ambivalents whose self-esteem is relatively low are likely to be angry or aggressive but not competitive in conventional, achievement-oriented ways. The combination of low self-esteem and low internal control leads to a sense of personal powerlessness and aimlessness. Such a person is chronically frustrated and depressed but occasionally will explode in violent aggression when directly frustrated.

Before, during, and after the riots of 1965 to 1968, McCord and his associates conducted a large-scale study of the variety of ways in which low-income urban blacks in the West and Southwest adapted to ghetto life.[12] Interviews were conducted with randomly selected blacks in Houston, Oakland, and Watts, mostly by low-income black interviewers. "Natural dialogue" interviews with Watts blacks supplied additional data. Specifically, these researchers examined seven life-style types, which appeared to represent the most common adaptations to "internal colonialism":

1. The "stoic" who is outwardly apathetic and accepting and finds some happiness in joining a traditional Negro church or simply by resigning himself to being an "invisible man."
2. The "defeated," who has been crushed by life and escapes from a reality which he can no longer tolerate into a world of drugs, alcohol, or psychotic hallucination.
3. The "exploiter"—the blockbuster, numbers man, mortician—who has a stake in maintaining the status quo in the ghetto.

4. The "achiever" who seeks to better his own lot in life but may have little concern for the collective condition of American Negroes.
5. The "rebel without a cause," who rejects existing society and expresses his rebellion through, say, delinquency, but who is not working toward any long-term social reform.
6. The "activist," who hopes to change society by reform measures.
7. The "revolutionary," who has rebelled militantly against American society and hopes to effect a total change in the Negro way of life.

Children who manifested submissive traits during the early 1960's were, in our judgment, most likely to adopt stoic or defeated life-styles during adolescence and young adulthood; the independents of the 1960's were more likely to gravitate toward rebel, exploiter, or revolutionary adaptations. Clearly, most mainstreamers seemed to be headed toward conventional achiever life-styles, with some opting for militant or revolutionary styles and others for exploiter types. The most common child type, the ambivalents, were likely to turn toward defeated, stoic, exploiter, or rebel adaptations.

From the perspective of history, we may hypothesize that, from 1967 or 1968 on, low-income black children began to be inundated with the rhetoric and philosophy of the black movement, so that their counterparts today share a new black mood. Before the 1967 riots, we suggest, blacks were more divided than they are today regarding the desirability of assuming active individual and group postures and strategies for black liberation and equality. The transformation of the black mood is reflected in a decrease in the normative acceptance by masses of urban blacks of passive-defeated life-styles and increasing pressure on black children and adolescents to adopt more active, achievement-oriented approaches to the urban black condition.

One indication of these changes is the transformation of the cultural concept of "soul." According to Hannerz, writing in 1968, soul then represented " 'the essence of Negroness' . . . a folk conception of the lower-class urban Negro's own 'national character.' "[13] Soul was a way of acting, a personal style and tempo, indicative of a certain constellation of lower-class black ethnicity. Teenagers and younger adults, especially males, were seen to have the most soul. Soul talk, music, and food, Southern in origin, had assumed special meaning as a black way of life in urban areas. Soul was partly religious in derivation; it came to life in the realm of feeling.

For urban blacks, Hannerz suggested, soul *content* reflected a perceived lack of control over one's environment, where the smart and tough survived, and a related instability in personal relationships, especially between the sexes. For most soul brothers, it represented the effort to erect a workable identity through rhetoric:

The *style* of soul alternates between aggressive, somewhat boastful behavior and plaintive behavior from an implicit underdog position. This style occurs in many situations and may itself be related to the unstable personal relationships. . . .

Soul is by [many ghetto dwellers'] definition superior, and the motive of the soul vocabulary, I believe, is above all to reduce self-doubt by persuading soul brothers that they are successful. Being a soul brother is belonging to a select group instead of to a residual category of people who have not succeeded. . . . By talking to others of his group [in the soul idiom], he identifies with them and confers the same role on them. Using soul rhetoric is a way of convincing others of one's own worth and their worth.

Our belief is that the soul vocabulary also entered into lower-class urban black life-styles and identity through attempts to deal with both shame and doubt. The cultural concept of "soul" is also related to the lower-class black's changing relationship to the social structure:

Soul has arisen at this point [1968] because of the Negro's increasingly ambivalent conceptions about the opportunity structure. Earlier, lack of achievement according to American mainstream ideals could easily be explained in terms of impermeable social barriers. Now the impression is gaining ground that there are ways out of the situation.

The young men, who come under particularly great strain if such a belief is accepted, must either achieve (which many of them are obviously still unable to do); explain that achievement is impossible (which is probably less true); or explain that achievement according to mainstream ideals is not necessarily achievement according to their *own* ideals. The emergence of soul goes some way toward meeting the need of stating alternative ideals, and also provides solidarity among those with such a need.[14]

Thus "soul" was and to some extent may still be a cultural device to deal with the ambivalence of low-income blacks, their need to shore up self-esteem, affirm cohesiveness, and grant dignity to identity.

We suggest that Hannerz's analysis captured some elements of the soul concept up until the late 1960's, although we feel that he has somewhat overstated the significance of soul in "marginal man" terms. We agree that soul has existed significantly because of the fears of young, lower-class urban black men *vis-à-vis* existing mainstream opportunity. But a marginal-man interpretation risks advancing a view of soul almost exclusively in terms of white referents, thereby diverting attention from it as an expression of black ethnicity that serves to highlight moral character, existential experience, and emphasis on feeling. In any event, we believe that soul has taken on a more active and politically significant meaning since Hannerz's interpretation in 1968.

Soul had lost some acceptance and validity for a while around 1968.

It even became passé for some conventionally achieving blacks, in part, perhaps, because blacks were becoming more politically sophisticated and active. They were also developing heightened group pride and self-esteem and more positive and actively oriented identities. Although the passive form of soul still appears to exist prominently in the Northern black population (as in soul music), it seems to have been joined by a version transformed in the direction of optimism—activism. The concept has been shedding some of its association with the older images of ambivalence, disappointment, fear of failure, passivity, and doubt while acquiring associations of pride, responsibility, solidarity, and political action. In various cultural and political contexts, the word "soul," the vocabulary of soul, and soul music are no longer associated almost exclusively with a feeling of lack of control over one's surroundings. "Soul" ideology has increasingly taken on the role of cultural motivator of a politically active black identity, active group support and organization, and positive self-images.

Changes in the black mood over the past decade may be related to the type of cultural change described by Wallace as a "revitalization movement": "deliberate, organized attempts by some members of a society to construct a more satisfying culture by rapid acceptance of a pattern of multiple innovations. . . . This process depends upon the formulation of a new utopian image of sociocultural organization."[15] For urban low-income black communities this image has tentatively been constructed in terms of ethnic cohesion, race pride, collective organization and action, and individual identity change. The appearance of Malcolm X as a prophet of a new black world during the early 1960's and his widening impact upon the urban black population may illustrate a beginning of a revitalization process from within the black community. Preaching a code of moral, psychological, and political transformation, he challenged and eventually energized many blacks to turn from fatalism to activism, discipline, and, finally, organization. His promise of personal transformation and salvation was unmistakable.

A latter-day black prophet, Maualana Karenga, has offered blacks at least an embryonic revitalization code for cultural, political, economic, and personal "overturning":

Umoja (unity)—to strive for and maintain unity in the family, community, nation, and race

Kujichagulia (self-determination)—to define ourselves, name ourselves, and speak for ourselves, instead of being defined and spoken for by others

Ujima (collective work and responsibility)—to build and maintain our community together, and to make our brothers' and sisters' problems our problems and to solve them together

Ujamaa (cooperative economics)—to build and maintain our own stores, shops, and other businesses and to profit together from them

Nia (purpose)—to make our collective vocation the building and developing of our community in order to restore our people to their traditional greatness

Kuumba (creativity)—to do always as much as we can, in the way we can in order to leave our community more beautiful and beneficial than when we inherited it

Imani (faith)—to believe with all our hearts in our parents, our teachers, our leaders, our people and the righteousness and victory of our struggle.[16]

These "seven principles" have been disseminated by the media directed at blacks during the past four years and in the black community at large. They hold the possibility of guiding the socialization of black children into constructive functioning within a black perspective and life-style; they open entry points for lower-class children and adolescents who might not otherwise gravitate toward the movement because they cannot wholeheartedly identify with the flamboyant, romanticized media images of the 1960's black militant.

Black children and adolescents today have available within their own communities more models of conventional achievement-oriented life-styles than used to be the case. In addition, they see some models who offer alternatives to street culture, on the one hand, and conventional individualistic strivings, on the other. Whether they identify with conventional achievers, with black nationalists of varying ideologies, with exciting street-culture types, with aspects of all these types, black children and youth today are much more likely to avoid passive-defeated life-style adaptations than was true a decade ago.

NOTES

1. Philip E. Kraus, *Yesterday's Children: A Longitudinal Study of Children from Kindergarten into the Adult Years* (New York: Wiley, 1973).
2. *Ibid.*, p. 142.
3. *Ibid.*
4. Benjamin S. Bloom, *Stability and Change in Human Characteristics* (New York: Wiley, 1964), p. 110. A Swedish longitudinal study also found that intelligence-test scores and teachers' ratings in the third grade were good predictors of pupils' future educational achievements. See T. Hussen, *Talent, Opportunity, and Career* (Stockholm: Amqvist & Wiskell, 1969).
5. The finding of Kraus's study is relevant:

    Most of the children reported as having adjustment problems in any one of the early grades remained problems and were subsequently reported by two or more teachers. Furthermore, all but three of those reported in the sixth grade had displayed their difficulties before the end of the third grade and continued to have problems in the junior high school and well beyond. [Kraus, *Yesterday's Children,* p. 144]

Kagan and Moss also point to the stability of behavioral patterns: "It would appear that for some children the first four years of contact with the school and peer environments (i.e., during ages 6 to 10) crystallize behavioral tendencies that are maintained through young adulthood." (Jerome Kagan and Howard A. Moss, *Birth to Maturity: A Study in Psychological Development* [New York: Wiley, 1962], p. 272.)

6. *Youth in the Ghetto* (New York: Haryou, 1964), pp. 189–95.

7. William Labov and C. Robbins, "A Note on the Relation of Reading Failure to Peer-Group Status in Urban Ghettos," *Teachers College Record,* 70 (1969): 395–405.

8. H. Laurence Ross and E. M. Glasser, "A Study of Successful Persons from Seriously Disadvantaged Backgrounds," final report, Office of Special Manpower Programs, U.S. Department of Labor, Washington, D.C.

9. For further documentation on this point see Eleanor B. Leacock, *Teaching and Learning in City Schools: A Comparative Study* (New York: Basic Books, 1969).

10. See Samuel Bowles, "Towards Equality of Educational Opportunity," *Harvard Educational Review,* 38 (1968): 89–99.

11. Robert L. Crain and Carlos S. Weisman, *Discrimination, Personality, and Achievement: A Survey of Northern Blacks* (New York: Seminar Press, 1972).

12. William McCord, John Howard, Bernard Friedberg, and Edwin Harwood, *Life Styles in the Ghetto* (New York: W. W. Norton, 1969).

13. Ulf Hannerz, "The Significance of Soul," in August Meier, ed., *Black Experience: The Transformation of Activism,* 2d ed. (New Brunswick, N.J.: Transaction Books, 1973), pp. 123–38.

14. *Ibid.,* p. 137.

15. Anthony F. C. Wallace, *Culture and Personality,* 2d ed. (New York: Random House, 1970), p. 188.

16. See Imamu A. Baraka (LeRoi Jones), *Raise Race Rays Raze* (New York: Random House, 1971), pp. 133–46.

11 / BLACK IDENTITY: FIXITY AND CHANGE

Cultural pressure to evolve new black life-styles has profoundly affected the nature of black identity and identity development in urban communities. In previous chapters we tried to show that many poor black children suffered intense feelings of shame and doubt largely as an outgrowth of early loss of adult emotional support, restrictions on autonomous strivings, and various manifestations of race and class discrimination. Later peer pressures, growing alienation from adults, and school failure combine to further hamper their ability to deal competently with middle-class social reality and institutions, thereby further diminishing the children's sense of pride, dignity, and self-confidence.

In recent years, however, growing numbers of black youth have come to take a more critical view of commonly accepted criteria for success and to judge themselves by newly evolving black American standards. The emergence and strengthening of ethnic organizations, the ascendance of highly visible and self-confident models, the impact of a black ideological rhetoric, efforts at local institutional control, the election of blacks to important public offices, the tendency of the media to focus more on black life and to portray black American life and culture more authentically—all these influences have been transforming Negroes into black Americans.

Before we turn to a consideration of black identity change, let us consider a study of identity development among low-income black adolescents in the 1960's. The data were collected from 1962 to 1967. It is unlikely that a replication of the study today would produce the same depressing portrait.

A study of twenty-two black and white working-class New Haven males during their last three years of high school found distinct differences between the two racial groups in identity development.[1] The blacks showed far less change in self-images over time. Hauser suggests that this reflects what Erikson has conceptualized as "identity foreclosure" and "negative identity." "Identity foreclosure" is a premature fixing of an individual's self-image that impedes the further development of other self-defining potentials and possibilities. The child does not become all he could be. "Negative identity" is similar to identity foreclosure, but identity is fixed upon the repudiated, the scorned, and the rejected identifications and roles that have in the past been pointed out as most "undesirable and dangerous."[2]

Hauser explains the lack of self-image change—an important aspect of identity foreclosure—among the black adolescents in part by their general situation. During four years of interviews held twice yearly, they complained of racial restrictions on employment, dates, recreation, and housing. Another apparent determinant was the scarcity of "heroes"—men who were sufficiently idealized to be considered worthy models. Most of the black adolescents said there was no one they wished to be like, now or in the future. But they named men they did *not* want to resemble—such "antiheroes" as bums, gangsters, drunkards, petty thieves, and often their own fathers.[3] The paucity of positive role models appears to account in part for the absence of both significant role experimentation and an evolving synthesis of personal and social identifications—reflected in the changelessness of the blacks' self-images as they grew older. In Hauser's view these environmental features, which produce restrictions and degrading experiences, push the black teenager toward self-limitation and steadily diminishing self-esteem.

Hauser also offers a developmental perspective to complement the contextual one. What in the black teenagers' personal histories might tend to close identity development prematurely? One possibility is the likelihood that assertiveness and initiative were not encouraged by their families or community. In addition, since childhood many of the boys perceived their fathers with much anger and disrespect. These perceptions sometimes were augmented by their mothers' expectations of failure and irresponsibility from their men, or perhaps from men generally. Recall the frequent admonitions to many Central Harlem boys by mothers, grandmothers, and aunts to "be good," while fearing or expecting them to "turn out bad," often "like their fathers." Remember, too, their warnings not to play or associate with "those bad boys," although they were helpless to prevent or sever such undesirable ties. Such developmental experiences may contribute to a constriction of initiative and role experimentation, beginning in the preschool years.

Hauser suggests that a narrowing of identity formation first occurs during the preschool and childhood years, when conscience and initiative theoretically emerge and interact as guilt begins to set limits on role experimentation and aggression. We believe that identity foreclosure is rooted in the even earlier childhood experience of personal shame and doubt, long before the child embarks on the stage of role exploration and is capable of experiencing guilt, and that such early experiences often contribute to enduring focal preoccupations concerning personal acceptability and competence. Identity problems of low-income black teenagers thus may originate in the frustration of their earliest efforts at self-assertion and self-regulation.[4]

Preoccupations with shame and restriction clearly played a role in the development of inferiority feelings among the Northern black schoolchildren we observed. Shame infiltrated the child's consciousness through parental socialization practices, modeling, sibling and peer rivalries and conflicts, and direct race and class discrimination. It was perpetuated through failure in elementary school and difficulties in finding work as a teenager. Heightened feelings of shame, which hindered self-assertion, self-direction, and initiative, interacted with feelings of inferiority and often inhibited striving for competence.

Thus we may pose a historically critical black American developmental dilemma: the conflict between the young child's striving for autonomy, initiative, and competence and his desire to escape the painful feeling of shame and socially imposed behavioral restrictions, which indirectly intensify the experience of shame by interfering with the development of a sense of competence. As we have seen, shame and restriction increase the tendency to face life suspiciously.

Ethnic solidarity may serve to energize the developmental process while assuaging developmental hurts and frustrations. One of the poignant problems of the low-income black mother has been how best to mitigate the undermining influences upon her child's trusting dependence as he is subjected to shame-oriented, restrictive socialization. As the ghetto child becomes more active, aggressive, assertive, and demanding, his sense of security is endangered. As we have tried to show, established trust and the lingering desire to remain dependent were hastily and often abrasively eroded by restrictions and shaming when the young child's active exploration and assertiveness began to tax his mother's resources or try her patience or make her fear for his future safety.

The increasing intensity of the early childhood dilemmas we have described as one moves downward in socio-economic class may account in part for the apparent difference between Hauser's "working class" adolescents, who said they hoped never to resemble their "antiheroes," and many of the lower-class black preadolescents and adolescents we knew, who were clearly, though often ambivalently, attracted to their relatively limited choice of street models. These models provided a vivid source of ethnic identity and escape from a home atmosphere of restriction, shame, and failing relationships. Although feelings of shame often were linked to these models, the desire to break from parental control and unrewarding home and school lives became sufficiently compelling to drive many children to behave with defiant shamelessness toward parents or teachers, siblings or peers,[5] and therefore to identify more or less enthusiastically with street models. Many of the children openly admired adolescents and adults who demonstrated resourceful control over the environment, including those who were objects of scorn and fear to mainstream America (as well as many of the children's parents).

Furthermore, some observers have argued that the black experience differs profoundly from white Anglo experience with regard to some identifications. According to Joseph White, a black psychologist:

> Nowadays the bad nigger is very much in vogue as the hero in the black community, yet white people continue to perceive this person as the villain and cannot understand why black folks are currently rejecting white people's favorite Uncle Toms. As a people we have to trust our own kinds of perceptions and not absorb white expectations of superheroes and villains.[6]

To underrate the appeal that "bad niggers" hold for many black children is to misunderstand the developmental and role issues the children face. Their attraction to individuals who successfully "mess with the system" is more an active adaptation to certain features of the ghetto scene than a manifestation of regret and despair.

In some children, of course, smoldering anger and resentments seemed to stimulate self-hatred and identification with the scorned. Yet other children were making commitments to roles and values regarded as undesirable by many in their neighborhood and in the broader society without self-loathing. The precocious independents are, of course, outstanding examples of street children and adolescents who cannot easily be characterized as "self-haters."

Historically blacks have lived with great contradictions and ambiguities in a context of high stress. But, despite the apparent harm these experiences can do to intellectual and social development, it is also possible that many low-income black children have achieved unique developmental complexity through being forced to tolerate these painful ambivalences. That low-income black children in general learn to adapt to these experiences is suggested by the large numbers of "ambivalents"—a somewhat adaptive though limiting personality type.

SHAME AND IDENTITY TRANSFORMATION

One way of explaining Hauser's findings is to postulate that his black working-class adolescent subjects may have been experiencing both class-related personal shame and group-related (race and class) shame. The white teenagers should have been able to assuage their class-related feelings of personal shame by falling back to their prideful group identification as white Americans. Thus, they could be expected to run less risk of evolving a foreclosed or negative identity. Nevertheless, white working-class youths have been described as sharing a narrowly defined and rigidly held identity relative to white middle-class youths.[7]

Previously we have considered socio-economic status and race as factors limiting behavioral adaptations, life-styles, and identity formation in children and adolescents. The emergence of a new black ethnic consciousness, beginning on a large scale in the mid-1960's, by now has transformed the racial identity of many black children and youth, bolstering individual self-esteem and personal (as well as racial) identity. Hauser's finding that the identity development of low-income black teenagers was fixed and limited may therefore be descriptive of the period just before large numbers of blacks had begun to alter their group and personal identities. His subjects were "Negroes"—those who had not yet been significantly affected by the emerging racial consciousness within the black community—and most of his data were collected before the 1967 Detroit and Newark riots, the murder of Dr. King, and the widespread outbreaks that took place in Chicago, Washington, and other cities after the assassination.[8]

On the basis of observations of a wide segment of the black community, psychologist William E. Cross, Jr., developed a model that describes a series of well-defined stages through which adolescents and young adults pass in moving through a Negro-to-black identity transformation.[9] At Stage 1, *Pre-encounter,* the person's view of the world is "nonblack, antiblack, or the opposite of black." Although the content differs, the "context" of the black experience is similar for lower- and middle-class blacks. Their behavior, self-attitudes, and attitudes toward blackness are "degrading." Black history is highly distorted. Ghetto blacks who operate as pre-encounter Negroes justify or even romanticize hustling or exploiting other blacks as "survival" adaptations. A "white aesthetic" prevails, as does political naïveté and belief in the Protestant ethic. Whites are regarded as superior, and integration or assimilation is the preferred strategy for race relations.

At Stage 2, *Encounter,* self-feelings and the perception of the black condition are radically altered because some event, such as the murder of Martin Luther King, media reports of racial events, or discussions with others, shatters the person's experience of himself and leads him to search for a black identity. The person feels more black and is forced to test newly acquired perceptions in his or her search for a black identity. Thus a black who is hostile or neutral toward the black movement is jolted out of his previous assumptions, perceptions, and attitudes about *his* blackness, the world and condition of blackness, and into a quest at some level—at the very least a questioning of these issues.

Cross suggests that the experience of black as beautiful leads to "guilt" for having deserted the race among middle-class blacks; the lower-class person becomes guilty for "degrading his blackness." This guilt (and/or shame) and the rage he feels toward whites and their culture for having indoctrinated him into being a Negro "combine to fling the person into a frantic, determined, obsessive, extremely motivated search for black identity."

In Stage 3, *Immersion-Emersion,* the individual demands that things of value be related to blackness. He bathes himself in a world of blackness in any of a variety of ways. Whites and their culture are seen as dehumanized; "immersion into blackness and a liberation from whiteness" are felt. Afro hairstyles or an African name may be adopted. Everything black is good and romantic; the person becomes an Afro-American, a black American, or, sometimes, an African.

The Encounter and Immersion-Emersion stages are reminiscent of what psychologists refer to as the experience of "self-discovery." The immersion is described as a "strong, powerful, dominating sensation." Whereas the motive forces for encounter were limited to guilt (shame) and rage, immersion is additionally energized by the inclusion of an emergent feeling of pride.

Reminiscent of a revitalization movement (process), there is

> [a] turning inward and a withdrawal from everything that is perceived as being or representing the White world. Yet, ironically, a need rushes forth to confront the "man" as a means of dramatizing, concretizing, or proving one's Blackness. The confrontation, especially for Black leaders, is a manhood (or womanhood) ritual—a baptismal or purification rite. . . . [A] "blacker than thou" syndrome intoxicates the minds of many people. Black people are classified as "Uncle Tom," "militant," "together," "soulful," "middle-class," "intellectual snob." . . . Labeling others helps . . . clarify . . . identity. . . . Not only are people stereotyped, but the person's cosmology is greatly simplified and tends to be racist.[10]

In sum, there is a concern during the immersion phase that one's new consciousness be "pure or acceptable." The rites and rituals of purification are fueled by guilt (shame), rage, and a new feeling of pride.

After immersion into a black consciousness, one may emerge from dead-end, either/or, racist oversimplifications. Black heroes at this juncture serve as exemplary models to guide one toward discarding or questioning "the simplistic components of the black is beautiful philosophy, especially the tendency toward reverse racism." (Malcolm X's turn away from black racism is perhaps the most outstanding contemporary historical illustration of how the white man is rehumanized in an advanced stage of black consciousness.) One becomes open to a more critical analysis of the black American experience in political, cultural, and socio-economic terms.

Although rage persists to some extent during Stage 3, guilt (shame) feelings are yielding a sense of pride. At this juncture, "accepted factors of the black experience" might be incorporated, and the person may focus on or be receptive to plans, strategies, and tactics of action "for the development (liberation) of the black community or the necessary transformations of the black life-style."

At Stage 4, *Internalization,* the possibility now exists for the person to focus on things other than himself and other blacks. This stage is the most problematic:

> During the immersion-emersion stage the individual develops an idealistic, superhuman level of expectancy toward practically everything "Black," in which case minimal reinforcement may carry the person into continued involvement (evolution into the internalization stage). Yet prolonged or traumatic frustration . . . of these high expectancy levels may produce a Black person more deeply rooted in *nihilistic* expectancies than witnessed in the behavior of individuals functioning at the pre-encounter level.[11]

The completion of Stage 3 may result in some slippage back to an earlier stage. The individual may remain overwhelmed with hate for whites. A low-income black will be most angry because, in addition to not being able to progress to Stage 4, he enjoys little respite from oppression.

The internalized person feels more secure and satisfied with himself. He becomes receptive to plans for action. If the person's development ends at this stage he has progressed toward acquiring a black identity. But as we interpret the model, it is his feeling about being a black person that has undergone the most changes: Commitment to a group-oriented plan of action and racial-ethnic cohesion are not yet complete.

The fullest expression of a black identity is found in Stage 5, *Internalization-Commitment,* among those who become committed to a plan to change their community. These persons go beyond rhetoric to action.

That Hauser found so little personal identity change among the black teenagers he studied as compared to their white peers may be due in part to social-class differences. The New Haven black teenagers may have been somewhat lower in class than their white working-class peers.

Evidence that black working-class youth were experiencing identity change by the 1970's is indirectly supplied by a study of Princeton University undergraduates.[12] On a series of sorting tasks, ninety black and ninety white students were able to distinguish distinct stages of black identity development in line with those conceptualized by Cross. The fact that the students were generally able to match twenty-eight statements hypothesized to be characteristic of the stages testifies to the apparent ability of black (and white) youth to identify different images and roles associated with contemporary blacks. Moreover, it implies that black identity has been changing.

In a study conducted early in 1973 in a New Jersey college with a population more representative of low-income blacks, 25 male and 25 female black students were asked by five black experimenters to define themselves by sorting the above-mentioned stage-related statements on a scale from most to least like themselves. They tended to rate themselves strongly among the most advanced stages.[13] Moreover, when they rated themselves on "the way you were" four (and then two) years ago, they demonstrated a clear perception of a significant transition away from a past Negro identity toward a present black identity.

SOCIAL FORCES AND IDENTITY TRANSFORMATION

What has influenced great numbers of poor black children to begin to turn from shame toward pride, from narrow or negative self-definitions toward a positively toned, active racial identity and even toward increased self-esteem and a more positive identity? We have already mentioned some explosive events that had a tumultuous impact on black youth. In addition, long-term historical forces began to converge in the late 1960's to produce black children who were more ready to respond actively-aggressively to socialization restrictions and white racism than were previous generations.

The possible importance of Northern urban socialization for black identity development is suggested by at least one study of the relationship between self-esteem and various social-background characteristics of Harlem and Bedford-Stuyvesant youths. The Bedford-Stuyvesant youths, who showed lower self-esteem than the Harlem youths, were less likely to have been born in the North and less likely still to have been born in New York City. Youths born in New York City were likely to have higher self-esteem than those born elsewhere. Thus self-esteem may be related to growing up in large Northern cities.[14]

Social-psychological factors may have encouraged black identity transformation. Sears and McConahay have found that major demographic changes in the black population—such as migration from the rural South to the urban North and the increasing youthfulness of the black population, as well as increased educational attainment—may have had the effect of encouraging feelings of increased relative deprivation and an increasingly aggressive, assertive stance toward the white world.[15] In general it appears that black children growing up in the North have been learning to want and expect more of the goods available in our country. Frustrated expectations fed their anger. Growing up in the North may also have enabled black children to cultivate greater self-esteem; perhaps their growing anger gradually sharpened their sense of dignity. Moreover, if being born and reared in the North makes one angrier, more aggressive, and more assertive and teaches one to expect more from life, it may also encourage in some a belief in the possibility of greater personal control over one's future.

In sum, Northern black children have been living with greater personal and psychological freedom than was experienced under Jim Crow, and they have been subjected to an increasingly active socialization with respect to whites—particularly through their increased immersion in aggressive and assertive street-based peer groups. In addition, Northern black children have been growing up in an atmosphere of rising feelings of deprivation, which may have served to increase discontent, anger, and assertiveness in the black community in general. Those who reach adolescence or young adulthood today are increasingly ready to think well of their race and themselves.

In noting some of the factors that may have contributed to making black children and adolescents angrier, prouder, more aggressive, and more self-confident, we might be enumerating some of the salient traits in the development of a radically different black man. Caplan, reviewing empirical studies on militancy in the ghetto, suggests the appearance in the late 1960's of a new ghetto man:

A black militant who is committed to the removal of traditional racial restraints by open confrontation and, if necessary, by violence; a ghetto man who is very different in his actions and sympathies from the Negro of the past and from the white ghetto dwellers of an earlier period in their country's history. He is a ghetto man whose characteristics are seldom recognized and understood by white Americans.[16]

Black consciousness may be the most important determining characteristic of the new black man.

Negroes who riot do so because their conception of their lives and potential has changed without commensurate improvement in their chances for a better life. In the midst of squalor and despair, Negroes have abandoned the traditional stereotypes that made non-achievement and passive adaptation seem so natural. Rather, they have developed a black consciousness and a desire for a way of life with which they can feel the same pride and sense of potency they now derive from being black. Without these changes in self-perception, the demands to be regarded and treated as an individual with the same liberties as white Americans would never have reached the intensity that they have today. If this interpretation of the research is correct, it could be argued that the riots and other forms of civil rights protest are caused by the self-discovery of the American Negro and his attempt to recreate himself socially in ways that are commensurate with this new image. This battle for greater personal rights can be expected to continue as long as the Negro's political, social and economic efficacy is not aligned with his new and increasing sense of personal potency.[17]

We believe that the urban black masses in the early 1960's were in a state of what Crawford and Naditch call "discontent fatalism."[18] By the late 1960's or early 1970's many of them may have come to feel more personally and socially efficacious, but still frustrated in an age of rising expectations. They continued to perceive that opportunities were at least partially blocked by environmental and social constraints.[19] At the same time, they began to develop increasing racial pride as well as self-esteem. These feelings coupled with feelings of deprivation are likely to make people angry and aggressive if they do not see themselves as advancing, or if they perceive that they are suffering socio-economic setbacks in relation to those groups to which they compare themselves.

The changes in black identity that emerged during the 1960's both reflect and are determined by the black social-protest movement. The aggressiveness of the movement, its orientation to black experience, and its black-nationalist and pan-African elements imply an interplay between social and cultural forces and the development of a new black identity. The black movement is possibly the single most powerful force today fostering the development of a new racial self-esteem and self-confidence in the children of the black underclass.

Even the ghetto riots of the 1960's and 1970's may be viewed as having a direct impact upon racial identity and, implicitly, upon personal identity development in adolescents and young adults. Feagin and Hahn conclude that the riots mirror a "politics of violence":

> The outbreak of rioting reflected the fundamental fact of urban segregation and the emergence of group political identity. Rioting was probably occasioned less by the impersonal, anomic or psychologically stressful conditions of urban life than by the concentration of large numbers of black residents in distinct sectors of the city, by their frequent interaction, by their developing cohesion and political consciousness, and ultimately by their mobilization for militant political action. This view, therefore, facilitates the linking of ghetto riots to closely related, and similarly motivated, black actions on a collective basis before and after the riots, ranging from electoral politics, to non-violent organization, to black power, and local control movements: it encompasses a recognition of the influences exerted by the electoral and civil disobedience forms of political expression that preceded rioting.[20]

All these political and social activities of the late 1960's stand in marked contrast to Northern black experience, which until about the mid-1960's had been characterized by pervasive lethargy in the face of Northern racism. Not until the early 1960's did the mass of urban blacks begin to sluff off subservient patterns and identities and adopt new conceptions of black life and potential. Thus, manipulated by ambiguous and vague Northern racism, the black masses had remained relatively fixed in narrowly defined or negatively toned personal and racial identities.

Nevertheless, they apparently were becoming more ambivalent, more discontented, and, later, angrier and more aggressive (although this aggression was and still is significantly directed at other blacks). They still were psychologically oppressed; they still restricted their children's linguistic and cognitive activities; they still stunted their children's pride. They were not yet fully confronting themselves positively as a black mass stigmatized within a white country. Therefore they were largely incapable of re-evaluating themselves individually and as a group; they were correspondingly incapable of re-evaluating whites, white institutions, and white culture. It would seem, then, that it took time for Northern experience, public events, changing demographic patterns, changing community and family socialization, and the black movement within encapsulated ghetto areas to create the necessary conditions and climate for a new cultural and group consciousness in the urban black population.

Rather than assume that a positive black consciousness has been evolving continuously, we might speculate that masses of Negroes have been periodically and unpredictably jolted into confronting their blackness. In order for large numbers of Negroes to be driven out of a lethargic state and toward group pride and positive self-awareness, they may have "needed" such events as a Harlem riot in 1964; the assassination of Malcolm X and his subsequent reappraisal; more and larger urban revolts, with wide media coverage; and perhaps the single most jolting event to throw countless blacks into an unavoidable confrontation with their blackness—the assassination of Dr. Martin Luther King, Jr.

At least one study appears to lend indirect support to this dramatic-event theory of identity change. Clarke and Soule found in data they collected within twelve days after the King assassination that 65 per cent of a sample of 217 black preadolescents and adolescents in Florida public schools wished revenge beyond punishment by law for King's assassination.[21] The older adolescents were somewhat less likely to express a wish for violent sanctions for the assassin (74 per cent of the seventh-graders versus 50 per cent of the eleventh-graders). Among a sample of 165 white students in the same schools, as grade level increased, King himself was increasingly blamed for his own assassination. Some 66 per cent of the white eleventh-graders attributed the blame to King.

It is possible that adolescent and young adult blacks across the nation became more politicized or "blacker" immediately following King's death. Thus it is possible that the major identity differences between Hauser's mid-1960's subjects and Cross's early 1970's black youth—or, more broadly, the differences between the old Negro identity and the emerging black or Afro-American identity—may be in part a reaction to a succession of such transforming historical events. Perhaps millions of blacks who experienced relatively sudden challenges to their self-images were driven into an active process of identity change. And perhaps millions of children were ushered into long-term political-racial-personal socialization processes, which have been motivating them to develop more positive racial images and self-concepts.

Since the late 1960's the black militant appears to have been undergoing noticeable transformation. Some militants have become less consumed by hatred of whites, and some have relied less on rhetoric and individualistic charisma as time passes and have become more strategy-oriented and committed to planned, organized action. Black militancy and identity transformation may not only have been developmentally interacting with each other, but each connotes a developmental progression of social-cultural-personal changes.

The act of rioting or vicarious identification with rioters may have served to involve or commit many young low-income blacks to new racial and personal identities. We have tried to show that the Northern urban peer group extracted at least transitory individual allegiance and influenced the attitudes, behavior, and sentiments of many children in return for fun, excitement, camaraderie, or support. A semi-autonomous youthful subculture arose, disposed to challenge authority. Street-based affiliations may have lent an aggressive style and tone to some features of the black liberation movement. They may have siphoned off some of the grievances and antagonisms of children and adolescents toward parents and other blacks into expressions of strong antiwhite and pro-black feeling. The alienated peer group, therefore, has probably contributed to a new urban black identity and rising militancy, as well as to antisocial or defeatist life-styles.

In sum, the interaction of demographic changes, long-term Northern experience and socialization, dramatic public events (such as demonstrations, riots, and assassinations), and, finally, the black movement itself has influenced the emergence of a radical Negro-to-black identity transformation. In this sense, the black movement as a relatively unguided process is still a major impetus to black consciousness and pride among low-income segregated children and adolescents.

Sherif and Sherif portray the black social movement in terms of a thrust toward the development of identity and pride.[22] The centrality of the search for identity is illustrated through the rhetoric, activities, and functions of many black power proponents, whose concerns are marked by a turning from white cultural referents, values, and institutions toward other nonwhites throughout the world. The dissociation from white referents and a quest for a black referent converts inferiority feelings and shame into guilt and anger, and finally into pride.

Feelings of personal efficacy and an altered self-concept are achieved by those who complete the process. The black movement then may be seen as containing a parallel but mutual process of identity change.[23] Obviously, many blacks have been participating, to varying degrees, in dif-

ferent wings and phases of the black movement and consequently experiencing varying degrees of racial and personal identity change. All this
is not lost on contemporary black youth and even children.

Models of identity transformation such as those of Cross and the
Sherifs appear to describe rapid identity change in adolescents and young
adults with attendant emotional intensity and marked behavioral
changes. The enhanced intellectual capacities that emerge in adolescence
—e.g., ability to consider the hypothetical, various possibilities in a situation including contrary-to-fact propositions; to conceptualize one's own
thought and to reason about one's own mental constructions, premises,
and logic; as well as to relate many factors simultaneously[24]—permit the
growth of an ideological imagination that can influence identity development. Although the ideology may be an oversimplification of history and
the future, at certain historical moments the youth may feel compelled
to assume an ideological stance that is counter to the dominant ideology,
and this may engender radically new commitments, including the possibility of militancy. "Youth needs to base its rejections and acceptances
'normally' on ideological alternatives vitally related to the existing alternatives for identity formation, and in periods of radical change, this essentially adolescent propensity comes to dominate the collective mind."[25]

TOWARD A CHANGING BLACK CHILD

The thrust toward community control coupled with the rise of ethnic
ideology in segregated neighborhoods and schools may ensure that many
contemporary low-income black children will enter adolescence believing in the need for ethnic cohesiveness. Guttentag found that a community-controlled school district in Harlem exerted a variety of positive
influences on children, teachers, and parents.[26] Afternoon, evening, and
weekend centers were open to the community in all these schools. Many
adults in the community assumed responsibility for part of an educational program. Face-to-face contact between staff and parents was far
more frequent than in the non-community-controlled district. As a result,
there was a stronger intellectual and expressive atmosphere in the community-controlled schools than in schools in a comparison neighborhood.
There was more positive teacher-pupil interaction in the classroom, suggesting a social climate whose power exceeded individual teacher characteristics. Teachers' responses to children were more positive than in the
comparison schools. In the community-controlled schools, more parents
came to school to observe a class, to attend PTA meetings or other organizational activities, or to assist in teaching children to read or in some
other school program.

The children in the experimental district vigorously responded to the
changed school climate, especially to the increased influence of teachers

and parents. Awareness of the increased power and responsibility of parents and teachers in these schools was correlated with higher pupil achievement. In fact, children in the community-controlled schools attributed their academic success (or failure) to parents, teachers, and the school rather than to their own traits.

Achievement in the community-controlled schools appeared to improve over the three years they were in existence. Pupils in one school were significantly above national norms for reading. Children who had been in the district during the three years showed significantly stronger reading and math scores than did others. Given our emphasis on the need for adult support, direction, and attention and for a reduction of strong peer-supported anti-adult sentiment, these findings are not surprising. Recall, too, that preschoolers in the experimental district showed increased racial preference for same-race dolls (see Chapter 4), in line with the recent trend toward a growing racial acceptance among low-income black children.

In addition to frequent parent-teacher interactions, the success of the community-controlled district was attributed to its small size, which facilitates visiting by parents and thus maximizes the potential for face-to-face contact between parents and school staff.

Another reason for the success of the district may have been the "powerful and shared ideological commitment" of people in the community. It began when community groups came "together to fight a common enemy"—the central school board—over the location of a proposed new junior high school. This initial dispute led to community-group demands for local autonomy for schools. Community resolve was maximized during the existence of the community-controlled district by "active parent participation and involvement" in the education of the district's children. The commitment of shared ideology, Guttentag believes, had far-reaching effects throughout the school structure.

Perhaps these findings imply that segregation can be transformed into separation, substituting for shame and fatalism group pride, active participation, and group self-determination. Even with respect to self-concept, as distinguished from racial pride, some recent studies have found black students to have a higher self-concept than their white counterparts.[27] The highest self-concept among the blacks was found in all-black segregated settings and among teenagers, who expressed the strongest black-power ideology.[28] It may be that the growth of racial pride is serving to spur segregated black children's self-esteem and personal-identity development. It may be that the black liberation movement and the climate it fosters are nearly sufficient to establish racial pride and even some degree of self-esteem in segregated low-income black children.

Sizemore has argued that separatism may be the necessary first stage in the development of full black participation. She further states that "the ultimate goal of inclusion for excluded or stigmatized groups depends upon self-respect and identity." These qualities may currently be more likely to appear in racially separated than in integrated schools. Like Guttentag, Sizemore concludes that "being educated in the emotionally supportive setting of a school operated by one's own religious or ethnic group may promote more self-acceptance and security and render the individual more capable of full social separation."[29]

In an apparent reversal of earlier findings, Arkley found that a racially segregated low-income school is associated with *active* political orientations among black schoolchildren and with *passive* political orientations among white schoolchildren.[30] Thus, in studying the relationship of a low-SES elementary school's "organizational climate to the political orientations and behavior" of fifth-graders, he found that the racial mix of the school explained most of the differences in political attitudes and participation. The data were collected in the spring of 1970 from eighteen inner-city, low-income elementary schools in Michigan containing 1,027 children. As the percentage of black fifth-graders increased in these schools, "the feelings of attachment to the American political community decreased. . . . The laws were perceived as ineffective, the policeman was perceived as threatening, and authority figures and institutions were seen as fallible and lacking in punitive power." As the elementary school became increasingly white, children showed a higher attachment to the political community.

Just as the death of Dr. King may have had long-range socialization effects for black children, so too may the drift toward separatism in segregated settings. If racial identity, self-esteem, and active political participation are engendered in various segregated settings, black children and adolescents may be better prepared to struggle as adults to reduce social and economic inequities.

Ideology may count as much in Michigan as it appeared to in the Harlem community-controlled schools. The passive political orientations of the low-income white Michigan schoolchildren, on the other hand, may stem from an acceptance of their place in society as legitimate because they cannot explain their low status as a consequence of racism. Perhaps because they lack a class-struggle ideology or any other "handle," they cannot evolve a basis for dissent; whereas many low-income black children, despite insufficient political and social organization in their communities, may become comparatively more politicized as adults because of largely fortuitous effects of the black liberation movement—a movement currently in search of increased organization.

ETHNICITY, COMMUNITY, AND SOCIALIZATION

Studies of ethnic and religious minority groups that have maintained positive group identity despite poverty and active discrimination indicate that such groups have developed their own differentiated economic and social organizations to meet needs of group members that were not being met by institutions of the larger society.[31] Such groups generally assumed communal responsibility for individuals who were unable to care for themselves, such as the ill, orphaned, or elderly; they created or controlled their own educational system; and they developed an exceptionally powerful group ideology, which contained references to the group's intrinsic superiority and to differences between its values and those of other groups.

Poor black communities appear to have some of these characteristics, but others are relatively undeveloped. As we have noted, mutual aid may be observed in these communities, but it often seems to be based more on immediate economic necessity than on an explicitly shared value system and group outlook and may have a catch-as-catch-can quality. Formal community institutions that augment the efforts of isolated families to survive are not well developed.

During the late 1960's and early 1970's there were small advances in the development of local community control over public schools and some creation of alternative schools in urban black communities.[32] However, effective community control over local public schools has been blocked for the most part by centralized boards of education, which still control the allocation of money to local districts. Some promising experiments in Harlem schools were essentially destroyed by the central Board of Education in spite of evidence that many children in these schools experienced real educational and psychological benefits.[33]

During this same period, a variety of pro-black (and sometimes anti-white) ideologies were developed and disseminated in urban black communities. Certain ideologies focused specifically on a black value system as an alternative to prevailing white, Western values (as witness Karenga's seven principles listed in Chapter 10). But, despite the wide acceptance of pro-black slogans in black communities, relatively few indigenous structures and programs have been created in inner-city black communities, rooted in a black value system, that could provide support for large numbers of children to develop characteristics different from those traditionally required for individual survival.

Lacking widely accepted alternative value systems, institutions, and structures in inner-city black communities, individuals are left to face the consequences of economic exploitation and racism with very little communal support or direction. Survival often is bought at the price of diminished group cohesiveness and heightened suspiciousness, mistrust, and status competitiveness in spite of heightened racial pride.

Of course, the black church has always played a significant role in meeting the social-welfare needs of black American families. Various church-related organizations and groups have tried to help children whose families were unable to care for them. A black child-welfare system, however, based on a black American value system and run by and for blacks, exists only in embryonic form at present.[34] Because older children find themselves largely on their own, with minimal adult direction and support, the course of their development is not yet under effective familial or community control.

Within individual families, it is noteworthy that, irrespective of class, black parents who express a greater degree of political consciousness, who tend to blame the white power structure rather than black people for their difficulties, who endorse collective action and pro-black ideology, and who tend to become involved in cultural and political activity seem to be more likely to produce children who manifest positive ethnic identification—that is, positive social valuation of black people, black friendship choices, and pro-black racial and color identification—than are those who lack political consciousness and who are alienated from their own community.[35]

Until recently, racial shame and a negative racial identity have hampered black organizational potential. Since the 1954 Supreme Court desegregation decision, increased black consciousness and pride and, to a lesser extent, individual self-esteem have enabled some blacks to see more clearly the potential benefits of a life built around group advancement through a highly developed ethnic consciousness and ideological strategy favoring black unity. Guttentag's position is not unlike that of the black cultural-nationalists:

> Black ideology acts as a force tending toward the breaking down of *within-group social-class barriers;* it is the only ideology which could do so, since it reverses the values of white society. The stress on common social actions and purposes and the emphasis on "blackness" both of which tend to lessen social class distinctions . . . result in: (a) a great increase in within-group cohesiveness; and (b) more sharply drawn boundaries between group and non-group members.[36]

Harold Cruse, a black social theorist writing from a nationalist perspective in 1967, argues for ethnic solidarity:

> America, which idealizes the rights of the individual above everything else, is, in reality, a nation dominated by the social power of groups, classes, in-groups and cliques—both ethnic and religious. The individual in America has few rights that are not backed up by the political, economic, and social power of one group or another. Hence, the individual Negro has proportionately very few rights indeed, because his ethnic group (whether or not he actually identifies with it) has very little political, economic, or social power (beyond moral grounds) to wield. Thus it can be seen that those Negroes, and there are very many of them, who have accepted the full essence of the Great American Ideal of individualism are in serious trouble trying to function in America.[37]

Karenga contends that a cultural conversion extending from changes in individual consciousness to the building of collective structures and institutions is necessary for blacks to survive in America. However, he sees certain "collective weaknesses" among blacks that hinder their development of such ethnic solidarity and collective action. One such weakness is "leaderism," a "sickness that comes from our poor self-concepts and/or the obvious lack of collective values. Leaderism and leadership struggles are widespread because of the feeling of powerlessness in relation to the external opposition, and so an internal enemy is identified and attacked."[38]

In order to replace deleterious effects of self-devaluation that have caused strife between cultural and political nationalists, as well as to overcome other expressions of leaderism (e.g., "styling for TV or liberals," and the imagined possession of charisma), Karenga asserts that collective decision-making must gain ascendancy.

Another example of the collective weaknesses that stand in the way of remaking a black culture is "groupism":

> National liberation requires organized and unified responses to oppression, and anything less than this leaves us at an almost total loss. We must . . . transform our needs into *collective structure* and *movement* and not be satisfied with a national system of slogans and other subjective formulations. . . . We must have permanent structures that engender lasting loyalties, not loosely knit clusters of brittle brothers that break under stress and never express anything more than episodic allegiances to both structures and our struggle. Organization implies common identity, purpose, and direction . . . and speaks of a visible and expansive structure.[39]

Malcolm X's conversion to the Black Muslims also illustrates the profound importance of fully confronting one's racial identity. His conversion, too, suggests a dramatic transformational process associated with Negro-to-black identity change. Malcolm's intense subjective experience is set off by a visit from his brother when he was in prison. Reginald tells him:

> You don't even know who you are . . . the white devil has hidden it from you that you are of a race of people of ancient civilization. . . . You don't even know your true family name, you wouldn't recognize your true language if you heard it.[40]

It seems likely that the frequency of convulsive transformations to black identity has passed its peak today. Black babies now are born into the heritage of a black social movement that has already converted countless Negroes to blacks in varying degrees. The major tasks of black-child socialization and development today may lie in planned efforts to orient children toward future commitments to their people through strategic, organized activities.

One may assume that the black militant of the 1960's was a new person essentially because of increased formal and informal education, which made him more aware than his predecessor of the condition of his life, more dissatisfied, and more determined to do something to change it.[41] Or one may view the better education of the new man as principally a means of acquiring knowledge about how to change that condition, of which he has long been aware,[42] by banding together with other blacks to enhance political influence.[43] It is likely that both collective political awareness and methods of banding together are expanding in the black community.

Ethnic cohesiveness can increase racial isolation, preventing people from appreciating their shared values, reducing intergroup communication, and leading to "uncorrected perceptual distortions of each other and the growth of vested interests within both groups for continued separation."[44] Ethnic cohesiveness also leads to stronger differentiation between the in-group and outsiders, which in turn fosters stereotyping. However, as Guttentag states:

> It is rather a question of the trade-offs between various group conditions, and the effect of each condition on the poor. The lack of ethnic group cohesiveness must be weighed against both the positive and negative of strong group cohesive forces among poor individuals.[45]

Certainly community organization in low-income black neighborhoods appears to be a possible strategy to bolster the individual's attempts to challenge or negotiate institutional barriers to his mobility. For the children to whom this book has been devoted, ethnic cohesion and organization imply a warm, supportive, and encouraging life-style, fostering psychological development. An ethnic ideology that cuts across social-class divisions in the black community may help in the pursuit of this goal.

Urban black children's group and individual identities are changing in large measure because of the black ethnic ideology, but they still have not been receiving enough community-based support for their development. They face many of the same problems their parents faced as children and adolescents. And in-group divisiveness still beclouds the Harlems of America. In addition to the prejudice and poverty they must deal with in white America, blacks still must live in considerable fear of other blacks in their own communities.

Black author Orde Coombs says:

> I, too, am afraid to walk in black neighborhoods. It's time for blacks to do something about it. . . . How did we get to this place, where we spend our lives shaking from fear of rapacious attacks by our brothers and sisters? Harlem, our community, has become one of the most dangerous places in the world. . . . Is it any wonder that a black woman who has been in Harlem politics for a quarter of a century and has more than her

share of spunk and bravery tells me that "After Nixon, the person I fear most in the world is the ghetto black teenager?"[46]

Coombs reflects: "It is . . . fatalism, the absolute belief that one stands alone in the face of one's attackers, that is most eroding to the spirit of all our Harlems. . . . How can we get together to spell out our political aims, to worship and to organize if every time a black man ventures out of his home he must look behind every garbage can for a potential ambusher?"[47]

How to increase political punch, freedom, and safety simultaneously is an important challenge for black ethnic politics. The way in which this challenge is addressed will influence the prospects of development for black babies born today.

Even without formal local control, black ethnic ideology and the potential of cohesion offers the individual child, teenager, and young adult a strategy for upward mobility. We have noted that group cohesiveness can generate out-group stereotypes, reinforcing prejudices and running a strong risk of intensifying racial polarity. Yet in the short run, low-income blacks might best be able to raise achieving, committed, and courageous children through ethnically oriented local organizations. A closer tie between black nationalism and the neighborhood church, school, and other local black institutions may help make a whole generation of black children secure enough to seek some values and goals in common with their white contemporaries in order that some form of integrated republic can eventually arise. On the other hand, unless whites are willing to share America with ethnically proud blacks, the country will remain racially divided.

NOTES

1. Stuart T. Hauser, "Black and White Identity Development: Aspects and Perspectives," *Journal of Youth and Adolescence,* 1 (1972): 113–30. See also *idem, Black and White Identity Development* (New York: Wiley, 1971).
2. Erik H. Erikson, "The Problem of Ego Development," *Psychological Issues,* 1, No. 1 (1959): 120; *idem,* "Growth and Crisis of the 'Healthy' Personality," *Psychological Issues,* 1, No. 1 (1959): 87; and *idem, Identity: Youth and Crisis* (New York: W. W. Norton, 1968), p. 131.
3. Hauser, "Black and White Identity Development," pp. 124–25.
4. If *shame* has played an important role in undermining the childhood roots of identity formation in Northern blacks, this stands in sharp contrast to the experience of middle-class white children, who have been observed to be early and intensely regulated by *guilt.* See Erik H. Erikson, *Childhood and Society,* 2d ed. (New York: W. W. Norton, 1953), p. 252.

5. Erikson points out that there is a limit to the child's endurance in the face of demands to consider himself bad and evil; he may be obliged to flee from adults who pass such judgments. See Erikson, *Childhood and Society,* p. 253.

6. Joseph White, "Toward a Black Psychology," in Reginald L. Jones, ed., *Black Psychology* (New York: Harper & Row, 1972), p. 47.

7. For example, it has been observed that white working-class families and communities are alienated from the rapidly changing middle-class world, which requires great personal flexibility. Their insularity may restrict the range of self-definitions and make it problematic for working-class youth to adjust to a broader set of values, expectations, and relationships. Life-styles and identity seem to be relatively fixed for many of these youth. (See William Simon, John H. Gagnon, and S. A. Bluff, "Son of Joe: Continuity and Change Among White Working-Class Adolescents," *Journal of Youth and Adolescence,* 1 [March, 1972]: 13–34.) However, we feel that unflattering characterizations of white working-class ethnics, as of low-income blacks, may be colored by middle-class chauvinism and insufficient recognition of the effect of the political economy, not merely their families, communities, or schools, on the white working-class teenager's adjustment to the broader society.

8. Through interviews with black college students, William E. Cross, Jr., has concluded that King's death was perhaps the single most important event of the 1960's in triggering identity transformation among black teenagers. Joe R. Feagin and Harlan Hahn, *Ghetto Revolts: The Politics of Violence in American Cities* (New York: Macmillan, 1973), pp. 147–49, offers an analysis of the precipitating events and patterning of the ghetto revolts following the spring, 1968, King assassination.

9. William E. Cross, Jr., "Discovering the Black Referent: The Psychology of Black Liberation," in Vernon J. Dixon and Badi G. Foster, eds., *Beyond Black or White: An Alternate America* (Boston: Little, Brown, 1971), pp. 95–110. Another version is *idem,* "Toward a Psychology of Black Liberation: The Negro-to-Black Conversion Experience," *Black World* (1971): 13–27. For a similar conception of identity change, see Charles W. Thomas, *Boys No More: A Black Psychologist's View of Community* (Beverly Hills, Calif.: Glencoe, 1971).

10. Cross, "Discovering the Black Referent," pp. 103–4.

11. *Ibid.,* p. 105.

12. W. S. Hall, Roy O. Freedle, and William E. Cross, Jr., *Stages in the Development of a Black Identity* (Iowa City: American College Testing Program, 1972).

13. Ronald Krate, Gloria Leventhal, and Barry Silverstein, "Self-Perceived Transformation of Negro-to-Black Identity," *Psychological Reports,* 35 (1974): 1071–75.

14. Melvin Herman and Stanley Sadofsky, *Study of the Meaning, Experience, and Effects of the Neighborhood Youth Corps,* New York University Graduate School of Social Work, Center for the Study of

Unemployed Youth, 1967; Robert L. Crain and Carol Sachs Weisman, *Discrimination, Personality, and Achievement: A Survey of Northern Blacks* (New York: Seminar Press, 1972); and Gary T. Marx, *Protest and Prejudice: A Study of Belief in the Black Community* (New York: Harper & Row, 1967), are representative of a large body of literature that relates Northern and Western socialization, urbanization, youth, and increased level of education to racial identification and black pride, self-esteem, anger, and militancy.

15. David O. Sears and John B. McConahay, "Racial Socialization, Comparison Levels, and the Watts Riot," *Journal of Social Issues,* 26, No. 1 (1970): 121–40. See also T. Crawford and M. Naditch, "Relative Deprivation, Powerlessness, and Militancy: The Psychology of Social Protest," *Psychiatry,* 33, No. 2 (1970): 208–23.

16. N. Caplan, "The New Ghetto Man: A Review of Recent Empirical Evidence," *Journal of Social Issues,* 26 (1970): 59.

17. *Ibid.,* pp. 71–72.

18. Crawford and Naditch, "Relative Deprivation," p. 217.

19. *Ibid.* See also J. R. Forward and J. R. Williams, "Internal-External Control and Black Militancy," *Journal of Social Issues,* 26, No. 1 (1970): 75–92, and Caplan, "New Ghetto Man."

20. Feagin and Hahn, *Ghetto Revolts* (n. 8 *supra*), p. 48. See also Hanes Walton, Jr., *Black Politics: A Theoretical and Structural Analysis* (Philadelphia: Lippincott, 1972), pp. 214–16. Kenneth Clark has often suggested that the ghettos are political, social, educational, and, above all, economic colonies, and that their residents are subject peoples, victims of the cruelty, greed, insensitivity, guilt, and fear of their masters. See Kenneth B. Clark, *Dark Ghetto* (New York: Harper & Row, 1965). In contrast to political perspectives, frustration-aggression theories and subculture-of-poverty theories are the most frequently offered explanations for violence among low-income groups.

21. J. W. Clarke and John W. Soule, "Political Socialization, Racial Tension, and the Acceptance of Violence: Reactions of Southern Schoolchildren to the King Assassination," in William J. Crotty, ed., *Assassinations and the Political Order* (New York: Harper & Row, 1971).

22. Muzafer Sherif and Carolyn W. Sherif, "Black Unrest as a Social Movement Toward an Emerging Self-identity," *Journal of Social and Behavioral Sciences,* 15 (1970): 41–52.

23. Gerlach and Hine offer another construction that argues that personal change and movement change "intersect." Commitment is viewed as the motivating force that links a movement with individual change. See Luther P. Gerlach and Virginia H. Hine, *People, Power, Change: Movements of Social Transformation* (Indianapolis, Ind.: Bobbs-Merrill, 1970), Chapter 5.

24. See Bärbel Inhelder and Jean Piaget, *The Growth of Logical Thinking from Childhood to Adolescence* (New York: Basic Books, 1958).

25. Erikson, *Identity* (n. 2 *supra*), p. 190. Some middle-class white youth, and some women, as well as some black youth and young adults during the 1960's, felt the need for commitment to alternative ideologies.

Cf. Richard Flacks, *Youth and Social Change* (Chicago: Markham, 1971), and Robin Morgan, *Sisterhood Is Powerful* (New York: Random House, 1970). Perhaps ideological imagination has been too closely tied by social psychologists to adolescent turbulance, thereby obscuring or blunting its critique of existing social orders.

26. Marcia Guttentag, "Children in Harlem's Community-controlled Schools," *Journal of Social Issues,* 28 (1972): 1–20.

27. E.g., P. A. Zirkel, "Self-Concept and the 'Disadvantage' of Ethnic Group Membership and Mixture," *Review of Educational Research,* 41 (1971): 211–25; Edward S. Greenberg, "Black Children, Self-Esteem, and the Liberation Movement," *Politics and Society,* Spring, 1972, pp. 293–307; G. J. Powell, "Self-Concept in White and Black Children," in C. V. Willie *et al.,* eds., *Racism and Mental Health* (Pittsburgh: University of Pittsburgh Press, 1973), pp. 299–318; and C. Reese, "Black Self-Concept," *Children Today,* March–April, 1974, pp. 24–26.

28. Zirkel, "Self-Concept and the 'Disadvantage' . . . ," and Reese, "Black Self-Concept." See also E. E. Lessing, "Self-Concept of Black High School Students Varying in Endorsement of Black Power Ideology," paper presented at the American Psychological Association meetings, Montreal, August, 1973.

29. B. A. Sizemore, "Separatism: A Reality Approach to Inclusion?" in Robert L. Green, ed., *Racial Crisis in American Education* (Chicago: Follett, 1969), p. 272. Black kindergartners and first-graders who were exposed to "pro-black" education in an all-black community-controlled school were significantly more likely to give pro-black responses in a Clark-type doll study than they did before the exposure and in comparison with similar black children who had not been in such a program. See P. L. Bunton and T. H. Weissbach, "Attitudes Toward Blackness of Black Preschool Children Attending Community-Controlled or Public Schools," *Journal of Social Psychology,* 92 (1974): 53–59; see also Guttentag, "Harlem's Community-controlled Schools" (n. 26 *supra*).

30. A. S. Arkley, "Political Orientations and Behavior of Fifth-Grade Students in Racially Segregated Low-socioeconomic-status Schools," paper presented at meeting of American Political Science Association, New Orleans, La., 1973. See also Arkley, "Black Participants and White Subjects: The Relationship of Elementary-school Racial Segregation to Fifth-Graders' Political Orientations and Behavior," paper presented at meeting of American Educational Research Association, Chicago, Ill., April, 1974.

31. Marcia Guttentag, "Group Cohesiveness, Ethnic Organization, and Poverty," *Journal of Social Issues,* 26 (1970): 105–31.

32. See Marilyn Gittell with Maurice R. Berube, Frances Gottfried, Marcia Guttentag, and Adele Spier, *Local Control in Education: Three Demonstration School Districts in New York City* (New York: Praeger, 1972).

33. Guttentag, "Harlem's Community-controlled Schools" (n. 26 *supra*).

34. See Andrew Billingsley and Jeanne D. Giovannoni, *Children of the*

Storm: Black Children and American Child Welfare (New York: Harcourt Brace Jovanovich, 1972), and also J. P. Comer, "Are We Failing Our Children?" *Ebony,* August, 1974, pp. 54–61.

35. See E. J. Barnes, "The Black Community as the Source of Positive Self-Concept for Black Children," in Reginald L. Jones, ed., *Black Psychology* (New York: Harper & Row, 1972), pp. 166–92.
36. Guttentag, "Group Cohesiveness," p. 123.
37. Harold Cruse, *The Crisis of the Negro Intellectual* (New York: William Morrow, 1967), pp. 6–7.
38. Ron Karenga, "Overturning Ourselves: From Mystification to Meaningful Struggle," *Black Scholar,* October, 1972, p. 9.
39. *Ibid.,* pp. 10–11. Maslow's study of "peak experiences" is reminiscent of much of the thrust of Karenga's writings. Cf.: "To have a clear perception . . . that the universe is all of a piece and that one has a place in it . . . can be so profound and shaking an experience that it can change the person's character and his Weltanschauung forever after." Abraham H. Maslow, *Religions, Values, and Peak Experiences* (Columbus: The Ohio State University Press, 1964), p. 59. See also Anthony F. Wallace, *Culture and Personality,* 2d ed. (New York: Random House, 1970), Chapter 5; Cross, "Discovering Black Referent" (n. 9 *supra*); and Thomas, *Boys No More* (n. 9 *supra*).
40. Malcolm X, *The Autobiography of Malcolm X,* ed. by Alex Haley (New York: Grove Press, 1964), p. 161.
41. Cf. Caplan, "New Ghetto Man" (n. 16 *supra*).
42. S. M. Moinant, James W. Raine, S. L. Burbeck, and K. K. Davison, "Black Ghetto Residents as Rioters," *Journal of Social Issues,* 28, No. 4 (1972): 45–62.
43. *Ibid.* See also Feagin and Hahn, *Ghetto Revolts* (n. 8 *supra*).
44. Thomas Pettigrew, "Racially Separate or Together?" *Journal of Social Issues,* 25, No. 1 (1969): 43–69.
45. Guttentag, "Group Cohesiveness" (n. 31 *supra*), p. 124.
47. Orde Coombs, "Fear and Trembling in Black Streets," *New York* Magazine, November 20, 1972, pp. 47–50.
48. *Ibid.*

INDEX